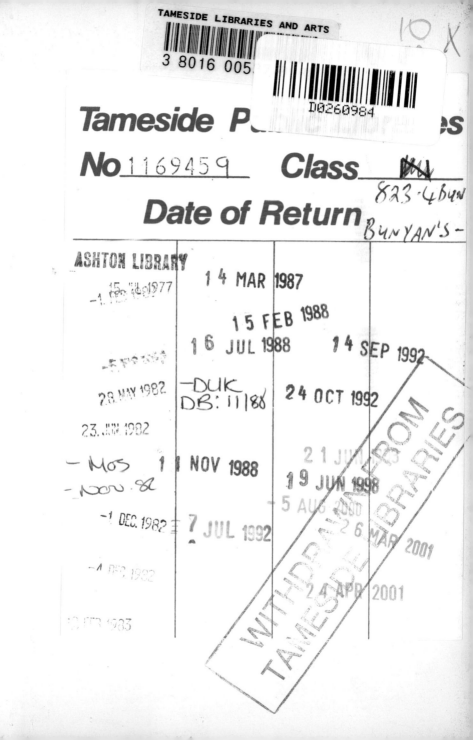

Shakespeare: *Richard II* NICHOLAS BROOKE
Shakespeare: *The Tempest* D. J. PALMER
Shakespeare: *Twelfth Night* D. J. PALMER
Shakespeare: *The Winter's Tale* KENNETH MUIR
Shelley: *Shorter Poems and Lyrics* PATRICK SWINDEN
Swift: *Gulliver's Travels* RICHARD GRAVIL
Tennyson: *In Memoriam* JOHN DIXON HUNT
Virginia Woolf: *To the Lighthouse* MORRIS BEJA
Webster: *'The White Devil' and 'The Duchess of Malfi'*
    R. V. HOLDSWORTH
Wordsworth: *Lyical Ballads* ALUN R. JONES AND WILLIAM
    TYDEMAN
Wordsworth: *The Prelude* W. J. HARVEY AND RICHARD GRAVIL
Yeats: *Last Poems* JON STALLWORTHY

TITLES IN PREPARATION INCLUDE

Jane Austen: *'Northanger Abbey' and 'Persuasion'* B. C. SOUTHAM
Jonson: *'Every Man in His Humour' and 'The Alchemist'* R. V.
    HOLDSWORTH
Peacock: *Satirical Novels* LORNA SAGE
Shakespeare: *Coriolanus* B. A. BROCKMAN
Shakespeare: *'Much Ado About Nothing' and 'As You Like It'*
    JENNIFER SEARLE
Shakespeare: *Troilus and Cressida* PRISCILLA MARTIN
Spenser: *The Faerie Queene* PETER BAYLEY

Bunyan

The Pilgrim's Progress

A CASEBOOK

EDITED BY

ROGER SHARROCK

M

First published 1976 by
THE MACMILLAN PRESS LTD
London and Basingstoke
Associated companies in New York Dublin
Melbourne Johannesburg and Madras

SBN 333 15498 3 (hard cover)
333 15499 1 (paper cover)

Printed in Great Britain by
THE ANCHOR PRESS LTD
Tiptree, Essex

CONTENTS

ACKNOWLEDGEMENTS

The editor and publishers wish to thank the following, who have kindly given permission for the use of copyright material: Robert Bridges, 'Bunyan's Pilgrim's Progress' from *Collected Essays of Robert Bridges*, 1934, by permission of the Oxford University Press; Sir Charles Firth, extract from the Introduction to *Pilgrim's Progress*, 1898, by permission of Methuen & Co. Ltd; Roland Mushat Frye, 'The Way of All Pilgrims' from *God, Man and Satan: Patterns of Christian Thought and Life in Paradise Lost, Pilgrim's Progress and the Great Theologians* (© 1960 Princeton University Press), reprinted by permission of Princeton University Press; T. R. Glover, extract from *Poets and Puritans*, 1915, by permission of Methuen & Co. Ltd; Maurice Hussey, 'Bunyan's "Mr. Ignorance"' from *Modern Language Review*, XLIV, 1949, by permission of the author and the editor; Arnold Kettle, 'The Moral Fable' from *An Introduction to the English Novel*, 1951, by permission of Hutchinson Publishing Group Ltd; John R. Knott Jr, 'Bunyan's Gospel Day' reprinted from *English Literary Renaissance*, III, 1973, by permission of the author and the editors; F. R. Leavis, extract from chapter II in *Anna Karenina and Other Essays*, 1969, by permission of the author and Chatto and Windus Ltd (and by arrangement with the New American Library Inc. published as the Afterword from 'The Pilgrim's Progress' by John Bunyan, © 1964 F. R. Leavis); C. S. Lewis, 'The Vision of John Bunyan' from *Selected Literary Essays*, 1969, by permission of Cambridge University Press; Roy Pascal, 'The Present Tense in Pilgrim's Progress' from *Modern Language Review*, LX, 1965, by permission of the author and the editor; Roger Sharrock, 'Women and Children' and 'Character and Dream' from *Bunyan: Pilgrim's Progress, Studies in English Literature*, 1966, by permission of Edward Arnold (Publishers) Ltd; George Bernard Shaw, extract from Epistle Dedicatory to *Man and Superman*, 1932, by permission of The Society of Authors on behalf of the Bernard Shaw Estate; Henri A. Talon, 'Space and the Hero in the Pilgrim's Progress', from *Etudes Anglaises*, xiv, 1961, by permission of his heirs and of Didier (Publishers), Paris.

GENERAL EDITOR'S PREFACE

Each of this series of Casebooks concerns either one well-known and influential work of literature or two or three closely linked works. The main section consists of critical readings, mostly modern, brought together from journals and books. A selection of reviews and comments by the author's contemporaries is also included, and sometimes comments from the author himself. The Editor's Introduction charts the reputation of the work from its first appearance until the present time.

The critical forum is a place of vigorous conflict and disagreement, but there is nothing in this to cause dismay. What is attested is the complexity of human experience and the richness of literature, not any chaos or relativity of taste. A critic is better seen, no doubt, as an explorer than as an 'authority', but explorers ought to be, and usually are, well equipped. The effect of good criticism is to convince us of what C. S. Lewis called 'the enormous extension of our being which we owe to authors'. This Casebook will be justified if it helps to promote the same end.

A single volume can represent no more than a small selection of critical opinions. Some critics have been excluded for reasons of space, and it is hoped that readers will follow up the further suggestions in the Select Bibliography. Other contributions have been severed from their original context, to which some readers may wish to return. Indeed, if they take a hint from the critics represented here, they certainly will.

A. E. DYSON

INTRODUCTION

John Bunyan is universally known as the author of *The Pilgrim's Progress*; a comparative minority of its English readers may know, or know of, his spiritual autobiography *Grace Abounding*, his other allegory *The Holy War*, or even his pseudo-allegory *The Life and Death of Mr Badman* (which is in spite of its allegorical naming an unconscious stumble into the realistic novel of social life). But *The Pilgrim's Progress* is a world book and the vast majority of its readers now and in the past have known nothing else about the author. It is interesting to speculate on what the judgement of history on Bunyan would have been if he had never written it. It seems likely that he would have left a reputation as a minister and preacher of a certain persuasion of Baptists and of a group of 'gathered churches' in Bedfordshire; there would still be almost sixty books by him, arousing discourses on divine grace and the bondage of the law, controversy and Biblical commentary, to be investigated from time to time by the scholars of Nonconformity. From what is known of his life a robust and forthright personality would still emerge. Perhaps he would be recorded as a leader of the sectarian religious life of the common people comparable in stature to Richard Baxter among the conservative and educated Puritans.

Looking thus on the whole career of Bunyan, and then back to his masterpiece, it is bound to seem to us a glorious accident, a sport. So much of the theological writings of the seventeenth-century English Puritans exists for us across an immeasurable divide, the divide created by the seventeenth-century revolution in favour of rationality, brevity, and the equation of words to things; yet *The Pilgrim's Progress* bridges this divide, makes passionate religious commitment seem a sober, matter-of-fact affair, and equates its words to things with more success than the fashionable would-be rational preachers of the Restoration, Tillotson and South. So critics of *The Pilgrim's Progress* have

tended either to dwell on the uniqueness of the work or to
examine the ways in which this apparent uniqueness may disguise the manner in which the book is nevertheless fed by the
Puritan tradition and Bunyan's experience of the life of a
sectarian community. Coleridge, one of the earliest critics of *The
Pilgrim's Progress* represented in this anthology, says that
Bunyan's 'piety was baffled by his genius, and Bunyan of Parnassus had the better of Bunyan of the conventicle'. On the other
hand Q. D. Leavis can see the work as the sustained expression
of the spirit of English Puritanism, for which Bunyan's voice is
merely a channel. Between these two opposing views falls the main
bulk of modern Bunyan criticism, illuminating from various
angles that contemporary debate concerning tradition and the
individual talent which is our twentieth-century version of the
problem of free will and predestination that vexed seventeenth-
century Protestants.

The copy for the First Part of *The Pilgrim's Progress* was
entered in the Stationers' Register on 22 December 1677 :

Nathaniel Ponder entered then for his Coppy by vertue of a license
under the hand of Mr. Turner, and which is subscribed by Mr.
Warden Vere, One Book or Coppy Intituled The Pilgrim's Progress
from this world to that which is to come, delivered in ye Similitude
of a Dream, by John Bunyan, vjd.

The book was entered in the Term Catalogue for the following
Hilary Term, 18 February 1678; it is likely that this was the date
of publication or only slightly preceded it. Its publisher Nathaniel
Ponder was to continue to print the work, twelve editions of the
First Part in Bunyan's lifetime, to make his fortune by it, and to
earn the title of 'Bunyan' Ponder. According to the early lives of
Bunyan and to local tradition in Bedford he wrote the book in
the town gaol on the bridge over the Ouse, where he was confined for refusing to conform to the laws against unlicensed
preaching. Bunyan suffered two imprisonments. The first lasted
for twelve years from 1660 to 1672, though there is evidence that
during many of these years confinement was not strict and that
there were frequent periods of parole. The other, about which less
is known, was a period of some six months in 1677. In both cases

the place of imprisonment is likely to have been the county gaol, and not the picturesque but tiny lockup on Bedford Bridge. At the beginning of *The Pilgrim's Progress* the place where the Dreamer lies down to sleep is glossed in the third edition 'The Gaol'. But in which imprisonment did Bunyan write? The older biographers assumed it was the first, but then they do not discriminate very clearly between the two imprisonments. Modern scholars have been divided; some have assumed too readily that because the book was published in 1678 it must have been written in a rapid burst in the second imprisonment. There are strong reasons for believing that a good half of the work at least was composed during the first imprisonment, that it was interrupted on Bunyan's release under the 1672 Declaration of Indulgence because of his fresh responsibilities as pastor of the Bedford congregation and the controversies he engaged in at that time with the London Baptists, and that it might well have been completed during the second, shorter, imprisonment. Halfway through the book the Dreamer says, 'Then I awoke and dreamed again'. In the verses prefixed to the First Part Bunyan speaks of asking the advice of others on whether he should print his manuscript and receiving conflicting opinions : the suggestion is of a substantial time of consideration, not of rushing the copy to Ponder for publication in two or three months.

The strongest evidence for earlier composition lies in the intimate relation between *The Pilgrim's Progress* and Bunyan's autobiography *Grace Abounding to the Chief of Sinners* (1666). *The Pilgrim's Progress* is an urgent, first-person narrative, a continuing echo of the existential cry with which it commences, 'What shall I do to be saved?' The rich gallery of human life, both mean and generous, which Christian meets along the road cannot obscure the fact that all the other persons in the work are to a great extent aspects of his own yearning and tormented consciousness. In *Grace Abounding* there is a similar spotlight continuously playing on the interior struggle of Bunyan himself. In his younger days Bunyan, like other Puritans who have left narratives of their spiritual development, laboured under a consuming sense of guilt and needed the assurance of the free grace of Christ, impossible to be earned by the 'filthy rags' of

any mere moral righteousness, to make him whole. His experience was exceptional on account of its pathological intensity; the
Calvinist doctrine that all men are foreordained either to salvation or to damnation presented itself in his mind in a simple and
terrible form; in fearful dreams and visions the accusing texts of
the Bible which his mind dwelt on assumed the sensuous form of
voices, blows and pinches : he tells how he was pulled and thrust
about by the demons who tormented him until he endured a
sensation 'as though my breast-bone would have burst asunder'.
Warning verses of Scripture 'lay like a mill-post upon my back'.
His greatest temptation was to blaspheme Christ, and thus, he
thought, to become guilty of the unpardonable sin; the same
temptation is encountered in the allegory in the Valley of the
Shadow of Death :

just when he was come over against the mouth of the burning pit,
one of the wicked ones got behind him, and stepped up softly to him,
and whisperingly suggested many grievous blasphemies to him which
he verily thought had proceeded from his own mind.[1]

The Pilgrim's Progress develops the tendency to personify and
dramatise already at work in the autobiography. Instead of the
empty, introspective space of *Grace Abounding*, Christian, the
spiritual pilgrim, moves through a peopled world. The menacing
texts become palpable demons. The fear of having committed the
sin against the Holy Ghost becomes a Giant Despair who locks
him in a dungeon. The authority of the Bible is embodied in the
character Evangelist, who keeps reappearing to guide an often
bewildered Christian back on to the King's Highway. Between
them the confessional work and the allegory describe a process
of self-discovery and self-adjustment which Bunyan underwent
during his time in prison : by reviewing his doubts and temptations of over ten years before he is able to arrive more securely,
because with a fuller understanding, at that final resolution of
doubt which enabled him to stand his ground before the
magistrates and go to prison for the sake of conscience.

As well as urgent personal involvement Bunyan shows an
artistic involvement in his fiction quite unlike the average
Puritan's severely utilitarian attitude to literature, and not to be

met with in his doctrinal and evangelical writings where trope
and metaphor are strictly controlled so as to contribute to some
simple, single Biblical idea. The prefatory verses are an account
of the creative process; they describe a spontaneous element taking over and asserting itself against the grain of the writer's conscious plan :

> And thus it was : I writing of the way
> And race of saints in this our Gospel-day,
> Fell suddenly into an allegory
> About their journey, and the way to glory,
> In more than twenty things, which I set down;
> This done, I twenty more had in my crown,
> And they again began to multiply,
> Like sparks that from the coals of fire do fly. . . .
> Thus I set pen to paper with delight,
> And quickly had my thoughts in black and white.
> For having now my method by the end,
> Still as I pulled it came, and so I penned
> It down, until it came at last to be
> For length and breadth the bigness which you see.

That Bunyan was a natural writer is clear from his very first
paragraph. The slow yet nervous rhythm, the unlaboured echo
and assonance, lead straight into the introspective crisis of
Christian, and then just as he is 'no longer able to contain', the
purely introspective mood is broken, the rhythm lightens, and a
story begins :

As I walked through the wilderness of this world, I lighted on a
certain place, where was a den; and I laid me down in that place to
sleep : and as I slept I dreamed a dream. I dreamed, and behold
I saw a man clothed with rags, standing in a certain place, with his
face from his own house, with a book in his hand, and a great burden
upon his back. I looked, and saw him open the book, and read therein;
and as he read, he wept and trembled : and not being able longer
to contain, he brake out with a lamentable cry saying, 'What shall
I do?'

There are similar plangent, musical rhythms in *Grace Abounding*, running through long sentences or whole paragraphs where

the first-person clauses are linked simply by parataxis. This is Bunyan's language of self-revelation. But when Christian looks outwards towards the Celestial City and sets out on his journey, Bunyan applies a cooler and more objective style, terser sentences, a vivid use of colloquial phrases ('he all-to-befooled me', 'Whither away, good fellow?', 'a very pretty man'), together with a wealth of proverbial illustration. 'His house is as empty of religion as the white of an egg is of savour' : in a sentence like this it is hard to distinguish between traditional proverb, the language of the folk imagination, and Bunyan's individual thought as a shrewd popular preacher.

The Pilgrim's Progress represents a highly idiosyncratic blending of personal experience transmuted into fiction, traditional form, dramatised theology, and earnest preaching to the reader with nothing imaginative about it. Bunyan is always ready to kill his fiction stone dead if an improving lesson may be rammed home at its expense. There is a peculiar blend of imaginative assurance, as in the exultant psalmody of the characters' crossing of the River of Death in Part Two, and sheer naïveté. Yet it would be false superiority to accuse Bunyan of artistic clumsiness : rather it is that he does not accept the aesthetic category and sees only the need for an unambiguous moral and religious meaning at all costs. This works in strange ways, and anti-art, as with some of its twentieth-century exponents, is not always incompatible with literary success.

For instance, Christian is treated as a hero of romance going on a quest. It is the compelling charm of romance that helps to explain the appeal of the book to many generations of children and to readers of many different cultures (there are illustrations to Japanese missionary editions showing Christian as a Samurai warrior). But this treatment is not consistent. Christian fights Apollyon, the demon of spiritual doubt, with sword in hand and armour on his back; but as he goes on through the Valley of the Shadow of Death we are told that 'he was forced to put up his weapon, and betake himself to another weapon called All-prayer; so he cried, in my hearing, "O Lord, I beseech thee, deliver my soul" '. The allegorical mode has been broken and we have a direct statement that prayer is the chief weapon against temptation. Something may be lost on the dramatic side of the narrative, but the dangers of an over-complex and mechanical allegory are avoided; instead, we are returned to the primary sources of allegory in metaphorical thinking about experience, in this case hostility from without, physical or spiritual, and man's need to defend himself from danger. Similarly, when Christian and Hopeful are imprisoned in the castle of Giant Despair the atmosphere is that of a folk-tale; as a boy before his conversion Bunyan had rejoiced in reading a ballad, a news-book, or George-on-horseback' – the latter being the tale of St George and the dragon, probably encountered in Richard Johnson's *The Seven Champions of Christendom*. Despair is a gross giant with a club, and we seem to be moving in the world of fairy-tale until Christian suddenly says to Hopeful, as they languish in the dungeon, that he remembers, 'I have a key in my bosom called Promise that will unlock all doors in Doubting Castle'. Once more the allegory has been sacrificed, this time for a purely theological point : the promises are those texts of Scripture which hold forth the promise of salvation to the faithful. Bunyan makes much of them in his account of his conversion in *Grace Abounding*. Yet even in this episode, apart from the theological level, the key works at the level of fantasy, like a magic ring in romance, or a potent ray in science fiction; of course we spoil it all if we ask ourselves why Christian did not remember he had the key before. Finally, the last incident in the First Part administers a different kind of shock to the reader. Ignorance, whose quality is that he knows nothing of twice-born religion and lives complacently in a world of theory, comes by the wrong road to the Celestial City and knocks at the gate; he is bound and taken away to a door in the side of the hill. 'Then I saw that there was a way to Hell, even from the gates of Heaven, as well as from the City of Destruction. So I awoke, and behold it was a dream.' Curiously enough, it is the modern infidel reader, who like Pope's Dean 'never mentions hell to ears polite', and does not believe in it, who is most likely to be shocked by the apparent brutality of this. However Bunyan is not being vicious to Ignorance as a person. 'Turn up my metaphors . . . look within my veil', he says elsewhere. He is conscious of what Ignorance stands for and he believes in the truth of his fable, the terrible urgency of man's struggle for life against death : he is indeed speaking to his readers, writing as if all he can do is to warn, and therefore is content to end on this grim note rather than with some comfortable celestial chorus.

In the blend of Bunyan's fiction there is humour and plain realism as well as romance adventure and the conversion crises of Calvinist theology. Often the most lively presentation of character is to be found in the studies of hypocrites and villains met along the way. Worldly Wiseman is a pompous bourgeois; By-Ends is his near relation, and his corruption is suggested by the air of social importance with which he invests himself :

My wife is a very virtuous woman, the daughter of a virtuous woman. She was my Lady Faining's daughter, therefore she came of a very honourable family, and is arrived to such a pitch of breeding, that she knows how to carry it to all, even to prince and peasant. 'Tis true we somewhat differ in religion from those of the stricter sort. . . .

There is realism in the setting of the journey itself, the muddy road like those of the seventeenth century, the traveller with a pack on his back and the constant danger from footpads. In the persecution of the pilgrims at Vanity Fair realism and mythology are blended : the dreadful death of Faithful recalls some of the martyrdoms of the early Christians which Bunyan would have read about in John Foxe's *Acts and Monuments* ('the Book of Martyrs'), whereas the previous trial scene observes English judicial procedure with a jury – a packed one – bringing in their verdict and an abusive judge resembling some of the judges before whom Nonconformists had to appear in Bunyan's day.

It may be asked now why this mixture of Calvinist theology, folk-tale reminiscence, personal psychology and realistic thumb-nail sketches achieves such a unity of effect, and only seems incongruous to readers jealous of preserving their sophistication. To say that the journey as an image of human life from birth to death is of universal appeal, is a partial answer. Certainly as Jung and his followers have demonstrated, and whether or not one subscribes to the Jungian theory of archetypes, the metaphor of the strange initiatory journey is pervasive in culture from *The Epic of Gilgamesh* to *The Ancient Mariner*. But theories of myth applied to religious language and parable, as by modern reductionist theologians, have the effect of classing very powerful stories or reports, which were once thought to embody truth in some fashion, as though they were constructed at a remove from actual experience and in a purely illustrative manner. If this is misleading, as I think it is, it might be better to regard these stories, and Bunyan's too, not from the point of view of form-criticism and the comparative study of myth, but outwards from the pattern of any individual human life as a human being reflects on it : for such reflection invariably produces a pattern that is narrative in form. As in the older novelists, but in a much stronger and simpler way, Bunyan's story reflects the form of human life itself from birth to death. 'Now the day drew on . . .', 'In process of time . . .' – the most ordinary chronological links of the narrative offer not the contrivance of fiction but the very image of living on the human scale.

The popularity of the First Part drew from Bunyan a Second Part in 1684. In it he tells the story of the pilgrimage of Christian's wife, Christiana, and her family. Women had been neglected in the masculine, crisis-ridden First Part. Now this omission is repaired and the result is a gentler, more leisurely work, which captures more of everyday Puritan social life, courtship, marriage, and ordinary conversation. The heroics are reserved for Greatheart, the guardian of this female pilgrimage, and for the splendid conclusion in which one after the other the pilgrims cross the River of Death, each echoing the poetry of the twelfth chapter of Ecclesiastes and speaking his or her last words in character. 'As he [Valiant-for-Truth] went down deeper, he said, *"Grave where is thy victory?"* So he passed over, and the trumpets sounded for him on the other side.'

Literary criticism of *The Pilgrim's Progress* may be said not to exist before the Romantic period. Perhaps the most informed comment, and one compatible with modern ideas of the individuality of the literary imagination, is that to be found in Bunyan's two sets of prefatory verses. In them we meet a sense of creative spontaneity and an acknowledgement of the idiomatic character of 'mine own native language' which none of his imitators can capture. Throughout the eighteenth century Bunyan carried the stigma of being a writer who was popular with the common people; he was an artisan writing in the language of the market-place and his work fell outside the Augustan canon of polite literature. While literary taste was largely guided by a standard approximating to that of social elegance, Bunyan had no hope of being taken seriously, in spite of the praise of Johnson and others (usually given, significantly enough, in offhand remarks and not in writing). There was also in the age of the Enlightenment an increasing resistance to Puritan dogma. James Foster, a liberal Nonconformist, spoke for a sceptical time when he declared that none of the characters in *The Pilgrim's Progress* spoke sense except Ignorance (*Gentleman's Magazine*, 1741).

The greater part of the writing about *The Pilgrim's Progress* in the eighteenth, nineteenth, and into the twentieth century, was in the nature of pious commentary and moral exhortation, much of it by writers in the Free Church tradition. For a book that lay in the window-seat with the Bible there was no possibility of pure literary criticism; that was only to come, like the concept of 'the Bible designed to be read as literature', in the decadence of the English religious tradition. In Alexander Whyte's *Bunyan Characters* (4 vols, Edinburgh, 1893) and John Kelman's *The Road: A Study of John Bunyan's Pilgrim's Progress* (Edinburgh and London, 1912) it may be seen how a devotional purpose could be combined with an understanding of the method of Bunyan's moral portraiture and his skill in building a scene. T. R. Glover's essay in his *Poets and Puritans*, from which extracts are here reproduced, profits from the inward sympathy of a fellow Nonconformist, supplementing the scholarly awareness of Bunyan's comparative status in the European literary tradition.

It was the Romantic age which first afforded special consideration to Bunyan as an imaginative writer and to *The Pilgrim's Progress* as a work of art. Bunyan's book seemed admirably fitted to demonstrate the romantic preference for the naïve and spontaneous over the studied and artificial (as in Schiller's

famous distinction between naïve and sentimental poetry). And
Bunyan's resolute and simple character seemed equally suitable
for the role of the hero as man of letters, alongside Burns and
the antique bards and ballad-singers (it may be surmised that it
was only his reaction against Calvinist orthodoxy that prevented
Carlyle from placing Bunyan in this category of hero beside
Rousseau and Burns in *Heroes and Hero-Worship*). The new
interest in Bunyan on the part of the educated public was con-
solidated by Southey's edition of 1830. The edition elicited
notable review-essays by Scott and Macaulay. The view of
Bunyan as a tinker-genius was reinforced by Whig ideology : he
was also an heroic individual citizen who had obeyed his conscience and resisted arbitrary power by going to prison and becoming a martyr for the toleration that was to be achieved after
the overthrow of the Stuarts. Two widely separated poles of the
nineteenth-century appreciation of the allegory may be seen in
two of the numerous illustrations of the period : John Martin's
nightmarish mezzotint of Christian going through the Valley of
the Shadow of Death (in Southey's edition) and Cruikshank's
bustling, crowded drawing of Vanity Fair (in an edition of
1838).

Following on the fashion of German scholarship there were
during the nineteenth century a number of inquiries into the
probable sources of *The Pilgrim's Progress*. The older literary
snobbery died hard and it appears to have been felt that an out-
standing work must have been in debt to educated writers.
Spenser and Guillaume De Guileville's *Le Pèlerinage de l'homme*
were strong candidates. This sort of investigation culminated in
the exhaustive work of J. B. Wharey, *The Sources of Bunyan's
Allegories* (Baltimore, 1904). Such an approach has come to be
seen as unsatisfactory, because even if it could be proved that
Bunyan had read the first book of *The Faerie Queene* and
remembered it when he wrote the episode of Christian's fight
with Apollyon, this leaves out of account the far more important
and less measurable influence of sermons heard every Sunday in
the year, oral folk-tales, and the particular tropes and rhetoric of
that improving discourse which was always going on in a godly
household or when the elders of a church like the meeting at

Bedford visited a sick, lapsed, or perplexed member. The static episodes of talk and exhortation in *The Pilgrim's Progress* may for us suspend the drama and go on too long, but they bring us to the bedrock of Protestant life before the Enlightenment, continuous searching of the Word and discourse about it.

Critical attention to Bunyan has increased in the twentieth century, especially since the last war; it is still far out of proportion to the importance of his masterpiece : one would expect the bibliography of Milton far to exceed that of Bunyan, the learned against the unbookish, but when the number of articles and books on Marvell and Rochester exceeds that on Bunyan one is made aware of a curious aberration in contemporary academic taste.

Modern critics have been able to look beyond the romantic concept of the natural, uneducated genius. *The Pilgrim's Progress* has been studied in relation to the background of English popular Puritanism, and literary interpretation has been aided by the new materials provided by the social and ecclesiastical historians. William York Tindall was a pioneer of this approach in his *John Bunyan, Mechanick Preacher* (New York, 1934); in that work Bunyan is studied as one sectarian lay preacher among others with the same message and the same prejudices. Unfortunately Tindall writes like an india-paper Voltaire and depicts Bunyan as a kind of religious huckster. There have always been readers for whom Bunyan's uncompromising strength, in speech and tone, bespoke coarseness and insensitivity. The essay in this collection by Robert Bridges gives a reasoned balance of the appreciative and the critical; Alfred Noyes's strident attack on the bad taste of *The Pilgrim's Progress* in his *The Opalescent Parrot* (London, 1929) seemed less worthy of preservation.

Sir Charles Firth, the historian of the Commonwealth and Protectorate, anticipates much of the best in more modern criticism in his long and informed essay originally written as an introduction to the work (1898) and later included in his *Essays Historical and Literary* (Oxford, 1936). Henri A. Talon's *John Bunyan, l'homme et l'œuvre* (Paris, 1948; translated into English by Barbara Wall, London, 1951) attempts to trace the 'inner biography' of Bunyan the visionary and makes illuminating comparisons with continental mystical writers in the Catholic tradition. In my own work, mainly *John Bunyan* (London, 1954, 1968) and the short study of *The Pilgrim's Progress* (London, 1966) I have tried to do justice both to the peculiar psychological pressures on Bunyan's genius, the prisoner driven to self-examination and then to self-projection, and to the manner in which *The Pilgrim's Progress* speaks for the Puritan tradition and echoes the structure of Puritan theology.

There are finely-written general essays by C. S. Lewis and F. R. Leavis, on the visionary and moral qualities of the work respectively; the latter is concerned with defining the particular quality of seriousness in Bunyan, what Leavis terms his 'resoluteness'.

Many writers have discussed the psychopathology of Bunyan's early terrors in relation to his writing, among them William James in his *Varieties of Religious Experience* (New York, 1902). A recent example of this approach, which is however by no means confined to psychological analysis, is a sympathetic book by an Anglican, Monica Furlong's *Puritan's Progress: A Study of John Bunyan* (London, 1975).

Much of recent criticism has endeavoured to analyse the narrative art of *The Pilgrim's Progress* in terms of the problems and contradictions of Calvinist belief and of Bunyan's evangelical purpose. Such an attempt is U. M. Kaufmann, *The Pilgrim's Progress and Traditions in Puritan Meditation* (New Haven, Conn., 1966). There is an even more subtle discussion of the narrative mode of the work in S. E. Fish, *Self-Consuming Artifacts* (Berkeley and Los Angeles, 1972) : there is a summary of his argument at the beginning of the article by John R. Knott, which concludes this collection.

There is still no modern edition of Bunyan's complete works. The gap will be filled by the Oxford edition of *The Miscellaneous Works of John Bunyan*, under the editorship of Roger Sharrock and others. Separate critical editions of *The Life and Death of Mr Badman* and *The Holy War* are in preparation under the collaborative editorship of Roger Sharrock and James F. Forrest. It is to be hoped that when all this material is available it may assist the critical understanding of *The Pilgrim's Progress*.

There are two sorts of critical evidence which this book has not been able to draw upon, but which should not be overlooked by the reader. One is the illustrations, a varied and interesting field from the crude woodcuts of the early editions onwards. The other type of evidence is provided by imaginative works which owe something to the inspiration of Bunyan's work and character. One might single out Browning's poem 'Ned Bratts' in his *Dramatic Idyls*, First Series (1879), and Hawthorne's story *The Celestial Railroad* (1843; collected in *Mosses from an Old Manse*, 1846), where he satirises the Transcendentalists and reformers of mid-nineteenth-century New England.

ROGER SHARROCK

NOTE

1. Quotations are taken from the Penguin English Texts edition of *The Pilgrim's Progress*, ed. Roger Sharrock (Harmondsworth, 1965).

BIOGRAPHICAL NOTE OF 1768

[The authorship is anonymous, but William Oldys has been conjectured as the probable author. – Ed.]

BUNYAN (JOHN), the celebrated author of the *Pilgrim's Progress*, was born at Elstow, within a mile of Bedford, in the year 1628. His extraction was very mean, his father being a tinker. His parents gave him an education suitable to their condition, bringing him up to write and read; but his natural disposition led him to all manner of wickedness, particularly cursing and swearing; in which course of iniquity he continued, not without some extraordinary checks, 'till thro' a gradual progress in the reformation of his life, he arrived at an high degree of that saintship, which prevailed in those times of enthusiasm. He became a soldier in the Parliament's army, and, in 1645, was present at the siege of Leicester; where being drawn to stand centinel, and another soldier of his company desiring to take his place, he consented, and thereby probably escaped being shot through the head with a musket ball, which took off his comrade. About the year 1655, he was admitted a member of a Baptist congregation at Bedford; and being soon after convicted at the sessions of holding unlawful assemblies and conventicles, he was sentenced to perpetual banishment, and committed to prison; where, though that sentence was never executed upon him, he was confined twelve years and a half. In the last year of his imprisonment, the Pastor of the congregation at Bedford dying, he was unanimously chosen to supply his place, the twelfth of December 1671. He was indebted to the compassion and interest of Dr Barlow, Bishop of Lincoln, for his enlargement; after which he travelled into several parts of England, to visit and confirm the brethren, which procured him the epithet of Bishop Bunyan. In King James IId's reign, when that Prince's declaration for liberty of conscience came abroad, Mr Bunyan, by the voluntary contributions of his followers, built a publick meeting-house at Bedford, and preached constantly to large congregations. He likewise frequently came to London, and

visited the congregations of Nonconformists there. He died in
London of a fever, the thirty-first of August 1688, aged 60, and
was buried in the new burying-place near the Artillery-Ground.
He had, by his wife Elizabeth, four children; one of whom,
named Mary, was blind; his wife did not long survive him, but
died in 1692. We shall give his character in the words of the
Continuator of his Life :

He appeared in countenance to be of a stern and rough temper; but
in his conversation mild and affable; not given to loquacity, or
much discourse in company, unless some urgent occasion required it;
observing never to boast of himself or his parts; but rather seem
low in his own eyes, and submit himself to the judgment of others;
abhorring lying and swearing; being just in all that lay in his
power to his word; not seeming to revenge injuries, loving to reconcile
differences, and making friendship with all : he had a sharp quick
eye; accomplished with an excellent discerning of persons, being of
good judgment and quick wit. As for his person, he was tall of
stature; strong-boned, tho' not corpulent; somewhat of a ruddy
face, with sparkling eyes; wearing his hair on his upper lip, after
the old British fashion; his hair reddish, but in his latter days time
had sprinkled it with grey; his nose was well set, but not declining
or bending, and his mouth moderate large; his forehead something
high, and his habit always plain and modest.

His works are collected together in two volumes in folio, London
1736, 1737.

PART ONE

Contemporary Prefaces

BUNYAN'S PREFATORY VERSES TO THE FIRST PART

The Author's APOLOGY
For His Book

When at the first I took my Pen in hand,
Thus for to write; I did not understand
That I at all should make a little Book
In such a mode; Nay, I had undertook
To make another, which when almost done,
Before I was aware, I this began.

    And thus it was : I writing of the Way
And Race of Saints in this our Gospel-Day,
Fell suddenly into an Allegory
About their Journey, and the way to Glory,
In more than twenty things, which I set down;
This done, I twenty more had in my Crown,
And they again began to multiply,
Like sparks that from the coals of Fire do flie.
Nay then, thought I, if that you breed so fast,
I'll put you by your selves, lest you at last
Should prove *ad infinitum*, and eat out
The Book that I already am about.

    Well, so I did; but yet I did not think
To shew to all the World my Pen and Ink
In such a mode; I only thought to make
I knew not what : nor did I undertake
Thereby to please my Neighbour; no not I,
I did it mine own self to gratifie.

    Neither did I but vacant seasons spend
In this my Scribble; Nor did I intend
But to divert my self in doing this,
From worser thoughts, which make me do amiss.

    Thus I set Pen to Paper with delight,
And quickly had my thoughts in black and white.

For having now my Method by the end;
Still as I pull'd, it came; and so I penn'd
It down, until it came at last to be
For length and breadth the bigness which you see.

Well, when I had thus put mine ends together,
I shew'd them others, that I might see whether
They would condemn them, or them justifie :
And some said, let them live; some, let them die :
Some said, *John*, print it; others said, Not so :
Some said, It might do good; others said, No.

Now was I in a straight, and did not see
Which was the best thing to be done by me :
At last I thought, Since you are thus divided,
I print it will, and so the case decided.

For, thought I; Some I see would have it done,
Though others in that Channel do not run;
To prove then who advised for the best,
Thus I thought fit to put it to the test.

I further thought, if now I did deny
Those that would have it thus, to gratifie,
I did not know, but hinder them I might,
Of that which would to them be great delight.

For those that were not for its coming forth;
I said to them, Offend you I am loth;
Yet since your Brethren pleased with it be,
Forbear to judge, till you do further see.

If that thou wilt not read, let it alone;
Some love the meat, some love to pick the bone :
Yea, that I might them better palliate,
I did too with them thus Expostulate.

May I not write in such a stile as this?
In such a method too, and yet not miss
Mine end, thy good? why may it not be done?
Dark Clouds bring Waters, when the bright bring none;
Yea, dark, or bright, if they their silver drops
Cause to descend, the Earth, by yielding Crops,
Gives praise to both, and carpeth not at either,
But treasures up the Fruit they yield together :

Yea, so commixes both, that in her Fruit
None can distinguish this from that, they suit
Her well, when hungry : but if she be full,
She spues out both, and makes their blessings null.

You see the ways the Fisher-man doth take
To catch the Fish; what Engins doth he make?
Behold ! how he ingageth all his Wits;
Also his Snares, Lines, Angles, Hooks and Nets :
Yet Fish there be, that neither Hook, nor Line,
Nor Snare, nor Nct, nor Engin can make thine;
They must be grop'd for, and be tickled too,
Or they will not be catcht, what e're you do.

How doth the Fowler seek to catch his Game,
By divers means, all which one cannot name?
His Gun, his Nets, his Lime-twigs, light and bell :
He creeps, he goes, he stands; yea, who can tell
Of all his postures? Yct there's none of these
Will make him master of what Fowls he please.
Yea, he must Pipe, and Whistle to catch *this*;
Yet if he does so, *that* Bird he will miss.

If that a Pearl may in a Toads-hcad dwell,
And may be found too in an Oister-shell;
If things that promise nothing, do contain
What better is then Gold; who will disdain,
(That have an inkling of it,) there to look,
That they may find it? Now my little Book,
(Tho void of all those paintings that may make
It with this or the other man to take,)
Is not without those things that do excel,
What do in brave, but empty notions dwell.

Well, yet I am not fully satisfied,
That this your Book will stand, when soundly try'd.
Why, what's the matter? *It is dark*, what tho?
But it is feigned, what of that I tro?
Some men by feigning words as dark as mine,
Make truth to spangle, and its rayes to shine.

But they want solidness. Speak man thy mind :
They drown'd the weak; Metaphors make us blind.

Solidity, indeed becomes the Pen
Of him that writeth things Divine to men :
But must I needs want solidness, because
By Metaphors I speak; was not Gods Laws,
His Gospel-laws in olden time held forth
By Types, Shadows and Metaphors? Yet loth
Will any sober man be to find fault
With them, lest he be found for to assault
The highest Wisdom. No, he rather stoops,
And seeks to find out what by pins and loops,
By Calves, and Sheep; by Heifers, and by Rams;
By Birds and Herbs, and by the blood of Lambs;
God speaketh to him : And happy is he
That finds the light, and grace that in them be.

Be not too forward therefore to conclude,
That I want solidness; that I am rude :
All things solid in shew, not solid be;
All things in parables despise not we,
Lest things most hurtful lightly we receive;
And things that good are, of our souls bereave.

My dark and cloudy words they do but hold
The Truth, as Cabinets inclose the Gold.

The Prophets used much by Metaphors
To set forth Truth; Yea, who so considers
Christ, his Apostles too, shall plainly see,
That Truths to this day in such Mantles be.

Am I afraid to say that holy Writ,
Which for its Stile, and Phrase, puts down all Wit,
Is every where so full of all these things,
(Dark Figures, Allegories,) yet there springs
From that same Book that lustre, and those rayes
Of light, that turns our darkest nights to days.

Come, let my Carper, to his Life now look,
And find There darker Lines, then in my Book
He findeth any. Yea, and let him know,
That in his best things there are worse lines too.

May we but stand before impartial men,
To his poor One, I durst adventure Ten,

That they will take my meaning in these lines
Far better then his lies in Silver Shrines.
Come, Truth, although in Swadling-clouts, I find
Informs the Judgement, rectifies the Mind,
Pleases the Understanding, makes the Will
Submit : the Memory too it doth fill
With what doth our Imagination please;
Likewise, it tends our troubles to appease.

    Sound words I know *Timothy* is to use;
And old Wives Fables he is to refuse,
But yet grave *Paul* him no where doth forbid
The use of Parables; in which lay hid
That Gold, those Pearls, and precious stones that were
Worth digging for; and that with greatest care.

    Let me add one word more, O Man of God !
Art thou offended ? doth thou wish I had
Put forth my matter in another dress,
Or that I had in things been more express?
Three things let me propound, then I submit
To those that are my betters, (as is fit.)

    1. I find not that I am denied the use
Of this my method, so I no abuse
Put on the Words, Things, Readers, or be rude
In handling Figure, or Similitude,
In application; but, all that I may,
Seek the advance of Truth, this or that way :
Denyed did I say ? Nay, I have leave,
(Examples too, and that from them that have
God better pleased by their words or ways,
Then any Man that breatheth now adays,)
Thus to express my mind, thus to declare
Things unto thee that excellentest are.

    2. I find that men (as high as Trees) will write
Dialogue-wise; yet no Man doth them slight
For writing so : Indeed if they abuse
Truth, cursed be they, and the craft they use
To that intent; but yet let Truth be free
To make her Salleys upon Thee, and Me,

Which way it pleases God. For who knows how,
Better then he that taught us first to Plow,
To guide our Mind and Pens for his Design?
And he makes base things usher in Divine.

   3. I find that holy Writ in many places,
Hath semblance with this method, where the cases
Doth call for one thing to set forth another :
Use it I may then, and yet nothing smother
Truths golden Beams; Nay, by this method may
Make it cast forth its rayes as light as day.

   And now, before I do put up my Pen,
I'le shew the profit of my Book, and then
Commit both thee, and it unto that hand
That pulls the strong down, and makes weak ones stand.

   This Book it chaulketh out before thine eyes,
The man that seeks the everlasting Prize :
It shews you whence he comes, whither he goes,
What he leaves undone; also what he does :
It also shews you how he runs, and runs,
Till he unto the Gate of Glory comes.

   It shews too, who sets out for life amain,
As if the lasting Crown they would attain :
Here also you may see the reason why
They loose their labour, and like fools do die.

   This Book will make a Travailer of thee,
If by its Counsel thou wilt ruled be;
It will direct thee to the Holy Land,
If thou wilt its Directions understand :
Yea, it will make the sloathful, active be;
The Blind also, delightful things to see.

   Art thou for something rare, and profitable?
Wouldest thou see a Truth within a Fable?
Art thou forgetful? wouldest thou remember
From *New-years-day* to the last of *December*?
Then read my fancies, they will stick like Burs,
And may be to the Helpless, Comforters.

   This Book is writ in such a Dialect,
As may the minds of listless men affect :

It seems a Novelty, and yet contains
Nothing but sound and honest Gospel-strains.
  Wouldst thou divert thy self from Melancholly?
Would'st thou be pleasant, yet be far from folly?
Would'st thou read Riddles, and their Explanation,
Or else be drownded in thy Contemplation?
Dost thou love picking-meat? or would'st thou see
A man i' th Clouds, and hear him speak to thee?
Would'st thou be in a Dream, and yet not sleep?
Or would'st thou in a moment Laugh and Weep?
Wouldest thou loose thy self, and catch no harm?
And find thy self again without a charm?
Would'st read thy self, and read thou know'st not what
And yet know whether thou art blest or not,
By reading the same lines? O then come hither,
And lay my Book, thy Head and Heart together.

JOHN BUNYAN

SOURCE: John Bunyan, *The Pilgrim's Progress*, ed. J. B. Wharey, rev. Roger Sharrock (2nd ed., 1968) pp. 1–7.

BUNYAN'S PREFATORY VERSES TO THE SECOND PART

Go, now my little Book, to every place,
Where my first *Pilgrim* has but shewn his Face,
Call at their door : If any say, *who's there?*
Then answer thou, *Christiana is here.*
If they bid the *come in*, then enter thou
With all thy boys. And then, as thou know'st how,
Tell who they are, also from whence they came,
Perhaps they'l know them, by their looks, or name :
But if they should not, ask them yet again
If formerly they did not Entertain
One *Christian* a Pilgrim; If they say
They did : And was delighted in his way :
Then let them know that those related were
Unto him : Yea, his Wife and Children are.
    Tell them that they have left their House and Home,
Are turned Pilgrims, seek a World to come :
That they *have* met with hardships in the way,
That they *do* meet with troubles night and Day;
That they have trod on Serpents, fought with Devils,
Have also overcome a many evils.
Yea tell them also of the rest, who have
Of love to *Pilgrimage* been stout and brave
Defenders of that way, and how they still
Refuse this World, to do their Fathers will.
    Go, tell them also of those dainty things,
That *Pilgrimage* unto the *Pilgrim* brings,

Let them acquainted be, too, how they are
Beloved of their King, under his care;
What goodly *Mansions* for them he Provides.
Tho they meet with rough Winds, and swelling Tides,
How brave a calm they will enjoy at last,
Who *to* their Lord, and *by* his ways hold fast.

    Perhaps with heart and hand they will imbrace
Thee, as they did my firstling, and will Grace
Thee, and thy fellows with such chear and fair,
As shew will, they of *Pilgrims* lovers are.

1   *Object*
But how if they will not believe of me
That I am truly thine,'cause some there be
That Counterfeit the Pilgrim, and his name,
Seek by disguise to seem the very same.
And by that means have wrought themselves into
The Hands and Houses of I know not who,

Answer
'Tis true, some have of late, to Counterfeit
My Pilgrim, to their own, my Title set;
Yea others, half my Name and Title too;
Have stitched to their Book, to make them do;
But yet they by their *Features* do declare
Themselves not mine to be, whose ere they are.

    If such thou meetst with, then thine only way
Before them all, is, *to say out thy say,*
In thine own native Language, which no man
Now useth, nor with ease dissemble can.

    If after all, they still of you shall doubt,
Thinking that you like *Gipsies* go about,
In naughty-wise the Countrey to defile,
Or that you seek good People to beguile
With things unwarrantable : Send for me
And I will Testifie, you *Pilgrims* be;
Yea, I will Testifie that only you
My *Pilgrims* are; And that alone will do.

2   *Object*
But yet, perhaps, I may enquire for him,
Of those that wish him Damned life and limb,
What shall I do, when I at such a door,
For Pilgrims *ask, and they shall rage the more*?

Answer
Fright not thy self my Book, for such *Bugbears*
Are nothing else but ground for groundless fears,
My *Pilgrims* Book has travel'd Sea and Land,
Yet could I never come to understand,
That it was slighted, or turn'd out of Door
By any Kingdom, were they Rich or Poor.
    In *France* and *Flanders* where men kill each other
My *Pilgrim* is esteem'd a Friend, a Brother.
    In *Holland* too, 'tis said, as I am told,
My *Pilgrim* is with some, worth more than Gold.
    Highlanders, and *Wild-Irish* can agree,
My *Pilgrim* should familiar with them be.
    'Tis in *New-England* under such advance,
Receives there so much loving Countenance,
As to be Trim'd, new Cloth'd & Deckt with Gems,
That it might shew its Features, and its Limbs,
Yet more; so comely doth my *Pilgrim* walk,
That of him thousands daily Sing and talk.
    If you draw nearer home, it will appear
My *Pilgrim* knows no ground of shame, or fear;
City, and Countrey will him Entertain,
With welcome *Pilgrim*. Yea, they can't refrain
From smiling, if my *Pilgrim* be but by,
Or shews his head in any Company.
    Brave Galants do my *Pilgrim* hug and love,
Esteem it much, yea value it above
Things of a greater bulk, yea, with delight,
Say my *Larks leg* is better than a *Kite*.
    Young Ladys, and young Gentle-women too,
Do no small kindness to my *Pilgrim* shew;

Their Cabinets, their Bosoms, and their Hearts
My *Pilgrim* has, 'cause he to them imparts
His pretty riddles in such wholsome straines
As yields them profit double to their paines
Of reading. Yea, I think I may be bold
To say some prize him far above their Gold.

The very Children that do walk the street,
If they do but my holy *Pilgrim* meet,
Salute him will, will wish him well and say,
He is the only *Stripling* of the Day.

They that have never seen him, yet admire
What they have heard of him, and much desire
To have his Company, and hear him tell
Those *Pilgrim* storyes which he knows so well.

Yea, some who did not love him at the first,
But cal'd him *Fool*, and *Noddy*, say they must
Now they have *seen & heard* him, him commend,
And to those whom they love, they do him send.

Wherefore my *Second Part*, thou needst not be
Afraid to shew thy Head : None can hurt thee,
That wish but well to him, that went before,
'Cause thou com'st with a Second store,
Of things as good, as rich, as profitable,
For Young, for Old, for Stag'ring and for stable.

3   Object
But some there be that say he laughs too loud;
And some do say his Head is in a Cloud.
Some say, his Words and Storys are so dark,
They know not how, by them, to find his mark.

Answer
One may (I think) say both his laughs & cryes,
May well be guest at by his watry Eyes.
Some things are of that Nature as to make
Ones fancie Checkle while his Heart doth ake,
When *Jacob* saw his *Rachel* with the Sheep,
He did at the same time both kiss and weep.

Whereas some say a Cloud is in his Head,
That doth but shew how Wisdom's covered
With its own mantles : And to stir the mind
To a search after what it fain would find,
Things that seem to be hid in words obscure,
Do but the Godly mind the more alure;
To study what those Sayings should contain,
That speak to us in such a Cloudy strain.

    I also know, a dark Similitude
Will on the Fancie more it self intrude,
And will stick faster in the Heart and Head,
Then things from Similies not borrowed.

    Wherefore, my Book, let no discouragement
Hinder thy travels. Behold, thou art sent
To Friends, not foes : to Friends that will give place
To thee, thy *Pilgrims*, and thy words imbrace.

    Besides, what my first *Pilgrim* left conceal'd,
Thou my brave *Second Pilgrim* hast reveal'd;
What *Christian* left lock't up and went his way,
Sweet *Christiana* opens with her Key.

4   *Object*

But some love not the method of your first,
Romance they count it, throw't away as dust,
If I should meet with such, what should I say?
Must I slight them as they slight me, or nay?

Answer

My *Christiana*, if with such thou meet,
By all means in all Loving-wise, them greet;
Render them not reviling for revile :
But if they frown, I prethee on them smile.
Perhaps 'tis Nature, or some ill report
Has made them *thus* dispise, or *thus* retort.

    Some love no Cheese, some love no Fish, & some
Love not their Friends, nor their own House or home;
Some start at Pigg, slight Chicken, love not Fowl,
More then they love a Cuckoo or an Owl.

Leave such, my *Christiana*, to their choice,
And seek those, who to find thee will rejoyce;
By no means strive, but in all humble wise,
Present thee to them in thy *Pilgrims* guise.

Go then, my little Book and shew to all
That entertain, and bid thee welcome shall,
What thou shalt keep close, shut up from the rest,
And wish what thou shalt shew them may be blest
To them for good, may make them chuse to be
Pilgrims, better by far, then thee or me.

Go then, I say, tell all men who thou art,
Say, I am *Christiana*, and my part
Is now with my four Sons, to tell you what
It is for men to take a *Pilgrims* lot.

Go also tell them *who*, and what they be,
That now do go on *Pilgrimage* with thee;
Say, here's my neighbour Mercy, she is one,
That has long-time with me a *Pilgrim* gone :
Come see her in her *Virgin* Face, and learn
Twixt Idle ones, and *Pilgrims* to discern.
Yea let young Damsels learn of her to prize
The World which is to come, in any wise;
When little *Tripping* Maidens follow God,
And leave old doting Sinners to his Rod;
'Tis like those Days wherein the young ones cri'd
Hosanah to whom old ones did deride.

Next tell them of old *Honest*, who you found
With his white hairs treading the Pilgrims ground,
Yea, tell them how plain hearted *this* man was,
How after his good Lord he bare his Cross :
Perhaps with some gray Head this may prevail,
With Christ to fall in Love, and Sin bewail.

Tell them also how Master *Fearing* went
On Pilgrimage, and how the time he spent
In Solitariness, with Fears and Cries,
And how at last, he won the Joyful Prize.
He *was* a good man, though much down in Spirit,
He *is* a good Man, and doth Life inherit.

Tell them of Master *Feeblemind* also,
Who, not before, but still behind would go;
Show them also how he had like been slain,
And how one *Great-Heart* did his life regain :
This man was true of Heart, tho weak in grace,
One might true Godliness read in his Face.

Then tell them of Master *Ready-to-halt*,
A Man with Crutches, but much without fault :
Tell them how Master *Feeblemind*, and he
Did love, and in *Opinions* much agree.
And let all know, tho weakness was their chance,
Yet sometimes one could *Sing*, the other *Dance*.

Forget not Master *Valiant-for-the-Truth*,
That Man of courage, tho a very Youth.
Tell every one his Spirit was so stout,
No Man could ever make him face about,
And how *Great-Heart*, & he could not forbear
But put down Doubting Castle, slay Despair.

Overlook not Master *Despondancie*.
Nor *Much-a-fraid*, his Daughter, tho they ly
Under such Mantles as may make them look
(With some) as if their God had them forsook.
They softly went, but sure, and at the end,
Found that the Lord of *Pilgrims* was their Friend.
When thou hast told the World of all these things,
Then turn about, my book, and touch these strings,
Which, if but touched will such Musick make,
They'l make a Cripple dance, a Gyant quake.
Those Riddles that lie couch't within thy breast,
Freely propound, expound : and for the rest
Of thy misterious lines, let them remain,
For those whose nimble Fancies shall them gain.

Now may this little Book a blessing be,
To those that love this little Book and me,
And may its buyer have no cause to say,
His Money is but lost or thrown away.
Yea may this Second *Pilgrim* yield that Fruit,
As may with each good *Pilgrims* fancie sute,

And may it perswade some that go astray,
To turn their Foot and Heart to the right way.

Is the Hearty Prayer of the Author
J·OHN BUNYAN

SOURCE: John Bunyan, *The Pilgrim's Progress,* ed. J. B. Wharey, rev. Roger Sharrock (2nd ed., 1968) pp. 167–73.

PREFACE TO THE FRENCH TRANSLATION OF 1685

Dear Reader,

It is not our desire to offer a long and carefully prepared preamble to this translation of a recent work; we would rather present it to you directly so that you can test by your own experience what is being provided for your Christian contemplation and judgment.

The author is *John Bunyan*, still a good and faithful minister in the English town of *Bedford*; a man of a singularly holy and devoted life, who like that *Demetrius* of whom *St John* speaks (3 *John* 12) hath a good report of all men : in this little book, no less than in his other writings, (which are numerous and among which many shew forth the like character as this one) he displays a singular wisdom, a wide experience of the soul, and a deep understanding of spiritual things.

The aim of our Author is simply to take the case of a penitent soul who is seeking God as he journeys towards Eternity. We learn how he turns away from evil and destruction, his former state, leaves his father's house, and directs his face and his steps towards the new *Jerusalem* that stands on high, what he meets on his journey, and how he finally accomplishes his pilgrimage, says farewell to the world, and arrives safely on the hither side of death among the joys of eternity. And at the same time the book deals also with some of the divergencies from the proper route, and with many of those persons who travel in a different fashion, who seek their own road which is no good one, and how they finally discover that their steps lead them down into hell, and that none of the pleasures they have found can preserve them from death.

We have no doubt that among those who turn the pages of this book in a pious frame, there will be some who will recognise themselves in some places, their hearts' fashion painted true like a portrait before their eyes, as they behold their own conduct in the carriage of another. Here a true citizen of *Sion* who has governed his heart to seek after the God of his fathers, is limned cunningly and to the life in the character of a wayfaring *Christian* with his companions *Faithful* and *Hopeful*; here are revealed the very motion and condition of his soul as he once knew them in his inward man when the Eternal One revealed himself to him for the first time, convinced him of his sins and miserable condition, and led him to Christ, laying his hand upon him to separate him from the world; here we see a number of his meetings with other characters, and God's manner of proceeding both to comfort and correct him; we see how he conducts himself towards those in his presence and also towards those who are invisible and hidden from his eyes. Alas, if a worldly man, a hypocrite, a soul without grace, could only have the eyes of his understanding sufficiently opened, how often would he not behold himself here under another name? how often would he not behold here the destruction of those foolish imaginings which he had conceived by studying the desires of his own heart for the ground of his salvation! They would see their hopes and all their efforts brushed away like a spider's web.

If any one thinks that the style and manner of presentation are not sufficiently serious or fitting for such sacred matters as are here represented under various figures and in the form of a dream, let him know that the author, having applied himself to this manner of writing, found himself from the beginning, against his original intention, strongly pressed to the point of persuasion by several persons of good judgment and sincere conscience, until finally he allowed the book to be printed and published, as an offering destined to win souls, cast into the world so that perhaps some soul might be moved and won by this pious fraud and added to Christ's flock.

We live in an age of refinement when things have to be subtly rendered in order to appeal to public taste. Our Bunyan treats his subject in the manner of an allegory so that divine truths may penetrate to the inmost heart. It might have appeared necessary to defend this agreeable, edifying, and succinct mode of exposition, if several theologians and spokesmen of God's people had not already set out grave and lofty truths in a figurative way, following in the footsteps of the great and sovereign doctor Jesus, who so often opened his mouth in parables, and never addressed his disciples without them, as likewise did his servants the Prophets. Now we believe that the Reader should take particular care of those things which are here presented under an allegory, and of the allegorical figures themselves, always to the extent that they express the intention of the writer.

Oh that the Reader may find himself a true Citizen of *Sion* and a *Christian* who has set his foot on the Royal Road, that he may be strengthened, comforted and instructed; may he find himself a lost sheep who can be brought back from false ways and set on the paths of peace to follow in the steps of Jesus' flock; may he be stirred by the loving-kindness of King Jesus, Lord of the Hill of incense, to take him by the hem of his raiment and say, We wish to go with thee. There is always provision in the book for such effects, if it is read with like appetite by Flemish people as would match the regard in which the English hold it, for among them it has been reprinted several times; and that might encourage the Translator to translate another treatise by this author, a second part describing the whole sinful career of a reprobate person, from his childhood through his whole life and conduct to his death, under the title of *The Life and Death of Badman in the Form of Dialogue.*

May God who has the power to raise you up and grant you the inheritance of the saints in splendour, place us among his heirs and set us upon his right hand, after he shall have guided us by his Spirit and counsel finally into his Glory.

SOURCE: Preface (unpaginated) to *Voyage d'un Chrestien vers l'Eternité. Ecrit en Anglois, par Monsieur Bunjon, F.M. en Bedtfort; Et nouvellement traduit en François. Avec Figures. à Amsterdam, Chez Jean Boekholt, Libraire près de la Bourse. 1685. Avec Privilège* [translated by the editor].

PART TWO

Eighteenth- and Nineteenth-century Opinion and Criticism

1. SHORT CRITICAL COMMENT

JOHN GAY (1715)

[A condemned man is offered a prayer book and, urged to make use of it, he cries out :]

> I will! I will!
> Lend me thy handkercher. 'The pilgrim's pro – ' [reads and
> weeps]
>
> (I cannot see for tears) *'pro-progress'* : Oh!
> *'The Pilgrim's Progress, eight edi-ti-on:*
> *Lon-don print-ed – for – Ni-cho-las Bod-ding-ton:*
> *With new ad-di-tions never made before'*:
> – Oh! 'tis so moving, I can read no more.   [drops the book]

SOURCE: John Gay, *The What-d'ye-call-it: A Tragi-Comi-Pastoral Farce* (1715) Act II, scene I. (Boddington's name first appeared on the title-page of the eighth edition, but the reference may be to the eighth edition of the Second Part.)

ANONYMOUS (1741)

I will add to these [*Hudibras* and *A Tale of a Tub*] an Original of an opposite Kind, the *Pilgrim's Progress* of honest *John Bunyan*, a Man, who, if he wanted Learning, wanted likewise any sort of Art or Fraud, and whose Expression, if it be homely, is at the same time so just and natural, and so exactly of a Piece with the Structure of his Tale, that, take it all together, there never was an Allegory better designed, or better supported. The Wits may perhaps take Offence at the Respect I pay to this

Religious Romance; but if we consider the universal good
Reception it hath met with both at home and abroad, we must
either allow that it has Merit, or that ourselves and our neighbours are void of Penetration and true Judgment. Besides, this is
not the only Book of its Kind; there have been many others published with the same view, tho' not in the same manner, which,
though written by learned and judicious Men, have yet met with
an indifferent Reception, compared with that afforded to the
Pilgrim's Progress of *Bunyan*. He hath, therefore, according to
the Rules, a Right to Fame. . . . Sense is Sense in all Languages.

SOURCE: *The Gentleman's Magazine* (1741) p. 488.

DAVID HUME (1757)

But though this axiom [that beauties exist in the mind which
contemplates them] by passing into a proverb, seems to have
attained the sanction of common sense; there is certainly
a species of common sense which opposes it, at least serves to
modify and restrain it. Whoever would assert an equality
of genius and eloquence between OGILBY and MILTON, or
BUNYAN and ADDISON, would be thought to defend no less an
extravagance, than if he had maintained a mole-hill to be as high
as TENERIFFE, or a pond as extensive as the ocean.

SOURCE: 'Of the Standard of Taste', originally published
in *Four Dissertations* (1757); here quoted from 2 vol. ed. of
1800, vol. I, p. 245.

ANONYMOUS (1765)

The late Mr. James Foster used to say that not one of the
characters in the *Pilgrim's Progress* talked sense except Ignorance, whom the author has conducted the back way to hell. As

a work of imagination, however, illustrating a particular set of religious principles, the *Pilgrim's Progress* is certainly a work of original and uncommon genius. . . . In a word, it contains a most excellent epitome and illustration of the *Calvinistic* divinity, under an allegory highly entertaining and affecting.

SOURCE: Review of *Some Account of the Imprisonment of Mr. John Bunyan*, in *The Gentleman's Magazine* (1765) p. 168.

SAMUEL JOHNSON (1773)

Johnson praised John Bunyan highly. 'His *Pilgrim's Progress* has great merit, both for invention, imagination, and the conduct of the story; and it has had the best evidence of its merit, the general and continued approbation of mankind. Few books, I believe, have had a more extensive sale. It is remarkable, that it begins very much like the poem of Dante; yet there was no translation of Dante when Bunyan wrote. There is reason to think that he had read Spenser.'

SOURCE: James Boswell, *The Life of Samuel Johnson, LL.D.* (1791), ed. R. W. Chapman (Oxford, 1953) p. 529. (Boswell recorded the remark on Friday 30 April 1773.)

WILLIAM COWPER (1784)

O thou, whom borne on *Fancy*'s eager wing,
Back to the season of life's happy spring,
I pleased remember, and while *Memory* yet
Holds fast her office here, can ne'er forget;
Ingenious dreamer, in whose well-told tale
Sweet fiction and sweet truth alike prevail;

Whose humorous vein, strong sense, and simple style
May teach the gayest, make the gravest smile;
Witty, and well employ'd, and like thy Lord,
Speaking in parables his slighted Word;
I name thee not, lest so despised a name
Should move a sneer at thy deserved fame,
Yet e'en in transitory life's late day,
That mingles all my brown with sober gray,
Revere the man whose PILGRIM marks the road,
And guides the PROGRESS of the soul to God.

SOURCE: *Tirocinium, or, a Review of Schools* (1784) lines
131–46.

GEORGE CRABBE (1826)

Caroline, now six years old, reads incessantly and insatiably. She
has been travelling with John Bunyan's 'Pilgrim', and enjoying
a pleasure never, perhaps, to be repeated. The veil of religious
mystery, that so beautifully covers the outward and visible
adventures, is quite enchanting. The dear child was caught reading by her sleeping maid at five o'clock this morning, impatient
– 'tis our nature – to end her pleasure.

SOURCE: Letter to Mary Leadbeater (1826) in *The Life of
George Crabbe, by his Son* (Oxford, 1932) p. 278.

S. T. COLERIDGE (1830)

I

. . . in that admirable Allegory, the first Part of the Pilgrim's
Progress, which delights every one, the interest is so great that in
spite of all the writer's attempts to force the allegoric purpose on

the Reader's mind by his strange names – Old Stupidity of the Town of Honesty, &c. &c. – his piety was baffled by his genius, and the Bunyan of Parnassus had the better of the Bunyan of the Conventicle – and with the same illusion as we read any tale known to be fictitious, as a novel, – we go on with the characters as real persons, who had been nicknamed by their neighbours.

The Pilgrim's Progress is composed in the lowest style of English, without slang or false grammar. If you were to polish it, you would at once destroy the reality of the vision. For works of imagination should be written in very plain language; the more purely imaginative they are the more necessary it is to be plain.

This wonderful work is one of the very few books which may be read over repeatedly at different times, and each time with a new and a different pleasure. I read it once as a theologian – and let me assure you that there is great theological acumen in the work – once with devotional feelings – and once as a poet. I could not have believed beforehand that Calvinism could be painted in such exquisitely delightful colours.

I know of no book, the Bible excepted, as above all comparison, which I, according to my judgment and experience, could so safely recommend as teaching and enforcing the whole saving truth according to the mind that was in Christ Jesus, as in the Pilgrim's Progress. It is, in my conviction, incomparably the best *Summa Theologiae Evangelicae* ever produced by a writer not miraculously inspired. June 14, 1830.

. . . I can find nothing homely in it but a few phrases and single words. The conversation between Faithful and Talkative is a model of unaffected dignity and rhythmical flow.

Source: *Coleridge on the Seventeenth Century*, ed. Roberta Florence Brinkley (Duke University Press, 1955) pp. 475–6.

II

Calvinism never put on a less rigid form, never smoothed its brow and softened its voice more winningly than in the Pilgrim's Progress.

> SOURCE: *Miscellaneous Criticism of S. T. Coleridge*, ed. T. M. Raysor (Cambridge, Mass., 1936) p. 326.

THOMAS ARNOLD (1836)

I hold John Bunyan to have been a man of incomparably greater genius than any of them [i.e. of the Anglican divines and theologians], and to have given a far truer and more edifying picture of Christianity. His Pilgrim's Progress seems to be a complete reflection of Scripture, with none of the rubbish of the theologians mixed up with it.

I cannot trust myself to read the account of Christian going up to the Celestial Gate, after his passage through the river of death. . . .

I have always been struck by [the work's] piety: I am now equally, or even more, by its profound wisdom.

> SOURCE: Letter to Mr Justice Coleridge, 30 November 1836, and passages from conversation, in *The Life and Correspondence of Thomas Arnold, D. D.*, by Arthur Penrhyn Stanley, D.D. (1877) vol. II, p. 57.

JOHN RUSKIN (1886)

I had Walter Scott's novels and the *Iliad* (Pope's translation), for constant reading when I was a child, on week-days: on Sunday their effect was tempered by *Robinson Crusoe* and the

Pilgrim's Progress; my mother having it deeply in her heart to make an evangelical clergyman of me. Fortunately, I had an aunt more evangelical than my mother, and my aunt gave me cold mutton for Sunday's dinner, which – as I much preferred it hot – greatly diminished the influence of the *Pilgrim's Progress*; and the end of the matter was, that I got all the noble imaginative teaching of Defoe and Bunyan, and yet – am not an evangelical clergyman.

S o u r c e : *Praeterita: Outlines of Scenes and Thoughts Perhaps Worthy of Memory in my Past Life* (1886) in *The Works of John Ruskin*, ed. E. T. Cook and Alexander Wedderburn, vol. xxxv (1908) p. 13.

2. CRITICAL STUDIES

Robert Southey (1830)

The rapidity with which . . . editions succeeded one another, and the demand for pictures to illustrate them, are not the only proofs of the popularity which the Pilgrim's Progress obtained, before the second part was published. In the verses prefixed to that part Bunyan complains of dishonest imitators.

> . . . some have of late to counterfeit
> My Pilgrim, to their own, my title set;
> Yea others, half my name, and title too,
> Have stitched to their books, to make them do.

Only one of these has fallen in my way, – for it is by accident only that books of this perishable kind, which have no merit of their own to preserve them, are to be met with : and this though entitled 'the Second part of the Pilgrim's Progress' has no other relation to the first than in it's title, which was probably a trick of the publishers. These interlopers may very likely have given Bunyan an additional inducement to prepare a second part himself. It appeared in 1684 with this notice on the back of the title page; 'I appoint Mr. Nathaniel Ponder, but no other to print this book, John Bunyan, January 1, 1684.' No additions or alterations were made in this part, though the author lived more than four years after its publication.

A collation of the first part with the earliest attainable copies has enabled me in many places to restore good old vernacular English which had been injudiciously altered, or carelessly corrupted. This has also been done in the second part; but there I had the first edition before me, and this it is evident had not been inspected either in manuscript or while passing through the press, by any person capable of correcting it. It is plain that Bunyan had willingly availed himself of such corrections in the first part; and therefore it would have been improper to have restored a certain vulgarism of diction in the second, which the Editor of the folio edition had amended. Had it not been for this consideration, I should perhaps have restored his own text. For Bunyan was confident in his own powers of expression; he says

> ... thine only way
> Before them all, is to say out thy say
> In thine own native language, which no man
> Now useth, nor with ease dissemble can.

And he might well be confident in it. His is a homespun style, not a manufactured one : and what a difference is there between its homeliness, and the flippant vulgarity of the Roger L'Estrange and Tom Brown school! If it is not a well of English undefiled to which the poet as well as the philologist must repair, if they would drink of the living waters, it is a clear stream of current English, – the vernacular speech of his age, sometimes indeed in its rusticity and coarseness, but always in its plainness and its strength. To this natural style Bunyan is in some degree beholden for his general popularity; – his language is every where level to the most ignorant reader, and to the meanest capacity : there is a homely reality about it; a nursery tale is not more intelligible, in it's manner of narration, to a child. Another cause of his popularity is, that he taxes the imagination as little as the understanding. The vividness of his own, which, as his history shows, sometimes could not distinguish ideal impressions from actual ones, occasioned this. He saw the things of which he was writing, as distinctly with his mind's eye as if they were indeed passing before him in a dream. And the reader perhaps sees them more satisfactorily to himself, because the outline only of the picture is presented to him, and the author having made no attempt to fill up the details every reader supplies them according to the measure and scope of his own intellectual and imaginative powers.

When Bunyan's success had raised a brood of imitators, he was accused of being an imitator himself. He replied to this charge in some of his most characteristic rhymes, which were prefixed to his Holy War, as an Advertisement to the Reader.

Some say the Pilgrim's Progress is not mine,
Insinuating as if I would shine
In name and fame by the worth of another,
Like some made rich by robbing of their brother.

Or that so fond I am of being Sire,
I'll father bastards; or if need require,
I'll tell a lye in print, to get applause.
I scorn it; John such dirt-heap never was
Since God converted him. Let this suffice
To shew why I my Pilgrim patronize.

It came from mine own heart, so to my head,
And thence into my fingers trickled;
Then to my pen, from whence immediately
On paper I did dribble it daintily.

Manner and matter too was all mine own;
Nor was it unto any mortal known,
Till I had done it. Nor did any then
By books, by wits, by tongues, or hand, or pen,
Add five words to it, or wrote half a line
Thereof : the whole and every whit is mine.

Also for *This* thine eye is now upon,
The matter in this manner came from none
But the same heart and head, fingers and pen
As did the other. Witness all good men,
For none in all the world without a lye,
Can say that 'this is mine', excepting I.

I wrote not this of any ostentation;
Nor 'cause I seek of men their commendation.
I do it to keep them from such surmize,
As tempt them will my name to scandalize.
Witness my name; if anagramm'd to thee
The letters make *Nu hony in a B*.

John Bunyan

SOURCE: 'Life of Bunyan', in *The Pilgrim's Progress*, ed.
Robert Southey (1830) pp. lxxxvi–xc.

Sir Walter Scott (1830)

The parable of *The Pilgrim's Progress* is, of course, tinged with the tenets of the author, who might be called a Calvinist in every respect, save his aversion to the institution of a regular and ordained clergy. To these tenets he has, of course, adapted the pilgrimage of Christian, in the incidents which occur, and opinions which are expressed. The final condemnation of Ignorance, for instance, who is consigned to the infernal regions when asking admittance to the celestial city, because unable to produce a certificate of his calling, conveys the same severe doctrine of fatalism which had well nigh overturned the reason of Bunyan himself. But the work is not of a controversial character, – it might be perused without offence by sober-minded Christians of all persuasions; and we all know that it is read universally, and has been translated into many languages. It, indeed, appears from many passages in Bunyan's writings, that there was nothing which he dreaded so much as divisions amongst sincere Christians.

Since you would know (he says) by what name I would be distinguished from others, I tell you, I would be, and hope I am, a *Christian;* and chuse if God should count me worthy, to be called *a Christian, a Believer,* or other such name which is approved by the Holy Ghost. And as for those factious titles of Anabaptists, Independents, Presbyterians, or the like, I conclude that they come neither from Jerusalem nor from Antioch, but rather from Hell and Babylon; for they naturally tend to divisions. You may know them by their fruits.

Mr. Southey, observing with what general accuracy this apostle of the people writes the English language, notwithstanding all the disadvantages under which his youth must have been passed, pauses to notice one gross and repeated error. 'The vulgarism alluded to', says the laureate, 'consists in the almost uniform use of *a* for *have*, – never marked as a contraction, e.g. might *a* made me take heed, – like to *a* been smothered.' Under favour, however, this is a sin against orthography rather than grammar : the tinker of Elstowe only spelt according to the pro-

nunciation of the verb *to have*, then common in his class; and
the same form appears a hundred times in Shakspeare. We
must not here omit to mention the skill with which Mr. Southey
has restored much of Bunyan's masculine and idiomatic English, which had been gradually dropped out of successive impressions by careless, or unfaithful, or what is as bad, conceited
correctors of the press.

The speedy popularity of *The Pilgrim's Progress* had the
natural effect of inducing Bunyan again to indulge the vein of
allegory in which his warm imagination and clear and forcible
expression had procured him such success. Under this impression, he produced the second part of his *Pilgrim's Progress*; and
well says Mr. Southey, that none but those who have acquired
the ill habit of always reading critically, can feel it as a clog upon
the first. The first part is, indeed, one of those delightfully
simple and captivating tales which, as soon as finished, we are not
unwilling to begin again. Even the adult becomes himself like the
child who cannot be satisfied with the repetition of a favourite
tale, but harasses the story-telling aunt or nurse, to know more
of the incidents and characters. In this respect Bunyan has contrived a contrast, which, far from exhausting his subject, opens
new sources of attraction, and adds to the original impression.
The pilgrimage of Christiana, her friend Mercy and her children,
commands sympathy at least as powerful as that of Christian
himself, and it materially adds to the interest which we have
taken in the progress of the husband, to trace the effects produced by similar events in the case of women and children.

'There is a pleasure,' says the learned editor, 'in travelling with
another companion the same ground – a pleasure of reminiscence,
neither inferior in kind or degree to that which is derived from a
first impression. The characters are judiciously marked : that of
Mercy, particularly, is sketched with an admirable grace and simplicity; nor do we read of any with equal interest, excepting that of
Ruth in Scripture, so beautifully, on all occasions, does the Mercy
of John Bunyan unfold modest humility regarding her own merits,
and tender veneration for the matron Christiana.'[1]

The distinctions between the first and second part of *The Pilgrim's Progress* are such as circumstances render appropriate;

and as John Bunyan's strong mother wit enabled him to seize upon correctly. Christian, for example, a man, and a bold one, is represented as enduring his fatigues, trials, and combats, by his own stout courage, under the blessing of heaven : but to express that species of inspired heroism by which women are supported in the path of duty, notwithstanding the natural feebleness and timidity of their nature, Christiana and Mercy obtain from the interpreter their guide, called Great-heart, by whose strength and valour their lack of both is supplied, and the dangers and distresses of the way repelled and overcome. . . .

Mr. Burder . . . remarks that Bunyan maintains his allegory by assigning to his characters such significant names as introduce them with singular propriety. This was a qualification in great request among the authors of fictitious composition, whether narrative or dramatic, in Charles the Second's days, and no doubt many artificers of plays and novels in our own time would be inclined to join Falstaff, though rather in a different sense, in his earnest wish that he knew where 'a commodity of good names was to be purchased'. A happily christened list of dramatis personæ is a key note for the easy introduction of the story, and saves the author the trouble of tagging his characters with descriptions, always somewhat awkward, of person and disposition. In some respects it answers the purpose which Texier was wont to achieve in another way. Those who remember, like ourselves, that distinguished reader of the French comedians (and such treats are not easily forgotten), cannot but recollect, that on first reading over the list of characters with the author's short description annexed, M. Texier assumed in each the voice and manner in which he intended to read the part, and so wonderful was his discrimination, that the most obtuse hearer had never afterwards the least difficulty in ascertaining who was speaking. A happy selection of names has somewhat the same effect in placing the characters who bear them before us in their original concoction.

It is no doubt true that this may be coarsely and inartificially attempted, so as at once to destroy the reality of the tale. When the thrice noble, illustrious and excellent princess, as the title-page calls her, the Duchess of Newcastle, produces on the stage

such personages as Sir Mercury Poet, the Lady Fancy, Sir
William Sage, Lady Virtue, and Mimic – the jest is as flat and
dull as that of Snug the joiner, when he acts the lion bare-faced.
On the other hand, some authors produce names either real or
approaching to reality, which, nevertheless, possess that resemblance to the character which has all the effect of wit; and
by its happy coincidence with the narrative greatly enhances the
pleasure of the reader. Thus, in the excellent novel of *Marriage*,
an elderly dowager, who deals in telling her neighbours disagree-
able truths, which she calls 'speaking her mind', is very happily
Mrs. *Downe Wright*. Anstey, also, whose genius in this line was
particular, gives us a list of company, of each of whom we form
a distinct and individual idea from the name alone : –

> With old Lady Towzer,
> And Marshal Carouser,
> Came the great Hanoverian Baron Panmouzer.[2]

We might also mention the Widow Quicklackit, with 'little Bob
Jerome, old Chrysostom's son', or the parties in the country-
dance where the contrasts of stature, complexion, and age, are
conveyed by little more than the names.

> Miss Curd had a partner as black as Omiah;
> Kitty Tit shook her heels with old Doctor Goliah;
> While little John Trot, like a pony just nicked,
> With long Dolly Louderhead scampered and kicked.[3]

Other, and those very distinguished authors, have not ventured
to push this resemblance between the names and characters of
their personages so far. An ominous and unpleasing epithet, a
jarring and boding collocation of consonants form the names of
their villains; as for instance, who could expect anything good
from a Blifil? The heroes and heroines, on the contrary, rejoice
in the softest, and at the same time the most aristocratic names,
such as aspirants to the actual stage select for a first appearance.
Without permitting our remarks on this head to lead us
further astray from the subject, we shall only observe that
Bunyan was indifferent to other points, so his names were ex-
pressive. Mr. Penny-wise-pound-foolish is not a happy name, and

still less Mr. Wise-in-the-hundred-and-fool-in-the-shire, but they serve to keep the allegory before the reader's mind. On the other hand, Mrs. Batt's-eyes, Mr. Ready-to-halt, and Much-afraid his daughter, Fair-speech, By-ends, and the rest, without being very improbable, have the same advantage of maintaining the reader's attention to the author's meaning. As an apology for the length and singular composition of such names as Valiant-for-the-truth, Dare-not-lie, and the like, the reader must remember that it was the custom of that puritanical age to impose texts and religious sentences, for examples of which we may refer to the rolls of Praise-God-Barebones' parliament.

In these observations we have never touched upon Bunyan's poetry − an omission for which the good man, had he been alive, would scarce have thanked us, for he had a considerable notion of his gift that way, though his present editor is of the opinion that John modelled his verses upon those of Robert Wisdom, a degree more prosaic than the effusions of Sternhold and Hopkins. His mechanical education prevented his access to better models; and of verse he knew nothing but the necessity of tagging syllables of a certain amount with very slovenly rhymes. Mr. Southey has revived some specimens of verses written by Bunyan (with great self-approbation, doubtless) upon the leaves of Fox's *Book of Martyrs.* These 'Tincker's tetrastics', as Southey calls them, may rank, in idea and expression, with the basest doggrel. But his later poetry excels this humble model : he had learned to soar beyond Robert Wisdom, when he was able to express himself thus in recommendation of *The Pilgrim's Progress.*

> Wouldst thou divert thyself from melancholy?
> Wouldst thou be pleasant, yet be far from folly?
> Wouldst thou read riddles and their explanation?
> Or else be drowned in thy contemplation?
> Dost thou love picking meat? Or wouldst thou see
> A man i' the clouds, and hear him speak to thee?
> Wouldst thou be in a dream, and yet not sleep?
> Or wouldst thou in a moment laugh and weep?
> Wouldst thou lose thyself and catch no harm,
> And find thyself again without a charm?

Wouldst read thyself, and read thou know'st not what?
And yet know whether thou art blest or not,
By reading the same lines? O then come hither!
And lay my book, thy head, and heart together. (p. 9)

In these lines, though carelessly and roughly formed, there are
both ideas and powers of expression. Another little sonnet, taken
in connexion with the scene of repose, in the prose narrative, has
a simplicity which approaches elegance. It occurs on the
entrance of the Pilgrim into the valley of Humiliation.

Now, as they were going along and talking, they espied a boy feeding
his father's sheep. The boy was in very mean clothes, but of a fresh
and well-favoured countenance, and as he sat by himself, he sung.
Hark, said Mr. Great-heart, to what the shepherd's boy saith! So
they hearkened, and he said,

> He that is down needs fear no fall;
>   He that is low no pride;
> He that is humble ever shall
>   Have God to be his guide.
>
> I am content with what I have,
>   Little be it or much!
> And, Lord! contentment still I crave,
>   Because thou savest such.
>
> Fulness to such a burden is,
>   That go on pilgrimage:
> Here little, and hereafter bliss,
>   Is best from age to age.

Then said their guide, Do you hear him? I will dare to say, this
boy lives a merrier life, and wears more of that herb called *heart's-
ease* in his bosom, than he that is clad in silk and velvet. (pp. 311,
312.)

We must not omit to mention, that this edition of *The Pilgrim's
Progress* is adorned with a great variety of woodcuts, designed
and executed with singular felicity, and with some highly finished
engravings after the rich and imaginative pencil of John Martin.
Thus decorated, and recommended by the taste and criticism of
Mr. Southey, it might seem certain that the established favourite

of the common people should be well received among the upper classes; as, however, it contains many passages eminently faulty in point of taste, (as, indeed, from the origin and situation of the author, was naturally to be expected,) we should not be surprised if it were more coldly accepted than its merits deserve. A dead fly can corrupt a precious elixir – an obvious fault against taste, especially if it be of a kind which lies open to lively ridicule, may be enough, in a critical age like the present, to cancel the merit of wit, beauty, and sublimity.

In whatever shape presented, John Bunyan's parable must be dear to many, as to us, from the recollection that in youth they were enduced with permission to peruse it at times when all studies of a nature merely entertaining were prohibited. We remember with interest the passages where, in our childhood, we stumbled betwixt the literal story and metaphorical explanation; and can even recall to mind a more simple and early period, when Grim and Slaygood, and even he

> Whose castle's Doubting, and whose name's Despair,

were to us as literal Anakim as those destroyed by Giant-killing Jack. Those who can recollect the early development of their own ideas on such subjects, will many of them at the same time remember the reading of this work as the first task which gave exercise to the mind, before taste, grown too fastidious for enjoyment, taught them to be more disgusted with a single error than delighted with a hundred beauties.

S O U R C E : Review of Southey's edition in *Quarterly Review*, XLIII (1830); reprinted in *Sir Walter Scott on Novelists and Fiction*, ed. Ioan Williams (1968) pp. 399–406.

NOTES

1. Introduction to *The Pilgrim's Progress*, ed. Robert Southey 1830) p. xciv.
2. C. Anstey, *A New Bath Guide* (1766) p. xiii.
3. C. Anstey, *An Election Ball* (1776) p. ii.

Thomas Babington Macaulay

The characteristic peculiarity of the Pilgrim's Progress is that it is the only work of its kind which possesses a strong human interest. Other allegories only amuse the fancy. The allegory of Bunyan has been read by many thousands with tears. There are some good allegories in Johnson's works, and some of still higher merit by Addison. In these performances there is, perhaps, as much wit and ingenuity as in the Pilgrim's Progress. But the pleasure which is produced by the vision of Mirza, the Vision of Theodore, the genealogy of Wit, or the contest between Rest and Labour, is exactly similar to the pleasure which we derive from one of Cowley's odes or from a canto of Hudibras. It is a pleasure which belongs wholly to the understanding, and in which the feelings have no part whatever. Nay, even Spenser himself, though assuredly one of the greatest poets that ever lived, could not succeed in the attempt to make allegory interesting. It was in vain that he lavished the riches of his mind on the House of Pride and the House of Temperance. One unpardonable fault, the fault of tediousness, pervades the whole of the Fairy Queen. We become sick of cardinal virtues and deadly sins, and long for the society of plain men and women. Of the persons who read the first canto, not one in ten reaches the end of the first book, and not one in a hundred perseveres to the end of the poem. Very few and very weary are those who are in at the death of the Blatant Beast. If the last six books, which are said to have been destroyed in Ireland, had been preserved, we doubt whether any heart less stout than that of a commentator would have held out to the end.

It is not so with the Pilgrim's Progress. That wonderful book, while it obtains admiration from the most fastidious critics, is loved by those who are too simple to admire it. Doctor Johnson, all whose studies were desultory, and who hated, as he said, to read books through, made an exception in favour of the Pilgrim's Progress. That work was one of the two or three works which he wished longer. It was by no common merit that the illiterate sectary extracted praise like this from the most pedantic

of critics and the most bigoted of Tories. In the wildest parts of
Scotland the Pilgrim's Progress is the delight of the peasantry.
In every nursery the Pilgrim's Progress is a greater favourite
than Jack the Giant-killer. Every reader knows the straight and
narrow path as well as he knows a road in which he has gone
backward and forward a hundred times. This is the highest
miracle of genius, that things which are not should be as though
they were, that the imaginations of one mind should become the
personal recollections of another. And this miracle the tinker has
wrought. There is no ascent, no declivity, no resting-place, no
turn-stile, with which we are not perfectly acquainted. The
wicket-gate, and the desolate swamp which separates it from the
City of Destruction, the long line of road, as straight as a rule can
make it, the Interpreter's house and all its fair shows, the
prisoner in the iron cage, the palace, at the doors of which armed
men kept guard, and on the battlements of which walked persons clothed all in gold, the cross and the sepulchre, the steep hill
and the pleasant harbour, the stately front of the House Beautiful by the wayside, the chained lions crouching in the porch, the
low green valley of Humiliation, rich with grass and covered
with flocks, all are as well known to us as the sights of our own
street. Then we come to the narrow place where Apollyon strode
right across the whole breadth of the way, to stop the journey of
Christian, and where afterwards the pillar was set up to testify
how bravely the pilgrim had fought the good fight. As we advance, the valley becomes deeper and deeper. The shade of the
precipices on both sides falls blacker and blacker. The clouds
gather overhead. Doleful voices, the clanking of chains, and the
rushing of many feet to and fro, are heard through the darkness.
The way, hardly discernible in gloom, runs close by the mouth of
the burning pit, which sends forth its flames, its noisome smoke,
and its hideous shapes, to terrify the adventurer. Thence he
goes on, amidst the snares and pitfalls, with the mangled bodies
of those who have perished lying in the ditch by his side. At the
end of the long dark valley he passes the dens in which the old
giants dwelt, amidst the bones of those whom they had slain.

Then the road passes straight on through a waste moor, till
at length the towers of a distant city appear before the traveller;

and soon he is in the midst of the innumerable multitudes of
Vanity Fair. There are the jugglers and apes, the shops and the
puppet-shows. There are Italian Row, and French Row, and
Spanish Row, and Britain Row, with their crowds of buyers,
sellers, and loungers, jabbering all the languages of the earth.

Thence we go on by the little hill of the silver mine, and
through the meadow of lilies, along the bank of that pleasant
river which is bordered on both sides by fruit-trees. On the left
branches off the path leading to the horrible castle, the court-
yard of which is paved with the skulls of pilgrims; and right on-
ward are the sheepfolds and orchards of the Delectable Mountains.

From the Delectable Mountains, the way lies through the fogs
and briers of the Enchanted Ground, with here and there a bed
of soft cushions spread under a green arbour. And beyond is the
land of Beulah, where the flowers, the grapes, and the songs of
birds never cease, and where the sun shines night and day.
Thence are plainly seen the golden pavements and streets of
pearl, on the other side of that black and cold river over which
there is no bridge.

All the stages of the journey, all the forms which cross or overtake the pilgrims, giants, and hobgoblins, ill-favoured ones, and
shining ones, the tall, comely, swarthy Madam Bubble, with her
great purse by her side, and her fingers playing with the money,
the black man in the bright vesture, Mr. Worldly Wiseman and
my Lord Hategood, Mr. Talkative, and Mrs. Timorous, all are
actually existing beings to us. We follow the travellers through
their allegorical progress with interest not inferior to that with
which we follow Elizabeth from Siberia to Moscow, or Jeannie
Deans from Edinburgh to London. Bunyan is almost the only
writer who ever gave to the abstract the interest of the concrete.
In the works of many celebrated authors, men are mere personifications. We have not a jealous man, but jealousy, not a
traitor, but perfidy; not a patriot, but patriotism. The mind of
Bunyan on the contrary, was so imaginative that personifications, when he dealt with them, became men. A dialogue between
two qualities, in his dream, has more dramatic effect than
a dialogue between two human beings in most plays. In this res-

pect the genius of Bunyan bore a great resemblance to that of a man who had very little else in common with him, Percy Bysshe Shelley. The strong imagination of Shelley made him an idolater in his own despite. Out of the most indefinite terms of a hard, cold, dark metaphysical system, he made a gorgeous Pantheon, full of beautiful, majestic, and life-like forms. He turned atheism itself into a mythology, rich with visions as glorious as the gods that live in the marble of Phidias, or the virgin saints that smile on us from the canvass of Murillo. The Spirit of Beauty, the Principle of Good, the Principle of Evil, when he treated to them, ceased to be abstractions. They took shape and colour. They were no longer mere words; but 'intelligible forms'; 'fair humanities'; objects of love, of adoration, or of fear. As there can be no stronger sign of a mind destitute of the poetical faculty than that tendency which was so common among the writers of the French school to turn images into abstractions, Venus, for example, into Love, Minerva into Wisdom, Mars into War, and Bacchus into Festivity, so there can be no stronger sign of a mind truly poetical than a disposition to reverse this abstracting process, and to make individuals out of generalities. Some of the metaphysical and ethical theories of Shelley were certainly most absurd and pernicious. But we doubt whether any modern poet has possessed in an equal degree some of the highest qualities of the great ancient masters. The words bard and inspiration, which seem so cold and affected when applied to other modern writers, have a perfect propriety when applied to him. He was not an author, but a bard. His poetry seems not to have been an art, but an inspiration. Had he lived to the full age of man, he might not improbably have given to the world some great work of the very highest rank in design and execution. But, alas!

ὁ Δάφνις ἔβα ῥόον ἔκλυσε δίνα
τὸν Μοίσαις φίλον ἄνδρα, τὸν οὐ Νύμφαισιν ἀπεχθῆ.[1]

But we must return to Bunyan. The Pilgrim's Progress undoubtedly is not a perfect allegory. The types are often inconsistent with each other; and sometimes the allegorical disguise is altogether thrown off. The river, for example, is emble-

matic of death; and we are told that every human being must
pass through the river. But Faithful does not pass through it. He
is martyred, not in shadow, but in reality, at Vanity Fair. Hopeful talks to Christian about Esau's birthright and about his own
convictions of sin as Bunyan might have talked with one of his
own congregation. The damsels at the House Beautiful catechize
Christiana's boys, as any good ladies might catechize any boys at
a Sunday School. But we do not believe that any man, whatever
might be his genius, and whatever his good luck, could long continue a figurative history without falling into many inconsistencies. We are sure that inconsistencies, scarcely less gross
than the worst into which Bunyan has fallen, may be found in
the shortest and most elaborate allegories of the Spectator and
the Rambler. The Tale of a Tub and the History of John Bull
swarm with similar errors, if the name of error can be properly
applied to that which is unavoidable. It is not easy to make a
simile go on all-fours. But we believe that no human ingenuity
could produce such a centipede as a long allegory in which the
correspondence between the outward sign and the thing signified
should be exactly preserved. Certainly no writer, ancient or
modern, has yet achieved the adventure. The best thing, on the
whole, that an allegorist can do, is to present to his readers a succession of analogies, each of which may separately be striking and
happy, without looking very nicely to see whether they harmonize
with each other. This Bunyan has done; and, though a minute
scrutiny may detect inconsistencies in every page of his Tale, the
general effect which the Tale produces on all persons, learned
and unlearned, proves that he has done well. The passages which
it is most difficult to defend are those in which he altogether
drops the allegory, and puts into the mouth of his pilgrims
religious ejaculations and disquisitions, better suited to his own
pulpit at Bedford or Reading than to the Enchanted Ground or
to the Interpreter's Garden. Yet even these passages, though we
will not undertake to defend them against the objections of
critics, we feel that we could ill spare. We feel that the story owes
much of its charm to these occasional glimpses of solemn and
affecting subjects, which will not be hidden, which force themselves through the veil, and appear before us in their native

aspect. The effect is not unlike that which is said to have been produced on the ancient stage, when the eyes of the actor were seen flaming through his mask, and giving life and expression to what would else have been an inanimate and uninteresting disguise.

It is very amusing and very instructive to compare the Pilgrim's Progress with the Grace Abounding. The latter work is indeed one of the most remarkable pieces of autobiography in the world. It is a full and open confession of the fancies which passed through the mind of an illiterate man, whose affections were warm, whose nerves were irritable, whose imagination was ungovernable, and who was under the influence of the strongest religious excitement. In whatever age Bunyan had lived, the history of his feelings would, in all probability, have been very curious. But the time in which his lot was cast was the time of a great stirring of the human mind. A tremendous burst of public feeling, produced by the tyranny of the hierarchy, menaced the old ecclesiastical institutions with destruction. To the gloomy regularity of one intolerant Church had succeeded the license of innumerable sects, drunk with the sweet and heady must of their new liberty. Fanaticism, engendered by persecution, and destined to engender persecution in turn, spread rapidly through society. Even the strongest and most commanding minds were not proof against this strange taint. Any time might have produced George Fox and James Naylor. But to one time alone belong the frantic delusions of such a statesman as Vane, and the hysterical tears of such a soldier as Cromwell.

The history of Bunyan is the history of a most excitable mind in an age of excitement. By most of his biographers he has been treated with gross injustice. They have understood in a popular sense all those strong terms of self-condemnation which he employed in a theological sense. They have, therefore, represented him as an abandoned wretch, reclaimed by means almost miraculous, or, to use their favourite metaphor, 'as a brand plucked from the burning'. Mr. Ivimey calls him the depraved Bunyan and the wicked tinker of Elstow. Surely Mr. Ivimey ought to have been too familiar with the bitter accusations which the most pious people are in the habit of bringing against them-

selves, to understand literally all the strong expressions which are
to be found in the Grace Abounding. It is quite clear, as Mr.
Southey most justly remarks, that Bunyan never was a vicious
man. He married very early; and he solemnly declares that he
was strictly faithful to his wife. He does not appear to have been
a drunkard. He owns, indeed, that, when a boy, he never spoke
without an oath. But a single admonition cured him of this bad
habit for life; and the cure must have been wrought early; for at
eighteen he was in the army of the Parliament; and, if he had
carried the vice of profaneness into that service, he would doubtless have received something more than an admonition from Ser-
jeant   Bind-their-kings-in-chains,   or   Captain   Hew-Agag-in-
pieces-before-the-Lord. Bell-ringing and playing at hockey on
Sundays seem to have been the worst vices of this depraved
tinker. They would have passed for virtues with Archbishop
Laud. It is quite clear that, from a very early age, Bunyan was
a man of a strict life and of a tender conscience. 'He had been',
says Mr. Southey, 'a blackguard.' Even this we think too hard
a censure. Bunyan was not, we admit, so fine a gentleman as Lord
Digby; but he was a blackguard no otherwise than as every
labouring man that ever lived has been a blackguard. Indeed
Mr. Southey acknowledges this. 'Such he might have been expected to be by his birth, breeding, and vocation. Scarcely
indeed, by possibility, could he have been otherwise.' A man
whose manners and sentiments are decidedly below those of his
class deserves to be called a blackguard. But it is surely unfair to
apply so strong a word of reproach to one who is only what the
great mass of every community must inevitably be.

Those horrible internal conflicts which Bunyan has described
with so much power of language prove, not that he was a worse
man than his neighbours, but that his mind was constantly
occupied by religious considerations, that his fervour exceeded his
knowledge, and that his imagination exercised despotic power
over his body and mind. He heard voices from heaven. He saw
strange visions of distant hills, pleasant and sunny as his own
Delectable Mountains. From those abodes he was shut out, and
placed in a dark and horrible wilderness, where he wandered
through ice and snow, striving to make his way into the happy

region of light. At one time he was seized with an inclination to work miracles. At another time he thought himself actually possessed by the devil. He could distinguish the blasphemous whispers. He felt his infernal enemy pulling at his clothes behind him. He spurned with his feet and struck with his hands at the destroyer. Sometimes he was tempted to sell his part in the salvation of mankind. Sometimes a violent impulse urged him to start up from his food, to fall on his knees, and to break forth into prayer. At length he fancied that he had committed the unpardonable sin. His agony convulsed his robust frame. He was, he says, as if his breastbone would split; and this he took for a sign that he was destined to burst asunder like Judas. The agitation of his nerves made all his movements tremulous; and this trembling, he supposed, was a visible mark of his reprobation, like that which had been set on Cain. At one time, indeed, an encouraging voice seemed to rush in at the window, like the noise of wind, but very pleasant, and commanded, as he says, a great calm in his soul. At another time, a word of comfort 'was spoke loud unto him; it showed a great word; it seemed to be writ in great letters'. But these intervals of ease were short. His state, during two years and a half, was generally the most horrible that the human mind can imagine. 'I walked', says he, with his own peculiar eloquence,

to a neighbouring town; and sat down upon a settle in the street, and fell into a very deep pause about the most fearful state my sin had brought me to; and, after long musing, I lifted up my head; but methought I saw as if the sun that shineth in the heavens did grudge to give me light; and as if the very stones in the street, and tiles upon the houses, did band themselves against me. Methought that they all combined together to banish me out of the world. I was abhorred of them, and unfit to dwell among them, because I had sinned against the Saviour. Oh, how happy now was every creature over I! for they stood fast, and kept their station. But I was gone and lost.

Scarcely any madhouse could produce an instance of delusion so strong, or of misery so acute.

It was through this Valley of the Shadow of Death, overhung by darkness, peopled with devils, resounding with blasphemy and lamentation, and passing amidst quagmires, snares, and pitfalls, close by the very mouth of hell, that Bunyan journeyed to that bright and fruitful land of Beulah, in which he sojourned during the latter period of his pilgrimage. The only trace which his cruel sufferings and temptations seems to have left behind them was an affectionate compassion for those who were still in the state in which he had once been. Religion has scarcely ever worn a form so calm and soothing as in his allegory. The feeling which predominates through the whole book is a feeling of tenderness for weak, timid, and harassed minds. The character of Mr. Fearing, of Mr. Feeble-Mind, of Mr. Despondency and his daughter Miss Muchafraid, the account of poor Littlefaith who was robbed by the three thieves, of his spending money, the description of Christian's terror in the dungeons of Giant Despair and in his passage through the river, all clearly show how strong a sympathy Bunyan felt, after his own mind had become clear and cheerful, for persons afflicted with religious melancholy.

Mr. Southey, who has no love for the Calvinists, admits that, if Calvinism had never worn a blacker appearance than in Bunyan's works, it would never have become a term of reproach. In fact, those works of Bunyan with which we are acquainted are by no means more Calvinistic than the articles and homilies of the Church of England. The moderation of his opinions on the subject of predestination gave offence to some zealous persons. We have seen an absurd allegory, the heroine of which is named Hephzibah, written by some raving supralapsarian preacher who was dissatisfied with the mild theology of the Pilgrim's Progress. In this foolish book, if we recollect rightly, the Interpreter is called the Enlightener, and the House Beautiful is Castle Strength. Mr. Southey tells us that the Catholics had also their Pilgrim's Progress, without a Giant Pope, in which the Interpreter is the Director, and the House Beautiful Grace's Hall. It is surely a remarkable proof of the power of Bunyan's genius, that two religious parties, both of which regarded his opinions as heterodox, should have had recourse to him for assistance.

There are, we think, some characters and scenes in the Pilgrim's Progress, which can be fully comprehended and enjoyed only by persons familiar with the history of the times through

which Bunyan lived. The character of Mr. Greatheart, the
guide, is an example. His fighting is, of course, allegorical; but
the allegory is not strictly preserved. He delivers a sermon on
imputed righteousness to his companions : and, soon after, he
gives battle to Giant Grim, who had taken upon him to back the
lions. He expounds the fifty-third chapter of Isaiah to the household and guests of Gaius; and then he sallies out to attack Slay-
good, who was of the nature of flesh-eaters, in his den. These are
inconsistencies; but they are inconsistencies which add, we think,
to the interest of the narrative. We have not the least doubt that
Bunyan had in view some stout old Greatheart of Naseby and
Worcester, who prayed with his men before he drilled them, who
knew the spiritual state of every dragoon in his troop, and who,
with the praises of God in his mouth, and a two-edged sword in
his hand, had turned to flight, on many fields of battle, the
swearing, drunken bravoes of Rupert and Lunsford.

Every age produces such men as By-ends. But the middle of
the seventeenth century was eminently prolific of such men. Mr.
Southey thinks that the satire was aimed at some particular individual; and this seems by no means improbable. At all events,
Bunyan must have known many of those hypocrites who followed religion only when religion walked in silver slippers, when the
sun shone, and when the people applauded. Indeed he might
have easily found all the kindred of By-ends among the public
men of his time. He might have found among the peers my Lord
Turn-about, my Lord Time-server, and my Lord Fair-speech;
in the House of Commons, Mr. Smooth-man, Mr. Anything, and
Mr. Facing-both-ways; nor would 'the parson of the parish, Mr.
Two-tongues', have been wanting. The town of Bedford probably contained more than one politician who, after contriving to
raise an estate by seeking the Lord during the reign of the saints,
contrived to keep what he had got by persecuting the saints during the reign of the strumpets, and more than one priest who,
during repeated changes in the discipline and doctrines of the
church, had remained constant to nothing but his benefice.

One of the most remarkable passages in the Pilgrim's Progress is that in which the proceedings against Faithful are described. It is impossible to doubt that Bunyan intended to satirise

the mode in which state trials were conducted under Charles the
Second. The license given to the witnesses for the prosecution,
the shameless partiality and ferocious insolence of the judge, the
precipitancy and the blind rancour of the jury, remind us of those
odious mummeries which, from the Restoration to the Revolution, were merely forms preliminary to hanging, drawing, and
quartering. Lord Hategood performs the office of counsel for
the prisoners as well as Scroggs himself could have performed it.

Judge. Thou runagate, heretic, and traitor, hast thou heard
what these honest gentlemen have witnessed against thee?
Faithful. May I speak a few words in my own defence?
Judge. Sirrah, sirrah! thou deservest to live no longer, but to be
slain immediately upon the place; yet, that all men may see our
gentleness to thee, let us hear what thou, vile runagate, hast to say.

No person who knows the state trials can be at a loss for parallel
cases. Indeed, write what Bunyan would, the baseness and cruelty
of the lawyers of those times 'sinned up to it still', and even went
beyond it. The imaginary trial of Faithful, before a jury composed of personified vices, was just and merciful, when compared
with the real trial of Alice Lisle before that tribunal where all the
vices sat in the person of Jefferies.

The style of Bunyan is delightful to every reader, and invalu-
able as a study to every person who wishes to obtain a wide
command over the English language. The vocabulary is the
vocabulary of the common people. There is not an expression,
if we except a few technical terms of theology, which would
puzzle the rudest peasant. We have observed several pages
which do not contain a single word of more than two syllables.
Yet no writer has said more exactly what he meant to say. For
magnificence, for pathos, for vehement exhortation, for subtle
disquisition, for every purpose of the poet, the orator, and the
divine, this homely dialect, the dialect of plain working men, was
perfectly sufficient. There is no book in our literature on which
we would so readily stake the fame of the old unpolluted English
language, no book which shows so well how rich that language
is in its own proper wealth, and how little it has been improved by
all it has borrowed.

Cowper said, forty or fifty years ago, that he dared not name John Bunyan in his verse, for fear of moving a sneer. To our refined forefathers, we suppose, Lord Roscommon's Essay on Translated Verse, and the Duke of Buckinghamshire's Essay on Poetry, appeared to be compositions infinitely superior to the allegory of the preaching tinker. We live in better times; and we are not afraid to say, that, though there were many clever men in England during the latter half of the seventeenth century, there were only two minds which possessed the imaginative faculty in a very eminent degree. One of those minds produced the Paradise Lost, the other the Pilgrim's Progress.

S o u r c e : review of Southey's edition of *Pilgrim's Progress*, in *Edinburgh Review* (1830); reprinted in *Critical and Historical Essays of Lord Macaulay*, ed. F. C. Montague, vol. 1 (1903) pp. 335–49.

NOTE

1. 'The waters closed over him whom the Muses loved, nor did the nymphs mislike him' – Theocritus, *Idylls*, ed, and trans. A. S. F. Gow, 1, 1 (Cambridge, 1950).

J. W. Hales (1893)

Certainly, in one way, Bunyan must ever be the chief wonder of our literature. No one has done so much with so little help from predecessors or contemporaries. Few works besides the Bible can be mentioned as seriously affecting or informing him. He owed something to the popularised *Romance of Chivalry*; he may have taken an idea or two from Foxe's *Book of Martyrs*; but, on the whole, Foxe probably did him more harm than good. But the Bible was, in fact, his library. The proverb tells us to beware of the man of one book; but proverbs are commonly one-sided and partial. Much depends on who the man is, and what the book. No one can overrate the literary or the spiritual influence of the Bible upon Bunyan. But, as we have just said, there are few other literary influences worth recording. And it is difficult to conceive how Bunyan could have been brought into contact with the literary culture of his time without being ruined. For it was altogether unfavourable to such intensity and fervour as characterise his nature. The genius of Milton, indeed, flourished, and flourished nobly, in that same age. But Milton's was a personality of almost scornful independence. His soul was 'like a star; it dwelt apart'. Not so Bunyan's. His was an eager, sympathetic spirit that would have withered in the atmosphere in which that other lived its own glorious life, lonely, exalted, supreme –

Unshaken, unseduced, unterrified.

Moreover, Bunyan was some twenty years the younger; and the magnificent inheritance of Elizabethan traditions, in which Milton in some sense shared, was well-nigh exhausted when Bunyan grew up. Milton belongs in many respects to the great Elizabethan race. If we take Butler or Dryden as more truly representing the age to which Bunyan belonged, we shall see reason to suspect that it might have gone ill with Bunyan had he moved into their circle. How could his fervid, passionate soul have thriven there? In the midst of cynics and satirists, how could it but have languished and died? Something of the ancient chivalrous spirit lived in the bosom of this Bedfordshire tinker;

he had a lingering love for knight errantry and its ways; to him were still dear the old ballads whose simplicity and artlessness had won them the contempt of the Restoration wits. Evidently, Bunyan could not have been Bunyan had he been so unfortunate as to rise in the social scale. One simply cannot imagine Mr John Bunyan, late of Elstow, sipping coffee at Button's!

Not that it is not to be regretted that he was no better educated. We will not be so disloyal to culture as not to believe it might not have vastly benefited and blessed him. But there is culture and culture; and what could have fostered and strengthened his genius was not then anywhere accessible for him.

One laudable service, for which let us ever be grateful, his age performed for him – it put him in prison. One could scarcely have expected from the Restorationists any proceeding so thoroughly sound and judicious. It may be that they did not altogether appreciate their own action; they thought, perhaps, they were taking measures to close his mouth; whereas they opened it. Supreme benefactors to Bunyan and to us, they were in fact preventing the lavish waste of his talents in sermons and such matters, and providing him with the leisure and the retirement necessary for a worthier expression of what his soul yearned to express, and must needs express, in one form or another. They to some extent silenced the preacher, but they gave immortal life and breath to the poet. Such a use of gaols seems now unhappily obsolete. It is impossible to say how many 'public men' of our time might not save their souls alive if only it could be revived – revived with some additional restrictions, such as, for instance, that the supply of writing-paper and of ink should be strictly limited. We all quote with much admiration Lovelace's lines about stone walls not making a prison, nor iron bars a cage; but we do not really believe them nowadays. In the seventeenth century they contained an accepted truth. And some of the most famous 'studies' of that period were prison cells. Famous in this way was Bunyan's place of confinement in Bedford, concerning the locality of which all that is fairly certain is that it was not the 'lock-up' of the bridge. There he was enabled to take council with himself, and depict with undying force the terrible struggles with which his 'little state of man' had been shaken and torn.

The secret of his success, as of all true success, is that he deals with realities. He could dispense with books, and such knowledge as they can give, because he could paint straight from nature. Few men that have lived have had experiences so intense, so protracted, so tremendous. Thus he found in his own history abundant material; and to give this shape became now an imperious desire. The creative instinct awoke in him, and the result was the first part of *The Pilgrim's Progress.* In the 'Author's Apology for his Book' he tells us in his own manner how he wrote it to relieve his overflowing brain. He was busy, he says, writing of 'the way and race of Saints' when he

> Fell suddenly into an allegory
> About their journey and the way to glory
> In more than twenty things which I set down;
> This done, I twenty more had in my crown,
> And they began again to multiply,
> Like sparks that from the coals of fire do fly.
>
> Thus I set pen to paper with delight,
> And quickly had my thoughts in black and white.
> For having now my method by the end
> Still, as I pulled, it came; and so I penn'd
> It down; until at last it came to be
> For length and breadth the bigness that you see.

It is the story of a true artist awaking to the consciousness of his gifts and to the joy of their application and use – of a creator feeling at his heart the first divine throbbings of creative energy and might.

SOURCE: *Folia Litteraria* (1893) pp. 252–5.

Sir Charles Firth (1898)

To contemporaries outside his own sect the author of the *Pilgrim's Progress* was nothing but a dissenting preacher with some little reputation among Nonconformists, a preacher, as a news-letter which mentioned his death remarked, 'said to be gifted in that way, though once a cobbler'. The literary fame of the author was a thing of growth as slow as the popularity of his book had been immediate. Addison cited Bunyan as a proof that even despicable writers had their admirers, Young compared his prose to Durfey's poetry, and when Cowper praised him he apologized for his praises :

> I name thee not, lest so despised a name
> Should move a sneer at thy deserved fame.

Yet before the eighteenth century ended the dictators of taste had begun to praise the work of the unlettered preacher. Swift wrote that he had been more entertained and more confirmed by a few pages in the *Pilgrim's Progress* than by a long discussion upon the will and the intellect. Johnson compared passages in it to Spenser and Dante, and told Boswell it was one of the three books which readers wished longer. It had great merit, he declared, 'both for invention, imagination, and conduct of the story', and when Bishop Percy's little girl confessed that she had not read it, he put her off his knee at once, and said he would not give a farthing for her. In 1830 the publication of Southey's edition of the *Pilgrim's Progress*, followed by Macaulay's essay, showed that the critics had at last accepted the verdict of the people on Bunyan's masterpiece, and in 1880, with the publication of Froude's life of the author, Bunyan was formally included in the roll of 'English men of letters'. It was not a dignity which he ever desired, and he would probably have classed most of his associates with Talkative the son of Saywell, who dwelt in Prating Row, and discoursed glibly of the history and mystery of things.

To explain the immediate popularity of the *Pilgrim's Progress* with Bunyan's contemporaries is more necessary than to trace the growth of his posthumous fame. A certain amount of success the very choice of his subject secured. Religious books were almost the only serious reading of the class for which Bunyan wrote. Any allegory which appealed to Puritans of the lower and middle classes, and represented in an imaginative form feelings they had experienced, struggles they had gone through, and ideals they cherished, was sure of a wide circle of readers. The inner meaning of Bunyan's narrative was plain enough, and a hundred pious commentators have pointed out the significance of every incident. But considered simply as a story, there was in what Bunyan terms 'the outside of my dream' much to explain its immediate popularity.

In the first place it was a great advantage that the idea on which Bunyan based his allegory was one with which people had long been familiar. Different commentators have pitched upon different books as containing the germ of the *Pilgrim's Progress.* A long list of such works is given in the preface to Mr. Offor's edition, and Guillaume de Guileville's *Pilgrimage of the Soule,* of which Caxton printed a translation in 1483, has been gravely republished as Bunyan's original. If Bunyan took the hint from any book it was from the Bible.[1] But the truth is the idea that life was but a pilgrimage through this world to the next was common property. In the Middle Ages the sight of the crowds of men who with staff and scrip and pilgrim's weeds travelled to the shrines of the Holy Land, had suggested to contemplative minds the obvious parallel. As late as the middle of the sixteenth century English pilgrims flocked to visit the shrines of St. Thomas of Canterbury or our Lady of Walsingham. The Middle Ages bequeathed the idea to the Protestants of the sixteenth and seventeenth centuries, and long after pilgrimages had ceased, the pilgrim of tradition –

> With his cockle hat and staff,
> And his sandal shoon

was a figure familiar to the minds of the people. To give the traditional equipment of the pilgrim a spiritual significance also was easy and natural. Sir Walter Raleigh, for instance, does so

in the poem called the 'Pilgrimage', which he wrote when he
was condemned to death.

> Give me my scallop shell of quiet,
>   My staff of faith to walk upon,
> My scrip of joy – immortal diet,
>   My bottle of Salvation,
> My gown of glory, hope's true gage,
> And thus I'll take my pilgrimage.

Emblem writers like Whitney and Quarles had popularized
the same idea in their pictures, and George Herbert had embodied it in one of the poems in his *Temple*.

Thus the fundamental conception of the *Pilgrim's Progress*
was one with which English readers were perfectly familiar, and
when Bunyan made it the basis of an allegory, their minds were
prepared to understand his hidden meaning.

Another cause of the book's success was its style. It addressed
the unlettered Puritan in a speech which unlettered Puritans
could understand. The people for whom Bunyan wrote were
illiterate people like his pilgrims themselves. Christian 'was a
scholar', and could read a notice board, but Hopeful could not
even do that. But they knew their Bible well, and were never at
a loss for a text. They could follow Bunyan in his highest flights,
and in his most serious theological arguments, because he used
the language of the Bible, and adopted its words, its phrases,
and its imagery. 'Bunyan's English', says Mr. J. R. Green, 'is the
English of the Bible. In no book do we see more clearly the new
imaginative force which had been given to the common life of
Englishmen by their study of the Bible.'

This is true, but it is not the whole truth. In the narrative part
of the *Pilgrim's Progress*, and in much of the dialogue, Bunyan
used everyday language of the seventeenth-century workman or
shopkeeper, which was a much more homely and less dignified
dialect than the language of the Bible.

As Macaulay remarks, the 'vocabulary of the *Pilgrim's Progress* is the vocabulary of the common people', and with the
limitation just pointed out the statement is correct. Hence come
the colloquialisms, the obsolete words, and the homely expres-

sions. For instance, when the pilgrims got to the top of the hill called Difficulty 'they were very willing to sit down, for they were all in a pelting heat'. When they reached their inn after a long day's walking, the host says to them, 'You have gone a good stitch, you may well be a-weary.' Their talk is full of proverbs and proverbial expressions. Christian says that the house of Talkative 'is as empty of religion as the white of an egg is of savour'. The common people that know Talkative say that he is 'a saint abroad and a devil at home'. When Hopeful says something Christian disapproves, Christian, in the words of the margin, 'snibbeth his fellow for unadvised speaking', and tells him he talks like a newly-hatched chicken. 'Thou talkest like one upon whose head is the shell to this day.'

Sometimes Bunyan drops into the language of his unregenerate days. Old Mr. Honest is described by Great-heart as 'a cock of the right kind' – an obvious reminiscence of a profane sport, which Bunyan had doubtless taken part in in the old times. There was a bad relapse in his account of the escape of the prisoners from Doubting Castle. Even when Christian had discovered the key in his bosom, he found the iron gate difficult to unlock, for 'that lock went damnable hard'. Scrupulous modern editors have often altered the adjective.

The colloquial language of the *Pilgrim's Progress* was not an accident. Bunyan purposely chose the style most likely to appeal to the readers he wished to reach. The fowler, he remarks, sometimes finds his gun and his net insufficient, and must pipe and whistle to catch his birds. The fisherman when hook and line fail him is driven to tickling for trout. In the same way the fisher of men must attract in order to capture.

A similar reason explains the introduction of the symbolical sights and pictures which the pilgrims see in the House Beautiful and elsewhere. The man with the muck rake, the parlour full of dust, the two little children in their little chairs, the robin with the great spider in its mouth, and the rest – these transparent parables were introduced by Bunyan because he was writing for the young and the unlearned. 'I make bold to talk thus metaphorically', explains Mr. Great-heart, 'for the ripening of the wits of young readers.' So when Mr. Interpreter led Mercy and

Christiana into his 'Significant Rooms' to see the hen and chickens and other moral spectacles, he condescendingly told them, 'I chose, my darlings, to lead you into the room where such things are, because you are women, and they are easy for you.'

These symbolical pictures also illustrate the way in which Bunyan made use of the popular literature of his time. For a century before his day emblem-books had enjoyed a wide popularity both in England and in Europe. The little pictures symbolically setting forth moral and religious truths, and accompanied by prose and verse explanations, were familiar to everybody. Hundreds of such works had been published both at home and abroad, both by Catholics and Protestants. The most popular of English emblem-writers, especially with the Puritans, was Francis Quarles, whose *Emblemes, Divine and Moral* appeared in 1635. No book was commoner in Puritan households, and it cannot be doubted that Bunyan knew a work so easy to meet with, and so valued by his party. He even tried his hand at composing emblems himself, and published in 1686 what he called *A Book for Boys and Girls, or Country Rhymes for Children*. It was republished in the next century under the title of *Divine Emblems*, and equipped with curious cuts. The sights which Mr. Interpreter shows the pilgrims are attempts to express in plain prose what Bunyan himself afterwards tried to express in rough verses, and what the emblem-writers had expressed in wood cuts or copper plates. Having taken a popular idea and made it the basis of his allegory, Bunyan now took a hint from popular literature, using it to embellish his story, and to make his moral purpose clearer.

But whatever suggestions Bunyan derived from literature, he drew more from the world around him than from books. One of the most remarkable qualities of his story is the faithfulness with which it pictures the life of the times. The road on which the pilgrims travel is as realistically described as the pilgrims themselves. It is like an old Roman road in some respects, for it goes up the hill called Difficulty, and across 'the delicate plain called Ease as straight as a rule can make it'. Sometimes there is a high wall by the side of it, and fruit-trees hang their branches over the wall to tempt the children. Dogs bark at the travellers as they pass by, and frighten the women 'with the great voice of their roaring'. Other travellers overtake them or meet them on the road; they see men lying asleep by the roadside; they see criminals hanging in irons a little way from it. Sometimes 'a fine pleasant green lane' comes down into the road; on one side of it there is 'a meadow and a style to go over into it', or a by-path such as that which leads Christian and Hopeful into the grounds of Giant Despair. It may be called the road to the Celestial City, but it is very like a common English seventeenth-century high-road. The dangers which beset the wayfarers are (in most cases) dangers which every seventeenth-century traveller had to face. Compare for instance Macaulay's description of an English road in the time of Charles II. 'It was only in fine weather that the whole breadth of the road was available for wheeled vehicles. Often the mud lay deep on the right and left, and only a narrow track of firm ground rose above the quagmire. It happened almost every day that coaches stuck fast until a team of cattle could be procured from some neighbour-ing farm to drag them out of the slough.' Does not this descrip-tion at once recall that 'very miry slough' named Despond, where Christian and Pliable 'wallowed for a time, being grievously be-daubed with the dirt', just because they missed 'the good and substantial stepping-stones in the middle'! A more serious danger than the mud was the frequent floods. Macaulay illustrates this from Ralph Thoresby's account of his journeys from Leeds to London. 'On one occasion he learned that the floods were out between Ware and London, that passengers had to swim for their lives, and that a higgler had perished in the waters. In conse-quence of these tidings he turned out of the highroad, and was conducted across some meadows where it was necessary for him to ride to the saddle skirts in water. In the course of another journey he narrowly escaped being swept away by an inunda-tion of the Trent.' In like manner Christian and Hopeful were surprised in By-Path Meadow by the sudden rising of the river. 'By this time the waters were greatly risen, by reason of which the way of going back was very dangerous. It was so dark, and the flood was so high, that in going back they had like to have been drowned nine or ten times.'

If the traveller escaped the mud and the waters, there was a third danger equally common and more terrible. The latter part of the seventeenth century was the golden age of the British highwayman. Then flourished Claude Duval, John Nevison, the Golden Farmer, Muldsack, and many others whose fame lives in the pages of Johnson's *Lives of Highwaymen and Pirates*. The open heaths and moors round London were their favourite hunting-grounds, or they lay in wait in the woods that bordered the great roads. Cambridge scholars on their way to London, says Macaulay, trembled as they approached Epping Forest. Oxford scholars for equally good reasons thanked God when they had passed Maidenhead Thicket. The mounted highwaymen attacked horsemen and coaches, the poor pedestrian was preyed upon by the footpads – gangs of sturdy rogues armed with cudgels, who assaulted and robbed the foot-traveller as he tramped on his weary way, and it was much if they spared his life. Such were the villains who attacked Valiant-for-truth, and plundered Little-Faith. Alter the names, and the robbery of Little-Faith reads like a page from the *Police News* of the period.

The thing was this : –
At the entering in at this passage, there comes down from Broadway Gate, a Lane called Dead Man's Lane; so called because of the murders that are commonly done there; and this Little-Faith going on pilgrimage as we do now, chanced to sit down there, and slept. Now there happened at that time, to come down the lane from Broadway Gate, three sturdy rogues, and their names were Faint-heart, Mistrust, and Guilt (three brothers), and they espying Little-Faith, where he was, came galloping up with speed. Now the good man was just awake from his sleep, and was getting up to go on his journey. So they came up all to him, and with threatening language bid him stand.
At this Little-Faith looked as white as a clout, and had neither power to fight nor fly. Then said Faint-heart, Deliver thy purse. But he making no haste to do it (for he was loathe to lose his money), Mistrust ran up to him, and thrusting his hand in his pocket, pulled out thence a bag of silver. Then he cried out, Thieves! Thieves! With that, Guilt with a great club that was in his hand, struck Little-Faith on the head, and with that blow felled him flat to the ground : where he lay bleeding as one that would bleed to death. All this

while the thieves stood by. But, at last, they hearing that some were upon the road, and fearing lest it should be one Great-grace, that dwells in the city of Good-confidence, they betook themselves to their heels, and left this good man to shift for himself. Now, after a while, Little-Faith came to himself, and getting up, made shift to scramble on his way. This was the story.

On the other hand, some of the perils the pilgrims meet with are not perils to which seventeenth-century travellers were usually exposed. They did not generally meet a dragon 'straddling quite over the whole breadth of the way', or a giant preparing to pick a passenger's bones, or seven devils carrying a man down a very dark lane. There is a romantic as well as a realistic element in the story, and for this romantic element Bunyan was indebted to the popular literature of the time. Dr. Johnson, discussing the *Pilgrim's Progress* with Boswell, observes, in his confident way, that there is reason to think that Bunyan had read Spenser. A recent editor, Mr. Venables, takes this hint, and works it out, trying to show from certain resemblances between the *Pilgrim's Progress* and the *Faery Queen*, that Bunyan was familiar with Spenser's epic. He compares the House Beautiful to Spenser's House of Holiness, Apollyon to the Dragon vanquished by the Red Cross Knight, and the cave of giants Pope and Pagan with the cave of Despair. Other parallels might be pointed out, but nevertheless it is very unlikely that Bunyan ever read a line of Spenser. The sources of Bunyan's literary inspiration are to be found, not in the books which were read by scholars and gentlemen, but in the literature of the people. Both Bunyan and Spenser were indebted to the romances of chivalry for their romantic machinery, their giants and dragons and enchanters. Spenser knew the romances in their literary form, and in the epics of Ariosto and other Italian poets. Bunyan knew them in their popular form, in the abridgements, the compilations, and the imitations which ballads and chapbooks had made familiar to Englishmen of the uneducated classes. They had been his favourite reading when he was unconverted. 'I remember', he says, speaking of a preacher, 'he alleged many a scripture, but those I valued not. The Scriptures, thought I, what are they? A dead letter, a little ink and paper,

of three or four shillings worth. Give me a ballad, a newsbook
that teaches curious arts, that tells of old fables; but for the holy
Scriptures I cared not.'

One of the best examples of these story books is Richard Johnson's *Seven Champions of Christendom*, originally published in
1607, which went through innumerable editions. It begins with
the life of St. George, and is doubtless what Bunyan refers to as
'George'. This book or some other of the same kind suggested
many of the incidents which happen to Bunyan's pilgrims. The
monsters in the *Pilgrim's Progress* are of two kinds. Apollyon
was a fiend somewhat of the nature of a dragon. He had 'scales
like a fish, wings like a dragon, feet like a bear, out of his belly
came fire and smoke, and his mouth was like the mouth of a lion'.
He made a 'yelling and a hideous roaring' all the time of the
fight, and when he spake he 'spake like a dragon'. Christian was
healed of the wounds he received by applying to them some of
the leaves of the tree of life. In the same way St. George in the
Seven Champions was healed of the wounds he got from the
Egyptian dragon, by the virtues of the fruit of a miraculous tree
that grew near the site of the battle.

In the encounters of the pilgrims with the giants the influence
of the romances is more plainly perceptible. The giants are of a
less complex nature than the monsters. Despair is only an
immense man. 'He had a cap of steel upon his head, a breast-
plate of fire girded to him, and he came out in iron shoes with
a great club in his hand.' Slaygood is not only a giant, but a
cannibal. 'He was of the nature of the flesh eaters', and is found
stripping Feeble-mind 'with a purpose after that to pick his
bones'. He resembles the giant thirty feet high 'who never eats
any meat but the raw flesh of mankind', whom St. George
vanquishes.

Giant Maul is perhaps the most typical of Bunyan's giants, and
his fight with Great-heart is the most minutely described. It begins, as these fights generally begin in the romances, by a
defiance and an exchange of taunts between the two champions.

Then the giant came up, and Mr. Great-heart went to meet him,
and as he went he drew his sword, but the giant had a club. So
without more ado they fell to it, and at the first blow the giant struck

Mr. Great-heart down upon one of his knees; with that the women and children cried out. So Mr. Great-heart recovering himself, laid about him in full lusty manner, and gave the giant a wound in his arm; thus he fought for the space of an hour, to that height of heat that the breath came out of the giant's nostrils as the heat doth out of a boiling caldron.

Then they sat down to rest them, but Mr. Great-heart betook him to prayer; also the women and children did nothing but sigh and cry all the time that the battle did last.

When they had rested them and taken breath they both fell to it again, and Mr. Great-heart with a full blow fetched the giant down to the ground. 'Nay, hold,' quoth he, 'and let me recover.' So Mr. Great-heart fairly let him get up; so to it they went again; and the giant missed but a little of narrowly breaking Mr. Great-heart's skull with his club.

Mr. Great-heart seeing that runs to him in the full heat of his spirit, and pierceth him under the fifth rib: with that the giant began to faint, and could hold up his club no longer. Then Mr. Great-heart seconded his blow, and smit the head of the giant from his shoulders.

The incidents of this fight have a general resemblance to the incidents of the battles recorded in the popular romances. Giants in these stories habitually fight with clubs, or even with whole trees. The giant Blanderon in his fight with St. Anthony employed an oak tree, 'and with his great oak he so nimbly bestirred him with such vehement blows that they seemed to shake the earth. And had not the politic knight continually skipped from the fury of his blow, he had been bruised as small as flesh unto the pot, for every stroke that the giant gave the root of his oak entered at least three inches into the ground.'

Another family characteristic of these giants is that, like Giant Maul, they get extremely hot, while the knight, who is always in good condition, keeps cool. Blanderon, for instance, grows so breathless that he is finally unable to lift his club above his head. 'The sweat of the giant's brows ran into his eyes, and by reason he was so extreme fat he grew so blind that he could not see to endure combat any longer.'

Great-heart is a most chivalrous fighter, and when the giant is knocked down allows him to get up again. St. Anthony is less generous to Blanderon, and refuses him the breathing time for which he petitions, but Guy of Warwick is as obliging as Great-heart. Colebrand, the giant whom Guy is fighting, becomes very thirsty, and says :

> Good Sir, an it be thy will
> Give me leave to drink my fill,
> For sweet St. Charity,
> And I will do thee the same deed
> Another time if thou have need,
> I tell thee certainly.

On which Guy agrees to wait till he has refreshed himself.

One must not exaggerate these resemblances between Bunyan's story and the stories in which he had once delighted, but it is plain that he was not uninfluenced by them. They suggested the adventures to which he gave an allegorical meaning, and his recollections of them sometimes supplied him with appropriate details.

There is the same mixture of realism and romance in Bunyan's description of the countries through which the pilgrims travel, and of the scenery through which the road passes. Here and there reminiscences of popular literature colour his pictures, or even suggest his scenes, but for the most part he draws what he had seen with his own eyes. Bunyan's feeling for natural beauty is very keen, but it is the landscape of his native Midlands, which pleased him most. From the roof of the House Beautiful Christian sees afar off 'a most pleasant mountainous country, beautified with woods and vineyards and fruits of all sorts; flowers also with springs and fountains very beautiful to behold'. But when he gets amongst rocks he is rather afraid of them. In the story they threaten to topple down on the traveller's head, or to give way under his feet. Woods and green fields, rich meadows and softly-sliding waters attract Bunyan's imagination most. In his ideal country, the land of Beulah, the air is 'sweet and pleasant', 'the sun shineth night and day'. 'They heard continually the singing of birds, and saw every day the flowers appear in the earth.' More mundane, because further from the celestial city, is the beauty of the Valley of Humiliation. It is empty and solitary; 'I love to be in such places where there is no rattling with coaches nor rumbling with wheels', exclaims Mercy. 'It consisteth much in meadows,' says Mr. Great-heart, 'and if a man were to come here in summer time as we do now, if he knew not anything before thereof, and if he also delighted himself in the sight of his eyes, he might see all that would be delightful to him. Behold how green this valley is, also how beautified with lillies.'

The shepherd boy feeding his father's sheep supplies the one touch necessary to complete the picture. 'The boy was in very mean clothes but of a very fresh and well-favoured countenance, and as he sate by himself he sung. . . . Then said their guide, Do you hear him? I will dare to say that this boy lives a merrier life, and wears more of that herb called Heartsease in his bosom, than he that is clad in silk and velvet.'

The song the shepherd sings is a song of content – a Puritan echo of a hundred similar songs of the Elizabethan poets – like in temper, if simpler in expression, to 'Art thou poor, yet hast thou golden slumbers', or 'My mind to me a kingdom is', or, 'How happy is he born and taught'. We are back in Arcadia, with Sidney's shepherds piping as if they would never grow old, or with the happy melodist of Keats 'forever piping songs forever new'. These fair lands of Bunyan's fancy are a kind of homely Arcadia – like the Arcadia of earlier poets, and yet different, a Puritan instead of a pagan Arcadia. Marlowe's passionate shepherd promises his shepherdess 'a thousand fragrant posies'. 'In the land of Beulah the children if the town would go into the king's gardens to gather nosegays for the pilgrims, and bring them to them with much affection.' In Marlowe's Arcadia there are 'shallow rivers to whose falls melodious birds sing madrigals'. In the grove outside the House Beautiful the birds sing with a 'most curious melodious note', but they sing the psalms of Sternhold and Hopkins.

Amidst these landscapes from Bedfordshire and the echoes of Arcadia appear once more the reminiscences of popular romance. One of the chief characteristics of romances is what Milton terms

> Forests and enchantments drear,
> Where more is meant than meets the ear.

Of this nature is Bunyan's Enchanted Land. 'By this time,' he says, 'they were got to the enchanted ground, where the air naturally tended to make one drowsy. And that place was all grown over with briars and thorns; excepting here and there, where was an enchanted arbour, upon which if a man sits, or in which if a man sleep, 'tis a question, say some, whether ever they shall rise or wake again in this world. Over this forest therefore they went.' In one of these arbours Great-heart and his band find Heedless and Too-bold in their unwaking slumbers.

Just so in the *Seven Champions*, when St. David ventured into the Enchanted Garden of the Magician Ormandine, 'all his senses were overtaken with a sudden and heavy sleep'. He fell flat on the ground, 'where his eyes were so fast locked up by magic art, and his waking senses drowned in such a dead slumber, that it was as impossible to recover himself from sleep as to pull the sun out of the firmament'. So he lay asleep for seven years. Further on in the same romance occurs an enchanted bed, which is not unlike one of Bunyan's arbours. 'Whoever but sat upon the sides, or touched the furniture of the bed, were presently cast in as deep a sleep as if they had drunk the juice of Dwaile or the seed of poppy.'

Even the conception of the Valley of the Shadow of Death, which Bunyan invests with so much spiritual significance, finds its parallels in these romances. St. George has to journey through an Enchanted Vale, when he hears 'dismal croaking of night ravens, hissing of serpents, bellowing of bulls, and roaring of monsters'. St. Andrew traverses in a land of continual darkness the Vale of Walking Spirits amid like sounds of terror. To say that here and elsewhere Bunyan's incidents were suggested by his recollections of popular romance, does not diminish the originality of the *Pilgrim's Progress*, but helps to explain its popularity. The man who, like Bunyan himself, turned from reading romances to thinking about his soul and its salvation, found in Bunyan's pages something of the charm he had found in the old fables of adventure.

When the pilgrims reach Vanity Fair we are once more amid scenes drawn from the life of the times. 'The Fair', Bunyan tells us, 'was an ancient thing of long standing, and a very great fair.'

He describes with the most vivid realism the rows of booths where all kinds of merchandise were sold, the shows where jugglings and plays and games of every kind were to be seen, and the noise of buyers and sellers in its streets. It is possible, as commentators suggest, that he had in his mind the actual fair which had been annually held at Elstow ever since Henry II had granted a charter for it to the nuns of Elstow Abbey. Or he may have recalled the greater fair held at Stourbridge, near Cambridge, which he must have seen in his travels, or perhaps the Bartholomew Fair held at Smithfield in London. In Ben Jonson's play on Bartholomew Fair he depicts the adventures of two Puritans who strayed into that scene. All the sights and sounds of the fair shock them. 'Walk on in the middle way,' cries the leader to his companion, 'turn neither to the right nor to the left; let not your eyes be drawn aside with vanity, not your ears with noises. The wares are the wares of devils, and the whole Fair is the shop of Satan.' Zeal of the land Busy – as Jonson's Puritan is named – becomes as uncontrollable as Mr. Fearing when his blood was up. He is moved in the spirit to protest against the abuses of the fair by throwing over a basket of gingerbread, and is put in the stocks for it.

Gifford, in his edition of Jonson, conjectured that Bunyan in the days of his youth read Jonson's play, and asserted that Jonson's drama was the groundwork of Vanity Fair. But nothing is less likely than that Bunyan had read Jonson's satire against the Puritans; similar incidents must have come to his knowledge, for they were not uncommon. The Quakers in the days of the Commonwealth habitually preached in fairs and markets, and suffered accordingly. 'On the market day,' writes George Fox in his journal, 'I went to Lancaster and spake through the market in the dreadful power of God, declaring the day of the Lord to the people, and crying out against all their deceitful merchandise.' In Vanity Fair and in the incidents which followed the arrival of Christian and Faithful, Bunyan is once more copying life, and not borrowing from literature.

Equally realistic is the trial of Christian and Faithful. It resembles, as Macaulay does not fail to point out, the parody of justice which was administered by hostile judges to accused Nonconformists. When Baxter was tried in 1685 for complaining in print of the persecutions of his brethren, Lord Jefferies behaved very like Lord Hategood. 'This is an old rogue,' said Jefferies, 'a schismatical knave, a hypocritical villain. He deserves to be whipped at the cart's tail.' When Baxter strove to argue in his defence, Jefferies rudely stopped him.

'Richard, Richard, dost thou think we will let thee poison the Court?'

'Richard, thou art an old knave. Thou hast written books enough to fill a cart, and every book as full of sedition as an egg is of meat. By the grace of God I'll look after thee.'

In the same manner Hategood addressed Faithful, saying, 'Thou Runagate, Heretick, and Traitor, has thou heard what these honest gentlemen have witnessed against thee?'

'May I speak a few words in my own defence?'

'Sirrah, Sirrah, thou deservest to live no longer, but to be slain immediately upon the place; yet that all men may see our gentleness towards thee, let us see what thou hast to say.'

The trial at the town of Vanity should be compared with the trials which took place at the town of Mansoul as related in the *Holy War*. There is a singular resemblance in the deliberations of the two juries, and when the good men have the upper hand they give the bad men just as short a shrift as Faithful received.

A comparison of the trials in these two books also brings out more clearly the influence which another species of popular literature had exercised upon Bunyan. Allegorical trials played a great part in English and foreign polemical literature. There are several anti-Catholic pamphlets of the time of the English Reformation in which the form of a trial is adopted. Such for instance is the *Examination of the Mass* published in 1547. In the seventeenth century the same device was often employed by controversialists on both sides. When the Presbyterians got the upper hand, and endeavoured to suppress the worship of the Independents, a bold Independent printed *The Trial of Mr. Persecution*. Under the Protectorate, when the Government was engaged in suppressing the old festivals of the Church, there came to its assistance a *Trial of Father Christmas* for corrupting the world by riotous living.

A Puritan divine, Richard Bernard, of Batcombe, employed this device of a trial for much the same purpose as Bunyan used it, that is for moral rather than for controversial purposes. Bernard's book, which was published in 1627, went through nine editions by 1634, and was very popular with Puritans of the class to which Bunyan belonged. The title of the book is *The Isle of Man, or the Legal Proceedings in Manshire against Sin. Wherein, by way of a continued allegory, the chief malefactors disturbing both Church and Commonwealth are detected and attacked, with their arraignment and judicial trial according to the laws of England.*

Manshire is the name of the county in which the trials take place. The assizes are being held at the county town which is called Soul. 'That worthy judge Conscience' presides, and before him the criminals appear one after another. The names of these offenders are Old Man, who represents what in theological language is called 'the old Adam', his wife, Mistress Heart, his servant, Wilful Will, Covetousness, and others. A few extracts from the trial of Old Man will supply a specimen of Bernard's method of handling his allegory. The indictment is set forth in the usual legal form.

'Old Man, thou art indicted here by the name of Old Man of the town of Eve's temptation, in the county of Adam's consent, that upon the day of Man's fall in Paradise when he was driven out, thou didst corrupt the whole nature of man.'

David and St. Paul bear witness against the Criminal, who argues in his own defence much as the Pelagians do vainly talk. He is condemned to death and prays for mercy. 'Good my Lord, I beseech you to be good unto me, and cast not away so poor an old man, good my Lord, for I am at this day 5564 years old.'

But his plea for mercy and his request to be allowed benefit of clergy are all in vain. He is sentenced to be hung, or rather, as the judge says, 'to be cut off with all his works'.

Bernard's handling of his allegory is awkward and cumbrous; he can neither tell a story, nor draw a character, and he has very little humour, though he apologizes for showing too much. But there are nevertheless certain resemblances between the *Isle of Man* and the *Holy War* which seem to show that Bunyan had read the work of the earlier allegorist. The town of Soul in the county of Manshire naturally suggests Bunyan's town of Mansoul. Bernard's Wilful Will is the prototype of Bunyan's Lord Will be Will. There are touches in the trials described by Bernard which remind the reader of incidents in those related by Bunyan. Lord Covetousness in Bunyan's book changes his name to Prudent-thrifty, and in the same way Bernard's Covetousness finds a flaw in his indictment, pleading that his real name is Thrift. And Judge Conscience addresses Covetousness much in the same manner that Judge Hategood addresses Faithful.

'Sirrah, Sirrah, thou that hast so impudently denied thy name here before the face of thy country; it being so clearly proved against thee every way, what canst thou allege for thyself that now the sentence of death should not be pronounced against thee?'

All I wish to show is that in introducing these trials in his two allegories Bunyan was adopting a literary device with which English readers were already familiar, and one which was specially popular with the readers for whom he wrote. In his hands the old idea received a new life, and the tedious abstractions of the allegorical courts became living persons. It is in this power of giving life to his characters that the supreme excellence of Bunyan as an allegorist lies. Whatever adventures his pilgrims pass through they are always flesh and blood Englishmen of the seventeenth century, speaking and acting as English Puritans of their class would have acted under the conditions which Bunyan's imagination created. The serious discourse with which Christian and Faithful while away their march is as true to life as the road or the fair through which they pass. Ellwood the Quaker tells us in his autobiography how he and his friend Ovy set forth to learn from Isaac Pennington the true principles of Quakerism.

'We met at Stokenchurch,' he says, 'with our staves in our hands like a couple of pilgrims, intending to walk on foot; and having taken some refreshment and rest at Wycombe, went on cheerfully in the afternoon, entertaining each other with grave and religious discourses, which made the walk easier.'[2]

It has often been said that the pilgrims in Bunyan's story are as individual as Chaucer's pilgrims. Coleridge goes so far as to complain that the allegory is so strongly individualized that it ceases to be allegory, the characters become real persons with nicknames. Bunyan's characters themselves seem to feel that they are not abstractions, but men. Mr. By-ends protests when he is addressed by his name, 'That is not my name, but indeed it is a nickname given me by some that cannot abide me.' Another character modestly explains that his name is too good for him.

' "Your name is old Honesty, is it not," asks Great-heart, . . . So the old man blushed and said, "Not Honesty in the abstract, but Honest is my name, and I wish that my nature shall agree to what I am called.' "

Bunyan conceives his characters so clearly that he gives them not merely the utterances, but the features and the gestures appropriate to their parts. Mr. Honest recognizes Mr. Feeble-mind by his likeness to Mr. Fearing. 'He was mine uncle,' answers Fearing, 'he and I have been much of a temper; he was a little shorter than I, but yet we were much of a complexion.' At which old Honest observes with awkward candour, 'I am apt to believe you were related to one another: for you have his whitely look, a cast like his with your eye, and your speech is much alike.' Old Honest indeed is a keen observer of the little tricks of manner and bearing in which character reveals itself. 'Madam Bubble,' he reflectively remarks to Mr Stand-fast when he hears her name mentioned.

'Madam Bubble, is she not a tall comely dame, something of a swarthy complexion?' 'Right, you hit it,' says Stand-fast, 'she is just such a one.'

'Doth she not speak very smoothly, and give you a smile at the end of the sentence?'

'You fall right upon it again, these are her very actions.'

'Doth she not wear a great purse at her side, and is not her hand often in it fingering her money as if that was her heart's delight.'

' 'Tis just so – Had she stood by all this while, you could not more amply have set her forth before me.'

It is curious that Bunyan's power of individualizing his personages seems for a moment to leave him when he gives them proper names. Christiana and Mercy are clearly drawn, but Matthew, Joseph, Samuel, and James are little better than lay-figures. Beyond the fact that one was fond of his catechism and another too fond of green plums, there is little to distinguish them. And this is stranger because in the second part – inferior as it is on the whole to the first part – Bunyan handles his allegorical characters with more freedom and ease than in the first. The most vivid and impressive figure in it is Great-heart, the servant of Mr. Interpreter. He is a combination of two persons mentioned in the first part – of Mr. Great-grace, who is 'excellent good at his weapons' and bears in his face the scars of former battles, and of the nameless 'man of a very stout countenance' who fights his way through the armed men into the palace, 'cutting and hacking most fiercely'. But Great-heart is not merely the strong man armed; he beguiles the journey of the pilgrims he protects by the charms of his conversation. He begins, it is true, by a lengthy discourse on justification by faith, but he soon becomes humanized, and tells humorous stories of the pilgrims he has known, such as Mr. Fearing, 'the most troublesome pilgrim that ever I met with all my days'.

To the children he is always kind and affable. He takes the little boy by the hand up the Hill Difficulty, and cheers the others on, 'Come, my pretty boys; how do you like going on a pilgrimage?'

He jokes with them because they run and get behind him when they meet the lions.

But when there is more real danger – when they go through the valley – he is first behind and then in front, saying to them : 'Be of good cheer – we shall be out by and by', or 'Let them that are most afraid keep close to me'.

A very pleasing and natural touch is his delight in pilgrims of his own temper. When they meet old Honest asleep he at first takes them for thieves.

'What would, or could you a done, to a helped yourself, if indeed we had been of that company,' asks Great-heart.

'Done,' answers Honest, 'why I would a fought as long as breath had been in me.'

'Well said, Father Honest, well said,' quoth the guide, 'for by this I know thou art a cock of the right kind.'

So, too, when they meet the man with his sword drawn and his face all bloody from a three hours' fight with three thieves, all the old soldierly instincts break out in Great-heart at his story. 'Then said Great-heart to Mr. Valiant-for-truth, "Thou hast worthily behaved thyself; let me see thy sword." So he showed it him.

'When he had taken it in his hand and looked thereon a while, he said, "Ha, it is a right Jerusalem Blade."'

'Mr. Great-heart was delighted in him, for he loved one greatly that he found to be a man of his hands.'

So vivid is the portrait, so characteristic the touches, that one thinks Bunyan must have had in his mind's eye when he drew it some real soldier, someone whom he had served under at Newport, or some scarred veteran of Naseby and Worcester, who had come back to live in Bedford and turned his sword into a reaping hook.

In the second part of the *Pilgrim's Progress*, which was published in 1684, six years after the first part, Bunyan handles his allegorical characters with more freedom. Sometimes he seems to forget the allegory for a moment, and to let the sense of humour, or the story-telling instinct, run away with him. Look, for instance, at two episodes in the second part.

Matthew's illness after his over-indulgence in plums is a little crudely described, but it is humorous as well as realistic. 'Pray Sir,' says the afflicted mother to the 'antient and well-approved physician', 'try the utmost of your skill with him, whatever it costs'; to which he replies with professional dignity, 'Nay, I hope I shall be reasonable.'

Matthew's reluctance to take his physic, and his mother's moving entreaties to him, are copied from the life. 'With that she touched one of the pills with the end of her tongue. "Oh, Matthew," said she, "this potion is sweeter than honey."' As to the pills themselves, 'he was to take them three at a time fasting, in half a quarter of a pint of the tears of repentance.'

In the end after the cure is wrought the antient physician praises his pills. 'It is a universal pill, it is good against all the diseases that pilgrims are incident to.' 'Pray Sir,' replies the provident parent, 'make me up twelve boxes of them'; and he does.

All this is, of course, allegorical, but the reader forgets all about its spiritual significance, and takes no notice of the texts in the margin. He may be edified by it in the end, but for the moment he is simply 'merry and jocund', as the pilgrims are when they dance in the road.

A page or two earlier comes the episode of Mercy's love affair. At the House Beautiful Mercy

had a visitor that pretended some goodwill unto her. His name was Mr. Brisk, a man of some breeding, and that pretended to religion; but a man that stuck very close to the world. So he came once or twice or more to Mercy, and offered love unto her. Now Mercy was of a fair countenance, and therefore the more alluring.

Her mind also was, to be always busying of herself in doing; for when she had nothing to do for herself she would be making of hose and garments for others, and would bestow them upon them that had need. And Mr. Brisk, not knowing where or how she disposed of what she made, seemed to be greatly taken, for he found her never idle. 'I will warrant her a good housewife', quoth he to himself. Mercy then revealed the business to the maidens that were of the house, and enquired of them concerning him, for they did know him better than she. So they told her, that he was a very busy young man, and one that pretended to religion; but was, as they feared, a stranger to the power of that which was good.

'Nay, then,' said Mercy, 'I will look no more on him; for I purpose never to have a clog to my soul.'

Prudence then replied that there needed no great matter of discouragement to be given to him, her continuing so as she had begun to do for the poor would quickly cool his courage. So the next time he comes, he finds her at her old work a-making of things for the poor. Then said he, 'What! always at it?' 'Yes,' said she, 'either for myself or for others.' 'And what can thou earn a day?' quoth he. 'I do these things,' said she, 'that I may be rich in good works, laying up in store a good foundation against the time to come, that I may lay hold on eternal life.' 'Why, prithee, what dost thou do with them?' said he. 'Clothe the naked,' said she. With that his countenance fell. So he forbore to come at her again; and when he was asked the reason why, he said, 'Mercy was a pretty lass, but troubled with ill-conditions.'

Mercy's comment puts the finishing touch to the whole pic-

ture. 'Mercy and Mr. Brisk', observes Prudence, 'are of characters so different, that I believe they will never come together.'
Then says Mercy, with an air of modest pride, and doubtless
with her usual blush, 'I might a had husbands afore now, tho' I
spake not of it to any; but they were such as did not like my
conditions, though never did any of them find fault with my
person.'

Here the allegory disappears altogether. We have simply an
incident in the life of a fair Puritan described with absolute
fidelity to nature; the actors are ordinary men and women of the
time, and the fact that their names have a moral significance
makes no difference to the story. We are passing, in fact, from
allegory to the novel with an improving tendency. Bunyan is
here the forerunner of Hannah More and a whole generation
of novelists who sought to combine realistic fiction and moral
teaching, while Mr. Brisk is the not very remote ancestor of
Coelebs in search of a wife. In the days when the English
novel did not exist, an allegory which was so like a story of
everyday life had a charm which it is not easy for us to appreciate
now. Bunyan was not merely the first of English allegorists;
he is one of the founders of the English novel and the forerunner
of Defoe.

It is time to sum up this analysis of the causes of the popularity
of the *Pilgrim's Progress*. Bunyan took a familiar idea as the
basis of his story, and told it in a language that was simple or
elevated just as the subject required. He put the essence of his
own life into the story; put into it reproductions of the life he
saw round him, and recollections of books he had read; made
his actors real men and women, and made his narrative by turns
satirical and enthusiastic, humorous and pathetic, realistic and
romantic. It was no wonder that 'the outside of his dream'
attracted his readers, but what united and harmonized all these
different elements was the inner spirit of his dream. That which
gives the book a lasting power is the ideal of life which underlies
it all – of life as the Puritan conceived it then and conceives it
still. The *Pilgrim's Progress* is the prose epic of English Puritanism; it contains much that is only temporary and local in its
application, but unlike Milton's epic it can be understood every-

where, and has been translated into most tongues. Its real foundation is not a doctrinal system but a moral conception. Omit a few theological discussions, and it appeals to the Puritan of all creeds and all races. Everywhere the seeker after personal holiness or ideal perfection turns his face from his own home, and sets forth on the same journey: let others stay by their farm or their merchandise, he must follow the light which he sees, or thinks he sees; happy if at last he beholds the shining spires of the city he travels to, glad if he catches by the way only a glimpse of the glory of it. Some may laugh at him as a fool, others may tell him there is no such city; like Bunyan he heeds them not, but dreams his dream and holds it true.

S o u r c e : the essay originally formed the Introduction to the Methuen edition of *Pilgrim's Progress* (London, 1898); published separately as *John Bunyan*, English Association Pamphlet, no. 19 (London, 1911); reprinted in *Authors and Poets: Bibliographies, Criticism and Comment. The English Association Pamphlets and a Presidential Address* (London, 1968) pp. 39–64.

NOTES

1. Hebrews 11 :13.
2. Ellwood's *Autobiography*, ed. H. Morley (1885) p. 113.

PART THREE

Twentieth-century Criticism

Robert Bridges

BUNYAN'S *PILGRIM'S PROGRESS* (1905)

The Oxford Press has given us *The Pilgrim's Progress*,[1] illustrated by Cruikshank in twenty-five woodcuts that are new to the public. The preface records Coleridge's judgment that this book is 'incomparably the best Summa Theologiae Evangelicae ever produced by a writer not miraculously inspired', while an advertisement proclaims the verdict of current anti-criticism, that this grotesque portrayer of suburban imaginations, the master of the comic almanacks, is its ideal illustrator. Παράδοξόν τιτοῦτο.[2] Certainly the second picture which shows the sin-burdened Christian possessed by the fear of Hell, as in headlong flight from the doomed city he leaves his little family to their fate, is an admirable presentation of the spirit of the text, and worthy of all praise; even the artist's broad method of shading, happening to stripe one of Christian's stockings lengthwise and the other bandwise, accentuates the distraction of the ragged enthusiast. Let us examine the situation.

Christian's adventures are Bunyan's spiritual experiences. Now the only occasion on which Bunyan can be said to have deserted his family was in November 1660,[3] when on being arrested he refused bail, and subsequently chose to continue in jail rather than promise not to gather the people together in unlawful assemblies. It is true that it was difficult for him to avoid this offence; but the magistrates, who had been unwilling to imprison him, made compromise easy. He, however, persisted that if he were let free he would wilfully break the law. Separation from his wife and children was painful; yet, having the choice between silence with imprisonment and silence with freedom, his conscience forced him to prefer the material fetters and leave his family to the charity of their friends. With so much knowledge of the facts we may now turn to the story.

One cannot look for perfected art, nor even for consistency, in a long allegory, and the right defence of Bunyan's rude technique is that it makes no attempt to satisfy artistic canons. However much the interest may lie in the picturesque adventures, the reader soon perceives that the several incidents are typical episodes of a spiritual experience, and that their meaning is their spiritual meaning, which a strict interdependence and sequence might embarrass. But Bunyan's artistic awkwardness is prodigious. There is a passage in the Gospel about a man hating his wife and children for the kingdom's sake, and he had lately found this to have a practical meaning for himself; but he was then far advanced on his pilgrimage, had indeed known all its experiences save only the very last; he was elect of God, a called apostle and preacher, who renounced his family rather than his high vocation; whereas Christian in the story is in a very different stage; he had not even found the way; nothing corresponds. The facts of the story are that a man learning that the town in which he lived was damned to destruction thereupon ran away and left his wife and children to their fate. That pious pagan Aeneas would have had them all on his back. It is a disastrous opening, for it deprives the hero of intelligent sympathy. And the story, being bad in itself, is not excused or sustained by the allegory. It is in the nature of things that 'babes' cannot share in spiritual convictions of adults, and therefore such convictions do not sever a man from his children, nor do they interfere with his duty of caring for them. The story asserts the opposite, and the only moral to be drawn from it is that a man should not marry if he would save his soul; but John Bunyan was married twice.

It were no sounder criticism to disparage Bunyan's remarkable book than it is to overpraise it, but the excessive laudations of it are replete with paradoxes, which invite discrimination. For instance, it is difficult to reconcile Froude's just condemnation of Bunyan's narrow theology with his assertion that all 'is conceived in the large wide spirit of humanity itself'. I propose to examine Talkative, whom he selects to praise, as 'one of the best figures that Bunyan has drawn'. Dean Stanley also says admiringly, 'We too, as he, have met Mr. Talkative'; and Canon

Venables approves the testimony. Now, when Mr. Talkative comes in with his label, the old friends of Miss Bates anticipate pleasure; but when, on being twice questioned, he replies in Bunyan's most succinct manner, they are left in blank disappointment. After this he makes, it is true, some effort in character; but instead of talking he tells us that he does talk, and that he loves talking, and he suggests subjects for talk. Then Christian sets Faithful at him, and poor Talkative is nowhere; he is fairly lectured off the stage; he is constrained to blush and withdraw. We now see that he is not talkative in the ordinary sense; and since Christian knew him at home, and gives a long account of him, we may gather the author's intention. These, then, are his characteristics. *That he talks about religion without practising it,* 'yea, and he will talk when he is on the ale-bench, and the more drink he hath in his crown the more of these things has he in his mouth. He is a saint abroad and a sinner at home. He rails at his family and servants. In trade he is a Turk and unjust.' I must beg leave to wonder whether Dean Stanley was really familiar with such a man; I cannot think that he exists. That he existed in Bunyan's time I believe, and that he is drawn from the life; but there is hardly such a man nowadays – a ruffian who discusses Justification and Prayer and Newbirth on the ale-bench. He was a monster of his day, sectarian, not human 'in the large wide spirit of humanity'.

The above criticism, in so far as it is just, hits Bunyan's admirers rather than Bunyan; and yet I am sure that I am held off from Bunyan by just such a warping or dwarfing of great human types and motives as we find here. With that picturesque, forcible handling for which he is so justly extolled, he will seize on some great human topic and cast it down naked before our eyes; and we in gratitude for his vivid nomenclature, the value of which it is sometimes difficult to exaggerate, may perhaps omit to reckon how much or how little more he has given us. Most men must have waded in the Slough of Despond, and none can have more readily used his name for it than I; but it has not escaped my attention that I never in my despondency found any assistance from Christian's adventure, where a man whose name was Help came and pulled him out, and told him that he should have tried

to find the steps, though no one could see them, nor are we informed of what nature they are. So again with Giant Despair –
who in my family was obstinately mistaken by the children for
the real hero – how well-named he is! But what is this key of
Promise by which prisoners escape from the Castle of Doubt?
Promise implies faith in the promise, and it is surely just the
eclipse or lack of faith that they are suffering from. Bunyan's
exact meaning is not plain, but judging from the relief which
comes on sunshiny days, and from the key being all the while in
Christian's pocket, I conclude that this Doubt and Despair are a
mood, which might pass off of itself as it seems to do. Now, in so
far as this mood is corporeal or mental, it has its corporeal and
mental medicine; or if Bunyan will regard it as spiritual, the
cure for those in this condition is sympathy with their fellow-
creatures and the activity of good works; and his key had been
better made of that metal. Again, nothing could be more happily
named than his Vanity Fair, but read his catalogue of fairings,
where he says, 'Therefore at this fair are *all such* merchandise
sold *as* . . . !' I could not bring my hand to copy his list. He will
take occasion of a fool's abuse of good things to calumniate goodness, and with indiscriminate vulgarity he confounds good and
bad in one category of evil. It must have been stumbling at such
ineptitudes that led William Cory, when he 'skimmed' the
Pilgrim's Progress, to record his downright opinion that it was
'wretched stuff'. The language of life seems to have been translated into a dialect by Bunyan and to need retranslation before
it can have any meaning for us.

Here is another paradox, which Froude shall state for himself. In his account of John Bunyan he introduces him as the
man 'whose writings have for two centuries affected the
spiritual opinions of the English race in every part of the world
more powerfully than any book or books except the Bible'. But
on p. 62 he drops the following remark : 'Unfortunately, parents
do not read Bunyan, he is left to the children.' Now this *obiter
dictum* is quite just, and the truth of it is undoubtedly for nothing so much as for the credit of Froude's main opinion – unless, indeed, what Mr. Froude meant was that his own generation was the first to neglect Bunyan : for children do not attend

to Christian's theology, nor would they understand it if they did; it has, of course, no influence on their spiritual opinions. 'All fables have their morals, but the innocent enjoy the story', and their love for it is mainly due to its being the consecrated means of their indulgence in adventures and fights with giants and fearsome monsters on a Sunday, when their favourite pastimes are forbidden. I hesitated to trust my private impression of general experience in this matter, and made some inquiry, with this result : Of forty-two persons representing various classes, conditions, and districts, whom I took by hazard, I found that nine had never read the *Pilgrim's Progress* at all, and one was doubtful whether he had ever seen the book. Of the thirty-two there were twenty-five who had not read it since childhood; and, of the seven remaining, three knew it only from reading it to their children. Returning now to the thirty-two who had read it, twenty-one repudiated the notion that they had ever got any good from it spiritually or morally. Of the remaining eleven there were three who admitted that they might have received an impulse for good actions; two were merely respectful towards it; three liked it, one for literary reasons only; and three disliked it.

II

As a child's Sunday story-book the *Pilgrim's Progress* has been almost universally read; but the notion that any sound educational use could be made of it seems to me wrong; for as a picture of Christian life it has this bad blemish, that it neglects the practical side of morals. Of faith, hope, and love, the greatest here is faith; and though Bunyan's theology supposes works to be of no account in themselves, and that they will flow sufficiently and spontaneously from faith, yet for his own pictorial purpose he should have seen that works make the true portraiture of faith, and that Christian's faith, painted without the works of love, is sometimes in danger of appearing very like Mr. Talkative's. (As an artist I should have thought that all that queer dogmatism about Christ's three or four righteousnesses – which is drawn out of Mr. Greatheart by Mrs.

Christian's silly questions as to how Christ can have any left for
himself, if he gives so much away – would have been well placed
in Mr. Talkative's mouth.) Christian, as we see him, is selfishly
seeking his own salvation; he cares for nothing else. St. Paul, we
can see, would have died for any man as readily as did his
Master; there is nothing in Christian of this sort of devotion. He
is set going by the fear of Hell; he leaves his family to destruction and pursues his way alone. Though he receives help from
many, he helps nobody; he finds fault with everybody; he lives
for himself and God, not for God and his neighbour. It would
seem a more generous and wholesome doctrine that we deny ourselves, not for ourselves, but for others; and the few instances in
which Christian shows even compassion for others are outweigh-
ed by the satisfaction with which the downfall of others is regarded. If Passion laughs at Patience in this world, yet Patience
'will have as much reason *to laugh* at Passion in the next',
whither she will apparently transplant the tempers of Vanity Fair;
and when God shall pass sentence on the ignorant and wicked,
it is one of Christian's celestial pleasures that he will 'have a voice
in that judgment'. Here is food for children! For myself I can
say that I disliked the man, and should have felt no concern had
he been drowned in that last river, though I wished Mr. Hopeful
well through.

It would be very unfair on Bunyan to find fault with his art
because it has failed in picturing what is not given to the mind of
man to perceive, much less to describe, and that he has not
imagined any tolerable conditions for an eternal Paradise. But
when he talks of his 'crowns of gold' and 'riding in an equipage
with the King of Glory' (*wie köstlich!*) he seems worse than
inadequate; for we cannot forget that these objects are of the sort
which arouse his anger and contempt in Vanity Fair; and
though it may be only an artistic awkwardness, yet this preference for eternal vanities above temporal ones is uncomfortable,
and needlessly throws a nasty suspicion on his whole scheme.

Bunyan's chief merit, besides the gift that I have already
praised, is his prose style, which is admired by all who prefer
the force of plain speech to the devices of rhetoric. I need describe it no further than to say that it is as direct as possible, and

well sustained. He seldom uses any but the simplest words and diction, τὰ ἐπιτυχόντα ὀνόματα,[4] and he makes use of his opportunities for colloquial expressions. He tells us somewhere that he could have commanded a more ornamental style had he preferred it, and an examination of his style should establish or demolish the truth of this assertion. Having myself read only his *Pilgrim's Progress* and *Grace Abounding*, I am not equipped for the task; but my impression is that he could not have done well in any other manner. The clumsiness of his verse alone seems to justify this opinion, and there is another general consideration, which follows from the necessity of explaining how a man so little educated should have surpassed all but the very best writers; for of this, which is generally considered a wonder, there is a simple account. His imagination, sincerity, and single purpose were as likely to be found in his station as in any other, and given these, and given also his habit of using language in its highest intention, that is to search for truth and convey it convincingly to hearers by word of mouth, then the fact that he knew only one book, the Bible, and knew that by heart, is exactly what was required to save him from the mistakes into which erudition, with its distracting knowledge of good and bad, involves all writers except the born artist. And if this simple account of his success be the true one, it negatives the probability that he could equally have mastered the more elaborate excellencies, the λόγοι κεκαλλιεπημένοι καὶ κεκοσμημένοι.[5] Those who most admire his style may well admit that it is capable of more beauty than he has put into it, his greatest beauties of diction being mainly transcribed from the Bible, and his original beauties being chiefly in the way of suggestion, where the sincerity and depth of his religious emotion taught him an eloquent and truly artistic reserve. But there are many indications, moreover, that his artistic sense was neither acute nor profound. His manner of naming his personages by the adjective which predicates their characteristic quality, like the *dramatis personae* of Congreve's plays, though often more than justified, is pushed to quite an ugly excess, and that a Mr. Wiseman should narrate a long history of a Mr. Badman, and be hearkened to by a Mr. Attentive, is not a mastery of narrative device. Such

names are more often tedious than amusing; they suggest a commonplace lack of resource, and also a certain priggishness and
self-complacency in the writer; an objection that any one may
feel and which criticism can explain, for this way of naming
characters is of the nature of comedy, and requires that the
characters should be treated kindly. In a treatise on ethics where
vices are sometimes thus handled, the persons are abstractions;
and you may be as hard upon them as you will; but if you attach
a vicious name to the actor in a story you are bound to treat him
good-humouredly and let him off; else you are guilty of having
first defamed him and then of judging him after. If the actor in a
story is to be condemned by the reader he should not be openly
prejudged by the writer; and likewise, if readers are to admire
him, their admiration should not be pre-engaged. And
wherever the author declares his intention he will divert judgement away from the actor on to himself. Bunyan's people are
neither abstractions nor human beings; and this condition may
be to some extent essential to the characters in an allegory. I
should be sorry to dogmatise about allegorical art; one consideration, however, seems persuasive to me, and that is that the
limitations of human knowledge suggest that the ὑπόνοια[6]
should be subordinated to the story. Here would appear the real
artistic opportunity, and the reason for the form. Bunyan's self-
security of opinion led him to the contrary method : I should
judge that error of presumption led him into errors of art, and
that therefore Macaulay made another of his magnificent
blunders when he styled him 'best of all allegorists, as Demos-
thenes was best of all orators'. A large part of the approval that
Bunyan has won has been purchased, like most popular suc-
cesses in art, by a neglect of proprieties which are less esteemed
by the public than the novel effects that can be obtained by their
contravention.[7]

It is pleasanter to write about Bunyan without reference to
his theology, though one is tempted to contrast him with that
thorough-going gospeller of our own day, Count Leo Tolstoi.
Bunyan himself would have been horrified to find that the secret
of his fame was literary excellence, yet without that he would
have perished long ago. In this regard his book is like Milton's

epic, which was at first esteemed for its plot and theological aspect, and is now read in spite of them. Having found so much fault, I shall not be reckoned an extravagant admirer of Bunyan, and I wrote what I have written in justification of a moderate admiration. Had he been as unsparingly decried as he has been extolled, I might have taken the other side. Overpraise will do his reputation no service; and his theology needs so much allowance that anything which dislocates him from his time does him vast injury; and this some of his warmest friends do not perceive, when they Victorianise his spelling and parade his Calvinism on shiny paper.

S O U R C E : first published in *The Speaker* (April 1905); reprinted in Bridge's *Collected Essays* (Oxford, 1934) pp. 115–29.

N O T E S

The version printed in *Collected Essays* is typeset in Bridge's system of phonetic orthography; here it is translated into conventional spelling. – Ed.

1. *The Pilgrim's Progress*, by John Bunyan, illustrated with 25 drawings on wood by George Cruikshank from the collection of Edwin Truman (Oxford, 1904).
2. 'What a paradox!' – Ed.
3. This and other facts in Bunyan's history are taken from the biographies, especially Venables and Froude.
4. 'Words that hit the nail right on the head.' – Ed.
5. 'A style decked in fine phrases and embellishments.' – Ed.
6. 'Hidden thought', 'true intent'. – Ed.
7. The best-told allegory in the world is (in my opinion) St. Luke's story of the *Prodigal Son*. He seems to have easily won the first place by an absolutely faultless piece of work.

George Bernard Shaw

FROM THE EPISTLE DEDICATORY
TO *MAN AND SUPERMAN* (1907)

That the author of Everyman was no mere artist, but an artist-
philosopher, and that the artist-philosophers are the only sort of
artists I take quite seriously, will be no news to you. Even Plato
and Boswell, as the dramatists who invented Socrates and Dr
Johnson, impress me more deeply than the romantic play-
wrights. Ever since, as a boy, I first breathed the air of the trans-
cendental regions at a performance of Mozart's Zauberflöte, I
have been proof against the garish splendors and alcoholic ex-
citements of the ordinary stage combinations of Tappertitian
romance with the police intelligence. Bunyan, Blake, Hogarth,
and Turner (these four apart and above all the English classics),
Goethe, Shelley, Schopenhauer, Wagner, Ibsen, Morris, Tol-
stoy, and Nietzsche are among the writers whose peculiar sense of
the world I recognize as more or less akin to my own. . . .
The comparison between Falstaff and Prospero is like the comparison between Micawber and David Copperfield. At the end
of the book you know Micawber, whereas you only know what
has happened to David, and are not interested enough in him
to wonder what his politics or religion might be if anything so
stupendous as a religious or political idea, or a general idea of
any sort, were to occur to him. He is tolerable as a child; but he
never becomes a man, and might be left out of his biography
altogether but for his usefulness as a stage confidant, a Horatio or
'Charles his friend' : what they call on the stage a feeder.
  Now you cannot say this of the works of the
artist-philosophers. You cannot say it, for instance, of the Pilgrim's Progress. Put your Shakespearian hero and coward,
Henry V and Pistol or Parolles, beside Mr Valiant and Mr Fearing, and you have a sudden revelation of the abyss that lies

between the fashionable author who could see nothing in the world but personal aims and the tragedy of their disappointment or the comedy of their incongruity, and the field preacher who achieved virtue and courage by identifying himself with the purpose of the world as he understood it. The contrast is enormous : Bunyan's coward stirs your blood more than Shakespear's hero, who actually leaves you cold and secretly hostile. You suddenly see that Shakespear, with all his flashes and divinations, never understood virtue and courage, never conceived how any man who was not a fool could, like Bunyan's hero, look back from the brink of the river of death over the strife and labor of his pilgrimage, and say 'yet do I not repent me'; or, with the panache of a millionaire, bequeath 'my sword to him that shall succeed me in my pilgrimage, and my courage and skill to him that can get it'. This is the true joy in life, the being used for a purpose recognized by yourself as a mighty one; the being thoroughly worn out before you are thrown on the scrap heap; the being a force of Nature instead of a feverish selfish little clod of ailments and grievances complaining that the world will not devote itself to making you happy. And also the only real tragedy in life is the being used by personally minded men for purposes which you recognize to be base. All the rest is at worst mere misfortune or mortality : this alone is misery, slavery, hell on earth; and the revolt against it is the only force that offers a man's work to the poor artist, whom our personally minded rich people would so willingly employ as pandar, buffoon, beauty monger, sentimentalizer and the like.

It may seem a long step from Bunyan to Nietzsche; but the difference between their conclusions is merely formal. Bunyan's perception that righteousness is filthy rags, his scorn of Mr Legality in the village of Morality, his defiance of the Church as the supplanter of religion, his insistence on courage as the virtue of virtues, his estimate of the career of the conventionally respectable and sensible Worldly Wiseman as no better at bottom than the life and death of Mr Badman : all this, expressed by Bunyan in the terms of a tinker's theology, is what Nietzsche has expressed in terms of post-Darwin, post-Schopenhauer philosophy; Wagner in terms of polytheistic mythology; and Ibsen in terms of mid-xix century Parisian dramaturgy. Nothing is new in these matters except their novelties : for instance, it is a novelty to call Justification by Faith 'Wille', and Justification by Works 'Vorstellung'. The sole use of the novelty is that you and I buy and read Schopenhauer's treatise on Will and Representation when we should not dream of buying a set of sermons on Faith versus Works. At bottom the controversy is the same, and the dramatic results are the same. Bunyan makes no attempt to present his pilgrims as more sensible or better conducted than Mr Worldly Wiseman. Mr W. W.'s worst enemies, Mr Embezzler, Mr Never-go-to-Church-on-Sunday, Mr Bad Form, Mr Murderer, Mr Burglar, Mr Co-respondent, Mr Blackmailer, Mr Cad, Mr Drunkard, Mr Labor Agitator and so forth, can read the Pilgrim's Progress without finding a word said against them; whereas the respectable people who snub them and put them in prison, such as Mr W. W. himself and his young friend Civility; Formalist and Hypocrisy; Wildhead, Inconsiderate, and Pragmatick (who were clearly young university men of good family and high feeding); that brisk lad Ignorance, Talkative, By-ends of Fairspeech and his mother-in-law Lady Feigning, and other reputable gentlemen and citizens, catch it very severely. Even Little Faith, though he gets to heaven at last, is given to understand that it served him right to be mobbed by the brothers Faint Heart, Mistrust, and Guilt, all three recognized members of respectable society and veritable pillars of the law. The whole allegory is a consistent attack on morality and respectability, without a word that one can remember against vice and crime. Exactly what is complained of in Nietzsche and Ibsen, is it not? And also exactly what would be complained of in all the literature which is great enough and old enough to have attained canonical rank, officially or unofficially, were it not that books are admitted to the canon by a compact which confesses their greatness in consideration of abrogating their meaning; so that the reverend rector can agree with the prophet Micah as to his inspired style without being committed to any complicity in Micah's furiously Radical opinions. Why, even I, as I force myself, pen in hand, into recognition and civility, find all the force of my onslaught destroyed by a simple policy of non-resistance.

In vain do I redouble the violence of the language in which I proclaim my heterodoxies. I rail at the theistic credulity of Voltaire, the amoristic superstition of Shelley, the revival of tribal soothsaying and idolatrous rites which Huxley called Science and mistook for an advance on the Pentateuch, no less than at the welter of ecclesiastical and professional humbug which saves the face of the stupid system of violence and robbery we call Law and Industry. Even atheists reproach me with infidelity and anarchists with nihilism because I cannot endure their moral tirades. And yet, instead of exclaiming 'Send this inconceivable Satanist to the stake', the respectable newspapers pith me by announcing 'another book by this brilliant and thoughtful writer'. And the ordinary citizen, knowing that an author who is well spoken of by a respectable newspaper must be all right, reads me, as he reads Micah, with undisturbed edification from his own point of view. It is narrated that in the eighteenseventies an old lady, a very devout Methodist, moved from Colchester to a house in the neighborhood of the City Road, in London, where, mistaking the Hall of Science for a chapel, she sat at the feet of Charles Bradlaugh for many years, entranced by his eloquence, without questioning his orthodoxy or moulting a feather of her faith. I fear I shall be defrauded of my just martyrdom in the same way.

S O U R C E : from 'Epistle Dedicatory to Arthur Bingham Walkley', *Man and Superman* (1907) pp. xxviii–xxxiii.

T. R. Glover

ON THE PERMANENCE OF
THE PILGRIM'S PROGRESS (1915)

Allegory is the hardest of all literary modes, harder than Tragedy, with less range and more pitfalls. There are inconsistencies and improbabilities in the *Pilgrim's Progress* as there are in the *Odyssey,* and still more in *Don Quixote* – perhaps even in *Robinson Crusoe.*[1] Some of them are accidents; others are inherent in the scheme. Of these some are 'outside the tragedy', as Aristotle put it in criticizing Sophocles' *Œdipus*; but, the improbabilities once thus admitted, the rest follows. Others are lost sight of in the general impression; the charm of the whole thing is too great. From the moment when we see 'a Man cloathed with Rags, standing in a certain place, with his Face from his own House, a Book in his hand, and a great Burden upon his Back', we accept everything as probable, we believe everything, with all the emotion that attends such belief – just as we believe the *Ancient Mariner,* an even more improbable story.

But what of the part 'outside the Tragedy'? Are the adventures of a soul stirred by the fear of hell a theme of enough nobility for a great story? Is the motive either noble, or true?

It depends on the value we set on the human soul. If we hold with Plato that this life is the 'study of death', or, in plainer terms, a preparation for another life of more moment; or if we hold with Kant that God, freedom, and immortality are the postulates of the practical reason – the preconceptions involved in every act, much as the law of gravitation is subconsciously assumed in all our actions which relate to matter; – then, whether hell is eternal, as Bunyan thought, or not, sin becomes a thing of real and enduring significance, and the pilgrimage of the soul toward 'the higher regions' is no idle or light theme. Today, under the influence of a rather unreflective charity and of scientific conceptions, lightly seized and ill understood, there is a tendency for men to underestimate the power of evil as a force in human affairs. In the endeavour to reach some sort of monism, evil is viewed from a distance which permits pleasant talk of its being a necessary condition for good, and so forth. But, when, in practice there results an easier ideal of conduct and a more genial tolerance of evil, so long as it is not physical pain, – can we say that it is sound thinking?

But, we are asked, can a work stand as a picture of the Christian life, in which the family and the city are discarded? The question implies some failure to realize the limitations of Allegory and some misrepresentation of what we read in the book. In the second edition Bunyan added the conversation with Charity, in which Christian with tears explains that he did all he could to bring his family with him and they refused to come; and in the Second Part we see that he had really done a great deal for them and for the people of his city. For a man's own inward state is the measure of all he does for men, is, in fact, – in a sense, – his chief contribution to society. His estimate of his own spiritual, intellectual and moral needs and possibilities sets a limit to what he will suppose other men to need and to what he will attempt for them. And even if the criticism were true, that family and city are abandoned, Bunyan knew, as we have seen, that sometimes a family has to be forsaken – and he knew the pain of it. If these views are right – and there seems to be historical as well as philosophic reason for supposing them so – Bunyan or any man might look far for a nobler motive for story or allegory, a truer or a more vital.

With the warrant of Scripture under his eyes, and with his own indelible memories of 'strong suggestions', it is not surprising that Bunyan does not speak of evil in the impersonal way, but personifies it. An illustration may help at this point. Christian, at one awful stage, goes through Bunyan's own experience; and, in looking back, Bunyan's sense enables him to clear things. He makes a free use of italics in printing his books, and this whole passage is italicized by him.

One thing I would not let slip, I took notice that now poor Christian

was so confounded, that he did not know his own voice; and thus I
perceived it; Just when he was come over against the mouth of the
burning Pit, one of the wicked ones got behind him, and stept up
softly to him, and whisperingly suggested many grievous blasphemies
to him, which he verily thought had proceeded from his own mind.
This put Christian more to it than anything he met with before,
even to think that he should now blaspheme him, that he loved so
much before; yet if he could have helped it, he would not have
done it; but he had not the discretion neither to stop his Ears, nor
to know from whence those blasphemies came.

Now, whether evil is to be regarded or not as a personal force or
a series of such forces, this episode of Christian's journey
through the Valley of the Shadow of Death is true to the human
mind and its experience; and if Bunyan's language is not what
we somewhat crudely call scientific, it lies close alongside of the
experience it is intended to describe. The horrible complications
of the mind at variance with itself, the co-existence within it of
velle and *nolle*, its subjection to a yoke which it feels to be
foreign, which it hates and yet rather likes and so much the more
detests – through all this Bunyan had been, like Augustine before him; and really, if the experience is to be put at all into
words, none seem adequate to express its horror but those which
attribute personality to the element or elements of evil. The error
in such an attribution is less than the opposite error, which over-
takes us, when, for the pedantry of a scientific dialect, we
sacrifice something of the truth of an experience, blunting its
edges to make it symmetrical with theory.

In any case Satan and Apollyon were among the necessary
preconceptions of a writer in Bunyan's day, and the terms, however grotesquely they may strike a modern ear, corresponded with
what he felt he had experienced; so that it seems fairer to accept
them as 'outside the tragedy', as 'given', and then without pre-
judice consider what Bunyan makes of his story as he works
within his limitations, as every artist must.

No one will suggest that Bunyan read Aristotle, yet the curious
coincidence of his method in story-telling with a famous dictum
in the *Poetics* may help us to understand something of his genius.
'The poet should speak as little as possible in his own person. . . .

Homer, after a few prefatory words, at once brings in a man, or woman, or other personage; none of them wanting in characteristic qualities but each with a character of his own.'

Let us take Mr *Worldly Wiseman* as an example. We are only told his name and that he comes from *Carnal Policy*, a very great town; and, Christian happening to cross his way, he had 'some guess of him' and spoke. He at once begins to reveal himself. 'How now, good fellow, whither away after this burdened manner?' The question has a superficial look of sympathy, and a suggestion of some want of it. Christian explains his errand, and Wiseman abruptly asks, 'Hast thou a wife and Children?' – a practical common-sense sort of thing to ask, though not very obviously his affair.[2] Then he has a happy idea – the originality of this kind of man is generally rather threadbare. He offers a practical suggestion. 'I would advise thee then that thou with all speed get thy self rid of thy Burden; for thou wilt never be settled in thy mind till then : nor canst thou enjoy the benefits of the blessing which God hath bestowed upon thee till then.' We need not follow the conversation; it is full of common-sense; but we do not yet know what Worldly Wiseman looked like. That we learn when Evangelist asks Christian about the man who advised him to leave the way – 'What was he?' 'He looked like a Gentleman, and talked much to me.'

Earle, in his *Microcosmographie*, also drew a 'World's Wise Man', whose 'tush! is greatest at religion'. There was much drawing of 'characters' about this period, and Earle's are full of humour and point – perhaps a little too full to be quite true. At any rate the archetypal wise man of this world would probably own Bunyan's as the better likeness, and no doubt would wonder that Bunyan, with so much wits about him as to understand the common-sense he puts into Worldly Wiseman's mouth, should yet reject it.

Let us take another instance, where verification comes from an unexpected source to confirm Bunyan's truth in portraiture. *Atheist* 'fell into a very great laughter', when Christian and Hopeful explained to him the purpose of their pilgrimage – they would only have their travel for their pains.

Chr. Why, man? Do you think we shall not be received?

Atheist. Received! There is no such place as you dream of in all this World!

Chr. But there is in the World to come.

Atheist. When I was at home in mine own Country, I heard as you now affirm, and from that hearing went out to see, and have been seeking this City twenty years, but find no more of it than I did the first day I set out.

Chr. We have both heard, and believe that there is such a place to be found.

Atheist. Had I not when at home believed, I had not come thus far to seek; but finding none, (and yet I should, had there been such a place to be found, for I have gone to seek it further than you) I am going back again and will seek to refresh my self with the things that I then cast away for hopes of that which I see not.

Fourteen centuries earlier Lucian had written his account of his argument with Hermotimus. 'I conceive Virtue', he said to his friend, 'under the figure of a City, whose citizens are happy, absolutely wise, all of them brave, hardly distinguishable from Gods. Their relations are all peace and unity. Their life is serene and blissful in the enjoyment of all good things.' Should not men seek such a city, asks Hermotimus, and never count the toil nor lose heart?

Certainly above all things else we should devote ourselves to it and let the rest go, nor pay any great heed to our country that is here; nor, though our children or parents (if we have any) cling to us and cry, ought we to yield, but, if we can, urge them also to take the same journey; and, if they won't or can't, then shake them off and go straight to that all-happy City – letting even one's coat go, if they lay hold of it to keep us back, and press on thitherward. For there is no fear that they will shut you out there, even if you come without a coat. I remember hearing a description of it all once before from an old man who urged me to go with him to the City; he would show me the way, and on my arrival, he would enroll me, and make me one of his own tribe and kin, so that I should share the universal happiness. But I would not hearken – through folly and youth – it was fifteen years ago; or by now I might have reached the suburbs and been at the gates. . . . If the city had been near at hand and plain for all to see, long ago (you may be sure) with never a doubt

I would have gone to it and been a citizen long since. But as the City (as you say) lies far away, it is necessary to seek the road to take you there and the best guide.

And then Lucian proves at great length how impossible it is to find either road or guide, and how absurd is the quest, and his elderly friend gives up a life-time's endeavour, resolved henceforth 'to live like an ordinary person without eccentric or vain hopes'. Lucian's antagonists, unlike Bunyan's, are generally puppets, easily bowled over. Bunyan's men, like Plato's Callicles in the *Gorgias*, walk away (on feet of their own) convinced that they are right and the Pilgrim wrong.

It is interesting to note that the city which Christian seeks is the same as that at which Lucian laughs. Lucian had read Plato, and Bunyan the Epistle to the Hebrews. The writer of that epistle was a man of Hellenistic culture – 'the most cultured Greek of them all'[3] – and he too as he wrote had his eye with Plato upon 'the place above the heavens'. If the glimpse of the Celestial City from the Delectable Mountains owes anything to the *Faerie Queene* (I, 10) – and there is resemblance – then we might say that Bunyan's City is connected with Plato's by a second line of ancestry. In any case Atheist and Lucian could change places. Atheist's words would fit the Greek story, and Lucian could have said nothing else to Christian.

Bunyan does not 'play' in writing his allegory, any more than when he wrote *Grace Abounding*, though he has of course more scope here for humour. He will not under-estimate the Christian's foes; the cost shall be faithfully counted, and no Pliable can accuse Bunyan of telling him only half the story as poor Christian did. But this is not all. As he wrote, he fairly saw his men and identified himself with them. Such a faculty is the outcome of experience and imagination. He had himself been Ignorance, for he too was 'a brisk talker'. He had looked down the street where Atheist lived (*cf. G. A.* §§ 97, 98). Worldly Wiseman had tried to let him a house in the village of Morality, where (as he very justly remarked in 1678) houses stood empty and were to be had at reasonable rates.[4] *By-Ends* – and that half-brother of his mother's, the Mr *Two-Tongues*, who was 'the parson of our Parish', holding on in spite of the Uniformity Act, like his much-harassed contemporary the Vicar of Bray, who was probably connected with that honourable family – the old gentleman Mr Legality, and the 'pretty young Man', his son Civility, with the 'simpering looks' – Bunyan had known them all. And now Imagination breathed upon them, and they lived and looked and spoke with their native accents. Dialogue is instinctive with Bunyan. Even in other works, where it is less obvious, he falls naturally into it. It is one of the most charming features of his Allegories – so full of ease is it, so free and natural and close to life. Its spontaneity and its homely phrase are not to be allegorized. When Christian 'snibbeth his fellow' and tells him he talks 'like one upon whose head is the shell', this is not allegory, it is character. It is such unstudied words, that bring us face to face with men as they talk. Austere and relevant persons delete such things; the man of genius puts them in – or rather, finds them in and cannot cut them out, and in consequence he is reproached for laughing too loud.

The *Pilgrim's Progress* is one of those permanent books which survive their own theories. Paul, Augustine, à Kempis, and Bunyan had their views of the world natural and spiritual, and many of these views are no longer held. But they put more into their books than views – they worked life and experience into them in such a way that no re-modelling of Theology or Philosophy will take away their value. They stand as part of the great inheritance of our race – the living records of lives that were lived in the fullest sense of the word, lives of which no fraction was lost, but all was realised and turned to account by minds specially gifted for living and for telling what life is.

Like all such books, Bunyan's *Pilgrim* takes us into new regions and opens up new avenues of experience. For many of us it is now the one great type of the Christian life, – begun with a burden and moving on to freedom and ever higher happiness – but hard and dangerous, full of Doubting Castles and Sloughs of Despond, with much of the Valley of Humiliation and the Shadow of Death. It gives us the unspeakable feeling which pulsed through Christian's mind, when 'he thought he heard the Voice of a man, going before him', and gathered from that 'That some who feared God were in this Valley as well as himself'. Above all it is a book of Victory. There is the Celestial City, with its bells ringing, at the end, but, what is more to the point for us just now, we see Christian wounded, shamed and fallen 'with a dreadful fall', with Apollyon 'sure of him' at last – and yet there and then consciously 'more than conquerour through him that loved us'. As Christian said elsewhere (with a smile), 'I think verily I know the meaning of this'. And, when the last page is read, how often has the word of the 'Man of a very stout Countenance' come to the reader's lips – 'Set down my name, Sir'? . . .

SOURCE: from 'Bunyan' in *Poets and Puritans* (1915) pp. 126–35.

NOTES

1. A biologist friend of mine has remarked on the quite improbable freedom of Crusoe from insect parasites in the Tropics, but perhaps two centuries ago Englishmen noticed these things less.

2. Charity, of course, asks the same question, but after they have invited him to stay in the Palace Beautiful.

3. J. H. Moulton in *Cambridge Biblical Essays*, ed. H. B. Swete (Cambridge, 1909) p. 472.

4. Pepys' Diary is a commentary on the gradual depopulation of this village. The place has looked up a good deal of late years, and, like Ottawa, Toronto, and other great towns, has changed its name. It is now called Social Righteousness.

Maurice Hussey

BUNYAN'S 'MR IGNORANCE' (1949)

'*Pilgrim's Progress* has no Deadly Sins and no Everyman among its *dramatis personae*.' Many readers might find it difficult to assent to this proposition, for the hundreds of parish lectures have brought few to understand the spiritual experience behind the book and to realize that Graceless, who becomes Christian, is anything more than a human soul after death. Juvenile readers leave the book behind and never return along its path again. To speak of the allegory as a religious classic without being able to find in it the marks of a Calvinist drama of predestination is, for more qualified readers, to tell half the tale, and to dilute Bunyan's work into a pleasant narrative of devils and angels. It is the aim of this essay to show how the original readers understood the message at a time before its literary merits were known to Dr Johnson, Southey or Macaulay. For, assumptions that are common to author and reader are, at any time, an indication of the strength and quality of the society that produced both, and in this instance it is a connexion which includes a vast amount of practice in deciding questions of theology and morality. Instead of appealing to sophistication in artistic matters alone, Bunyan was sensing appreciation of moral theology: it was the combination of these interests that produced this masterly allegory.

The doctrines that are involved in the interpretation of the book are those of Reprobation and Election. To attempt to comprehend it without knowing how the original public felt about these points is to make a puerile affair of it, to fit it for the inattentive reading it must now receive, which sees it as a general account of life and death suitable for all creeds. The stages of the journey fit precisely into the Calvinist scheme of faith; they are no more than pleasant episodes when stripped of it. Christian

was not Everyman but one of the Lord's few chosen souls, and in
the presence of this theology communal religious spirit must
yield to personal interpretation of the Scriptures and the private
salvation of a few. Bunyan's contemporaries read the book
and saw it, I believe, in this fashion, approving the climax
in the last section of the pilgrimage not because the hero
is there rewarded, but because the last devil is swept into
Hell. Sentimental readers have misunderstood the drastic treatment of the subject of this essay, and regretted that Hell mouth
gaped for him. No true friend of the author would have found
him unjust in punishing this form of Ignorance instead of pitying
it, for he would have agreed that Ignorance was pernicious
and was there to demonstrate a commonplace of Puritan
theology: 'Most sins of men in these daies of light are not
for *want* of knowledge, but *against* knowledge, admonition and
conscience.'[1]

There is abundant evidence to confirm this, to show that the
ministers of God's word were at one. It is perhaps only necessary here to add that the conception of Mr Ignorance came from
another source, from Arthur Dent's *The Plaine Mans Path-Way
to Heaven*, where he appears as Antilegon, the caviller, under
a name far more uncompromising than that which Bunyan was
to give him. The insistence upon the state of soul is indispensable to the Puritan expositor, and in many books intended mainly
for ministers to read we may discover methods of answering that
most important question : What of those who are not elected?
The reply was that they lose nothing, for eternal rewards were
proofs of a superabundance in God's excellence. Nothing that
man can do could merit so great a blessing. Reprobates therefore lose no common inheritance in Calvinist theology; the
Catholic emphasis had been mistaken. The question was a difficult one, as the divine knew, and the caviller was frequently
baffled by these doctrines and in resisting the preacher's word was
only obstructing God's own decree with carnal objections. Mr
Ignorance fits into this framework as the Hypocrite and a
wealth of literary allusion might be adduced to prove the case.
The preachers drew their examples from the Bible and were
most fond of the names of Esau, Ananias and Sapphira, who

are mentioned by the Shepherds of the Delectable Mountains.
A more subtle point at issue here was that the wicked are unable to feel their reprobation since it is never finally revealed :
'Though the Godly may by their calling know their Election, yet
none can know in this life their Reprobation.'[2]

There is a mass of contemporary evidence whereby the reader
might detect a hypocrite. Chaucer's Pardoner and Fals-Semblant
are English forerunners of a long race, but the Catholic doctrine
of Grace freely given did not raise the problem of multitudes who
might try to creep into the fold without a hope of forgiveness.
Relying upon the sound religious education of his readers, Bunyan made his points without undue elaboration, and since all
who read were largely devoted to popular moral theology, his
audience was perfectly attuned to his discussion of such intimate
problems.

The Preacher is the most important instrument in the salvation of a soul which was predestined to find a reward. It was
only from sermons that the elected adult could come to feel his
good fortune. Every document tells this tale. Samuel Clarke's
Lives of 32 English Divines is a useful harvest of Puritan custom.
The lives of these preachers are very similar to Bunyan's own
account, *Grace Abounding*. Of one divine, Clarke says : 'The
Lord·was pleased to work upon him in the primrose of his life,
though he certainly knew not, either the Preacher or the
Sermon whereby he was converted.'[3] All writers attribute their
initial realization to a preacher. Bunyan, no less, to John Gifford, his Evangelist. Wherever the preacher occurs in the
Progress there is some corresponding phase of conversion to account for him. At first he explains and shows the way; later he
rebukes Christian for turning aside. The Interpreter assumes
some of his responsibility when he lightens Christian's troubles
with further support from Biblical promises. When Christian is
strong enough to stand on his own feet (not without several
mishaps) he needs no Evangelist; we find the latter catching up
the two neophytes to congratulate them on facing up to their
own problems successfully. In the last section, the ministerial
function is assumed by the Shepherds of the Delectable Mountains, who no longer assure the pilgrims of their reward but show

it through their perspective glasses, which act as a device to look into the future and to connect the episodes.

Eternal punishment is as essential as eternal reward, and the Shepherds perform a most important function in the book when they open Christian's eyes to a cavern from which the devils and crackers of the medieval drama pour out : 'This is a by-way to hell, a way that hypocrites go in at; namely, such as sell their birthright, with Esau; such as sell their master, with Judas; such as blaspheme the gospel, with Alexander; and that lie and dissemble, with Ananias and Sapphira his wife.'[4] In the conversation that follows, readers are informed that these sinners of the Bible had held out for several weary miles of pilgrimage, because they had deceived themselves with their true intentions, and were still full of vain hope. Immediately after this, there comes on to the scene one who strides carelessly through the countryside to join at the very last stage the strait path, which has been so laborious a journey for Christian and his friends. This man is Ignorance. He explains his hopes and reeks of carnal security to their regenerate souls. Christian faces the challenge and brushes him off, in precisely the way of Theologus with the caviller Antilegon in *The Plaine Mans Path-Way to Heaven.*[5] Such carnal confidence was too offensive for a contemporary to pass unrebuked. Bunyan's audience would have been taught by ministers who subscribed to the explanations offered in Thomas Taylor's *The Parable of the Sower and the Seed* (1621). Here, but at excessive length, this case is clarified in such a way as to make Bunyan's interpretation inevitable. Taylor treats of the need of hearing sermons – 'Faith is by hearing, and salvation by faith' – and the importance of being good ground to receive heavenly assistance.[6] He then goes on to delineate the soul of the hypocrite as one 'which likes Heaven well, but not the way to it' : which is actuated to religion by policy and science instead of conscience. Taylor is not out to comfort : 'It is no certaine marke of a childe of God, willingly to heare Sermons, nor to delight in the hearing, nor to receive the doctrine with ioy, no nor in many things commendably to practise . . .' (p. 121). The Christian must love Jerusalem above his chief joy and must humble himself. Here we may recall Christian's penitential words at the wicket-gate, 'Here is a poor burdened sinner' and compare them with the pervasive tone of Ignorance, if we care to learn the author's intention of emphasizing the need for humility and guidance. We may also compare the wordiness of Talkative with the longer passages of edifying conversation that are the fitting accompaniment for such a journey as Christian's. These are reported at length in two sessions – one more intimate and personal in its address than the other – which debate the duties of the Christian and the union between God and the soul after regeneration has been achieved. These ideas spring from homiletic sources, common to Bunyan, Taylor, Dent and many more. In blending in the mind of the creative dramatic artist they became the character Ignorance; in such comparisons we see how the religious writer prepared his ground, and in what way Bunyan was galvanizing and popularizing works with a narrower and more academic public.

Many writers have been satisfied that Ignorance represents an attack upon the Quaker trust in Inner Light. One ingenious detailed study[7] offered fuller proof of a case which does not necessarily invalidate the one offered here. Christian seizes at once upon the fact that the interloper has not chosen the true path. The excuse he offers does not alleviate Christian's wrath: 'I know my Lord's will, and I have been a good liver; I pay every man his own; I pray, fast, pay tithes, and give alms, and have left my country for whither I am going.'[8] – which was not written without a knowledge of the same sources as were open to Taylor: 'I thanke God, he might say, I am no Recusant, I come to Church, I heare good Sermons, and if any could tell me a better way to heaven, I would surely take it.'[9] The preacher would have unveiled the pride of the hypocrite and show that, in spite of apparent good deeds which impress the neighbourhood, he might be damned: 'He is a right honest Man, a substantiall man, a iolly housekeeper, a quiet neighbour, a welldealing man, and well-beloved of his neighbours, a man good to the poor.'[10] Similar phrases are used in Dent's *Path-Way*, when the Plain Man is not content to hear himself respected in the parish, since he knows, from the powerful exhortation of the divine, Theologus, that social life may be taken as no guide to the state of the soul, and that the carriage to the 'world-ward' is unimportant beside the conduct to 'God-ward'. The same notion appears in the scene where Worldly Wiseman requests Christian to give up the pilgrimage and to settle in the town of Morality: 'There shalt thou live by honest neighbours, in credit and in good fashion.' (p. 20)

Such collusion in three writers suggests a common traditional interpretation of human character, which is a facet of the seventeenth century's adherence to religious standards in general conduct. Biographers of the period summed up their subjects in certain ways; men might be praised for their humility, innocence, but not for their cultivation of the superficial or sentimental social virtues: 'But withal he was a person of great *gravity*, his *mildness* did not degenerate into fondness or levity, nor his *gravity* into moroseness, or austerity, but a *kindly* mixture of *mildness*, *Majesty* and attractive *sweetness*, but such an *awful reverence* into his countenance, as did at once banish impudent *profaneness*, and animate religious *modesty*.'[11] The words in italics are taken into speech from the categories of the pulpit, and suggest that men were valued for their conduct to 'God-ward' in society by all who were qualified to pronounce. That such judgements were general may be proved by the inspection of any similar document: Clarendon's portraits offer a gallery of religious portraiture with subjects taken from a large field.

To revert to the text, Ignorance, affronted by their scorn, leaves the two pilgrims; when he comes before our view again, he offers an excuse, which also condemns him': 'I take my pleasure in walking alone, even more a great deal than in company, unless I like it the better' (p. 172). In this passage a contemporary reader would have found not only scoffing at the holy ones, but also sinful self-reliance and security which is tantamount to a rejection of the advice of the elect. The dialogue grows heated, although it does not reach the warmth of Antilegon's abuse in Dent's book, permitted there to intensify the reader's disgust. Christian exposes the faults in his reasoning, and is answered: 'I have not in my head so many whimsies as you.' In this manner he swings away from the pair, full of false confidence. He is no

longer the personification of Ignorance alone; he is one who has
flown wilfully in God's face. The last that we see of him concludes the whole allegory very properly. On the last page the
elect look down and see him come up to the gate without his roll
of election :

. . . so he fumbled in his bosom for one, and found none. Then said
they, Have you none? But the man answered never a word. So they
told the King, but he would not come down to see him, but commanded the two Shining Ones that conducted Christian and Hopeful to the city, to go out and take Ignorance, and bind him hand and
foot, and have him away (p. 194).

He goes to join the others who prosper in their hypocrisy for a
short time, and who answer to the description offered in Robert
Bolton's *Foure Last Things*, even down to the Ferry of Vain-
Hope which brought him up to the gate : 'How many go to hell
with a vaine hope of heaven; whose chiefest cause of damnation
is their false perswasion, and groundlesse presumption of salvation.'[12]
   Because this problem worried readers, many tracts devoted
space to its explanation, and no book of the time is complete
without showing its readers their spiritual state. Dent's *Path-Way*
was undertaken to show whether 'a man bee saved or damned',
and all its successors had interpretations to offer. Bunyan was
not content to leave the matter in dramatic form; he amplified
his ideas in his tract, *The Pharisee and the Publican*. Here
he compares two attitudes to prayer; one that of a Publican con-
sorting with harlots and drunkards, the other of one proud that
he is of a higher class, and who stands in contempt of the
Publican who will not approach the altar in shame. This
Publican is the 'sinful commoner' who is to be preferred to one
who 'would carry the bell and wear the garland for religion', and
like it most, with By-Ends, when it went in its silver shoes. The
words of the Pharisee – 'I fast, give alms' – are the source for
those of Antilegon and Ignorance, and Bunyan's judgement is :
'What, though he was not like the publican, yet he was like, yea,
a downright hypocrite; he wanted in those things wherein he
boasted himself, sincerity.'[13] Deeper inspection proves to the com-

mentator that this profession of faith omits many sins that he committed in his pride, and will not humbly acknowledge. He also attributes to his own qualities the abilities he owes to God alone, which is, in a manner, putting food into a trencher at a heavenly banquet. The self-bemoaning publican is preferred, and accepted as a worthy pilgrim. The distinction to be drawn between these men tells again the attitude of the true believer who is never satisfied with himself, and of the hypocrite who is secure: 'We are not such Atheists, or so profane, but wee have believed ever since wee were borne: wee have ever trusted in Christ, and made account of him as our Saviour.'[14] Of the Pharisees, Bunyan concludes that 'at the end of their way is death and hell': and even to the end he counts on a reward, 'when indeed he was going down to the chambers of death', to the fate of the one who fell at the end of the celestial pilgrimage.

Spiritual education was highly prized by the Puritan divines, and it seemed impossible to them that sinfulness could be due to anything other than wilful ignorance. The poor 'lewd' and un-instructed man was a different case, and as such he stands out in the pages of popular theology, whether as the Poor Caitiff or as the Plain Man. His humility was recognized and his innocence protected from the falsifiers of God's Word, the 'Hypocrites and Sepulchres painted over', as Thomas Taylor called them, who are inwardly 'full of filthie pride and covetousness' yet who attend all the functions of Christian religion.[15] To distinguish was indeed difficult and all the Puritan ministers were engaged in this attempt throughout the century, independently yet with phrase-ology and manner alike. The Biblical quotation from which their attitude develops is one which Bunyan himself uses in the case of Ignorance, as the doctrinal basis for his dramatization; it is from St John, and appears in Christian's denunciation:

But thou camest not in at the wicket-gate that is at the head of this way; thou camest in hither through that same crooked lane, and therefore, I fear, however thou mayest think of thyself, when the reckoning day shall come, thou wilt have laid to thy charge that thou art a thief and a robber, instead of getting admittance into the city.[16]

The Parable of the Man without the Wedding-Garment is threaded into this great narrative, since his sin also was wilful resistance to God's Word. He was not prepared for the feast and was cast out into exterior darkness to provide another attractive moralization for the expository theologian seeking concrete formulations for the problems of appearance and reality in religious observance. Henry Smith, the celebrated preacher, chose the parable as the text for a sermon : 'Some put on Christ as a cloak, which hangeth upon their shoulders, and covereth them : when they go abroad to be seen of men, they can put on the cloak of holiness, and seem for a while as holy as the best : but so soon as they come home the cloak goeth off, and the man is as he was, whose vizard was better than his face.'[17]

Readers of any of these works and hearers of any of these sermons knew well that there were hypocrites abroad, and all Bunyan's devils are presented for that purpose, and offered as a clear and exact lesson. Without the benefit of his religious training and the traditional inheritance which he and all his predecessors and contemporaries imbibed in their early days, many have mistaken his aim. They need the attentions of the Evangelist to correct them when they find the treatment of Ignorance the flaw in the book. To proceed no nearer to our century than Hannah More's tracts of the 1790's and to suggest no invidious modern parallels we find, instead of subtlety, a moral obtuseness that needs such speeches as this from a rich man to stir it into life : 'It is customary for everybody to repeat the general confession . . . though every respectable person must know they have no particular concern in it, as they are not sinners.'[18] This, in its blatancy, seems almost a caricature of one of the seventeenth-century originals. Popular theology at this period of Evangelical Revival achieved its effects by presenting the outrageously false which could have misled no wavering Saint. Bunyan's readers knew well why Mr Ignorance was damned. The contemporaries of Dent, Smith and Taylor had taught them to distinguish well. All writers assented to this interpretation (although some thought the Hypocrite capable of regeneration),[19] and knew that the pilgrimage was a difficult one in which some would be debarred from making acquaintance with its terrors. Anyone who was blithely whistling along a green lane, happy about the state of his soul on that particular morning in his life, would find no open gates at the other end.

SOURCE: *Modern Language Review*, XLIV (1949) pp. 483–9.

NOTES

1. Thomas Taylor, *The Practice of Repentance* (London, 1632) p. 79.
2. *Diaries and Letters of Philip Henry, M.A.*, ed. M. H. Lee (London, 1882) p. 33.
3. *The Life of Dr Robert Harris*, in Samuel Clarke, *32 English Divines* (London, 1677) p. 328.
4. Everyman Edition, p. 144.
5. Quotations will be found in an article in *Modern Language Review*, XLIV (January 1949) pp. 26–34.
6. Cf. Evangelist's 'I have sowed and you have reaped' (ed. cit. p. 102).
7. J. W. Draper, 'Mr Ignorance', *Modern Language Review*, XXII (1927).
8. *Pilgrim's Progress*, p. 146.
9. *The Parable of the Sower and the Seed*, p. 172.
10. Taylor, *The Practice of Repentance*, p. 267.
11. Oliver Heywood, *Life of John Angier of Denton*, ed. W. Axon (Manchester, 1937) p. 81. Italics mine [i.e. Hussey's – Ed.].
12. Robert Bolton, *Foure Last Things* (London, 1635) p. 26.
13. *The Pharisee and the Publican*, in *Works*, ed. G. Offor, II (Glasgow, Edinburgh and London, 1862) p. 224. I choose this tract, but the phrases and ideas appear in almost all his minor works.
14. Bolton, *Foure Last Things*, p. 64.
15. Bunyan's religious Communion was unusually broad, which gave him opportunities of studying the manners of the Reprobate in quality and in detail.
16. Ed. cit. p. 147. This is built up from : 'Qui non intrat per ostium in ovile, sed aliunde, fur est et latro.'
17. Henry Smith, 'The Wedding Garment', in *Sermons*, I (London, 1866) p. 157.
18. *Two Wealthy Farmers*. This is included in the collections of Hannah More's tracts, but has been also ascribed to Mrs Trimmer.

The *Tales for the Common People* were issued anonymously, and
were all written after a pattern which makes identification of author
impossible.

19. Anglican writers have been omitted from this study, but
Bishop Hall offers excellent descriptions of the genre.

Arnold Kettle

THE MORAL FABLE (1951)

Almost every household in eighteenth-century England in which any member was literate must have possessed a copy of *The Pilgrim's Progress*. Lady Wishfort in *The Way of the World* might be cynical about Bunyan but her cynicism was in itself a tribute to the universality of his book, even apparently among that small, fashionable section of London society that had arrogated to itself the title of the 'world'.

The quality in *The Pilgrim's Progress* and *Mr. Badman* that gives such force and solidity to their allegory and makes them a part of the tradition of the English novel is what we have already defined as realism, a concern with the actual, unimaginary problems of living besetting the average man and woman of the time. And the realism emerges not only from the unsuspecting detail (like Mr. By-ends' great-grandfather, merely a waterman 'looking one way and rowing another') but from the very texture of Bunyan's prose. This prose has too often been described simply as 'biblical'. Obviously the influence of the Bible is there and the Authorized Version itself was no dead work of academic translation; but to over-emphasize Bunyan's debt to the Bible may easily lead to an underestimation of his debt to his own ear.

> *Christian* : And what did you say to him?
> *Faithful* : Say! I could not tell what to say at first.

The tone of that 'Say!' is not the tone of the Bible. Nor is it sufficient to attach the label 'biblical' to this conversation between Faithful and Talkative :

> *Faithful.* . . . for what things so worthy of the use of the tongue

and mouth of men on Earth, as are the things of the God of Heaven?

Talkative. I like you wonderful well, for your saying is full of conviction; and I will add, what thing is so pleasant, and so profitable, as to talk of the things of God?

What things so pleasant? (that is, if a man hath any delight in things that are wonderful) for instance? If a man doth delight to talk of the History, or the Mystery of things; or if a man doth love to talk of Miracles, Wonders, or Signs, where shall he find things recorded so delightful, and so sweetly penned, as in the holy Scripture?

Faithful. That's true : but to be profited by such things in our talk should be that which we design.

Talkative. That is it that I said; for to talk of such things is most profitable, for by so doing, a man may get knowledge of many things; as of the vanity of earthly things, and the benefit of things above : (thus in general) but more particularly, By this a man may learn the necessity of the New birth, the insufficiency of our works, the need of Christ's righteousness, &c. Besides, by this a man may learn, what it is to repent, to believe, to pray, to suffer, or the like : by this also a man may learn what are the great promises and consolations of the Gospel, to his own comfort. Further, by this a man may learn to refute false opinions, to vindicate the truth, and also to instruct the ignorant.

Faithful. All this is true, and glad am I to hear these things from you.

Talkative. Alas, the want of this is the cause that so few understand the need of faith, and the necessity of a (work) of Grace in their Soul, in order to eternal life; but ignorantly live in the works of the Law, by which a man can by no means obtain the Kingdom of Heaven.

What brings this little scene so splendidly to life is the way Bunyan captures the colloquial note of the speech around him, so that Talkative becomes not a dim personification, not a stock figure of allegory, but a genuine flesh-and-blood person, a real next-door-neighbour. It is a very subtle passage not because Talkative is a subtle character or his shallowness hard to see through, but because the precise nature of that shallowness is revealed to us with a remarkable economy of words and without any extraneous comment. The difference between his view of 'profit', for instance, and Faithful's could not be more effectively conveyed, nor could the quality of his interest in 'the History, or the Mystery of things'. Even the glib near-rhyme has its contribution to make.

The Pilgrim's Progress is allegory. Bunyan himself significantly calls it a Dream. It is an allegorical representation of the individual Christian's struggle to achieve salvation. He abandons life (including his unfortunate wife and family) and seeks death. But the desire for death in *Pilgrim's Progress* has little in common with the death-wish of later literature. Christain's aim is not to cease upon the midnight with no pain. On the contrary his progress is one of constant struggle and conflict and the words, 'Life, Life, Eternal Life' are on his lips. True this identification of life with death leaves Bunyan with some unsolved problems, some loose ends to his pattern – Christian's wife in the first part, her children in the second – and to the modern reader the picture of Mr. Greatheart and Mr. Valiant playing for joy upon the well-tuned cymbal and harp while the children weep is inadequate and indeed repulsive. But the essential point is that, though he cannot wholly evade the consequences of a world-picture which sees death as more important than life and salvation as a matter concerning the individual as an isolated entity, in spite of this basically life-denying philosophy Bunyan manages to infuse a living breath into his fable. As Mr. Jack Lindsay has put it :

The impression conveyed by the allegory is the exact opposite of what it literally professes. The phantasms of good and evil become the real world; and in encountering them the Pilgrim lives through the life that Bunyan had known in definite place and time. The pattern of his experience, the fall and resolute rising-up, the loss and the finding, the resistance and the overcoming, the despair and the joy, the dark moaning valleys and the singing in the places of the flowers – it is the pattern of Bunyan's life. There are comrades and enemies, stout-hearts and cravens, men who care only for the goal of fellowship and men of greed and fear; and these are the men of contemporary England. The Celestial City is the dream of all England, all the world, united in Fellowship . . .

I think Mr. Lindsay is wrong to identify in too facile a way Bunyan's Celestial City with the modern man's goal of fellowship. Bunyan believed in a life after death and there is no point in insinuating that, had he known better, he would have believed in something else. What is important is that the positive quality of Bunyan's belief in a life after death and the actual tensions of mortal struggle which (as Mr. Lindsay excellently brings out) give the prose its muscular, colloquial vitality, these qualities go far to negate the anti-humanist, defeatist character of the myth itself. And the power to transform the myth in this way into something positive and vital comes from Bunyan's profound and disciplined participation not only in the folk-mythology of his day, which he made new, but in the life of his time – he the jailed dissenting tinker – and in the actual problems which racked seventeenth-century England.

The Pilgrim's Progress, at once allegorical and colloquial, is the link between the medieval allegory and the moral fable of the eighteenth century. The austere yet unsophisticated (though by no means unsubtle) Puritan morality of Bunyan may have little that is obviously in common with the worldly and bitter satire of Swift, but essentially *The Pilgrim's Progress* and *Gulliver's Travels* are of the same *genre*.

The difference in tone springs to a large degree from the differences in background of the authors. Whereas from every page of Bunyan's book there emerge the attitudes and hardships of the humble but independent 'small-man', the honest, upright, morally desperate journeyman, the tone of *Gulliver* is that of the supremely intelligent and sensitive member of the ruling class who has behind him, despite his lack of 'politeness', all the sophistication of a polite society in which, on one level at least, he is very much at home. His very capacity to shock his world comes from Swift's own inclusion in it. So does the lack of good advice. Unlike Bunyan he is not addressing an audience desperately desiring to know how to cope with their crushing burdens. And so his shock-tactics, though not less intense, are entirely different. Above all he is concerned to tell his readers that their world is not in the least like what they think it is. Not wickeder but worse. It is not the

Puritan soul seeking salvation but England in the reign of Queen Anne that is Swift's subject, and his weapon is his human indignation.

SOURCE: from 'The Moral Fable', in *An Introduction to the English Novel*, vol. 1 (1951) pp. 43–8.

R. M. Frye

THE WAY OF ALL PILGRIMS (1960)

Moving from transhistory into history, we find that the life of the archetypal man, Adam, gives way to the life of the archetypal Christian. The full vision of Christianity, presented in *Paradise Lost* through symbol and accommodation, sets the stage for all human thought and experience. The movement in Milton's epic is from divine reality to human situation, and the method is the accommodation, by vital symbols, of transcendent truth to human understanding. In *The Pilgrim's Progress*, the vision is implemented in the way, the faith caught up in works, and the movement is from the city of man to the city of God. The method of allegory in Bunyan's work is broad, so that all Christian life is set forth in, and explained by, the lives of his pilgrims. Milton carries us from the heavenly city to the earthly situation, and Bunyan reverses the course, taking us 'from this world to that which is to come'. Between the two works, the cycle is completed and the union of faith and life made explicit.

I DEPARTURE AND MOTIVES

Pilgrim's Progress opens with the vision of a man clothed in rags, symbolic of the ultimate poverty of humanity, and weighed down by the burden of guilt which he carries on his back. His first words are, 'What shall I do?' (9)[1] Knowing only the misery of man's condition, he finds no way of escape; he sees only part of the vision – man's evil – and from this he seeks release. As his understanding deepens, he adds three significant words to his earlier question: 'What shall I do *to be saved*?' (10) By these words, Bunyan indicates his protagonist's comprehension of the necessary distinction between escape and rescue, a distinction we have already treated (Part 1, Chap. 4). Knowing his sin, and his inability to escape unaided, without entering into even greater sin, the pilgrim is now prepared for the meeting with Evangelist, who points to the way of Christ and directs the pilgrim to the Wicket Gate.

The Gate by which the pilgrim enters upon the way is Christ, according to the symbolism by which Jesus had declared, 'I am the door.'[2] This identification of Christ with the Gate is explicit in Part II ('the Gate which is Christ') of *The Pilgrim's Progress* (197–204), but is clearly implicit here, so that the Christian begins with the incarnation and moves on toward God. Men tend to assume they can know God as he is, often judging Christ by his conformity to a prior human image of God. Christianity, however, denies that finite and sinful creatures can know God, with any great clarity, apart from Christ. Bunyan thus indicates that the pilgrim knows virtually nothing of God until he enters the Gate which God has provided, and that henceforth, his knowledge increases as he advances along the route of pilgrimage.

Pilgrim's Progress consists of two parts, each complete in itself. The first recounts the full journey of the pilgrim, who was called Graceless and is now known as Christian, from the City of Destruction to the Celestial City. Concerned as it is with the individual, this first part presents one facet of the Christian life, and does not deal primarily with the larger life of the Christian community. The second part of the allegory supplies the perspective of the Church, the body of Christians moving over the same ground that Christian had earlier covered. At first there is Christian's wife, Christiana, who had abandoned him to his journey alone, but who now sets out to follow him with their four sons and a charming young girl named Mercy. Others are added to this group as the pilgrimage proceeds, and finally there is a large company of diverse members who complete the journey together. By the device of two juxtaposed narratives, Bunyan provides a stereoscopic view of the Christian life, fully three-dimensional and vital in its perspectives, expressing both the individual and the corporate aspects of the pilgrimage.

From the total number of the pilgrims in both parts of the allegory, we see the various types of Christian life and the problems, temptations, and joys incident to each. Not all the pilgrims set out for the same reason, and each has a somewhat different experience of the way. Christian leaves the City of Destruction because of a compelling sense of doom, and a sort of numinous fear, so that he sets out with less sense of his goal than of his need. Christiana, on the other hand, begins her journey in response to a specific invitation from the King of Heaven, and with a clear sense both of favorable destiny and of destination. Further, it is at the invitation of Christiana, rather than of God, that young Mercy begins her pilgrimage, while Hopeful joins Christian on his lonely way after the martyrdom of Christian's earlier companion, Faithful. Others leave for equally appropriate and personal reasons, but all go through the same Gate, and over the same way. As Augustine put it, 'Christ as God is the fatherland where we are going; Christ as man is the way by which we go.'[3] The way is the same, but the wayfarers differ and, therefore, so does the wayfaring. Each learns for himself and in terms of his own character 'how to act faith' (213), to use the words of Christiana, and each increases in the love for God and for God's people, which is the only ultimately satisfactory motive for acting the Christian faith.

The pilgrims who complete the journey from destruction to fulfillment do so out of 'the love that they bear to the King of this place' (172), and they continue in the way only because, like Christian, they prefer the person, company, and servants of Christ over the enticements of Apollyon (61–2). No other motivation is ultimately sufficient to sustain the pilgrims in the completion of so difficult a way. Each who perseveres does so in order that, as young Samuel puts it, 'I may see God, and serve him without weariness; that I may see Christ and love him everlastingly; that I may have that fulness of the Holy Spirit in me, that I can by no means here enjoy' (238). Heaven is sought not because it is 'a palace and state most blessed', but because God is the center of heaven, and it is only for that reason that heaven is the palace and state most blessed (238).

The love of God, then, is clearly central. Without it, man's alienation cannot be overcome, or his fulfillment attained. We have developed in some detail, in Chapter 3, the threefold alienation from which Adam suffers, as his sin sets him at odds with

God, with his neighbor, and with himself. This isolation of the self is overcome, as we have seen, only by reconciliation with God, and this reconciliation comes in its turn only through the action of God himself, in and through Christ. In Christ, God acts so that his justice and mercy, his power and his love, are at one, and it is only through such divine action that man can be rescued from imprisonment to his own self-critical or self-satisfied self. No merely human efforts will suffice, for, as Hopeful says of himself, man commits enough sin in one duty to seal his own isolation; Augustine says, our greatest virtues are but splendid vices (149). Man, then, must enter through the one Gate.

Along the way, there are a number of pseudo-pilgrims who have entered over the wall rather than through the Gate, and they contend that their entry is effective enough, since it has put them on the road in a manner best suited to their own conditions; it is, in other words, more convenient for them. Of the convenient, Kierkegaard writes that it should be applied 'wherever it can be applied, in relation to everything which is in such a sense a thing that this thing can be possessed irrespective of the way in which it is possessed, so that one can have it either in this way or the other; for when such is the case, the convenient and comfortable way is undeniably to be preferred'. Such a 'convenient and comfortable' view of the way is held by those who enter it apart from the Gate, and who never complete the journey. Kierkegaard aptly continues: 'But the eternal is not a thing which can be had regardless of the way in which it is acquired; no, the eternal is not really a thing, but is the way in which it is acquired. The eternal is acquired in *one* way, and the eternal is different from everything else precisely for the fact that it can be acquired only in a single way.'[4] Eternal life, then, *is* 'the way in which it is acquired', and that way is the Christ-Gate, which provides the only ultimate means of reconciliation.

This reconciliation, though primarily with God, is also with other selves and with the individual self. Once the self is properly related to its creator, it is ready for a proper relation with other creatures and with itself as a part of creation. These relations are expressions of love, which Augustine defines as 'a motion of the soul whose purpose is to enjoy God for his own sake, and ourselves and our neighbor for the sake of God'.[5]

Contradicting the operation of this love, it is one function of the demonic agents along the route of the pilgrims to set up 'a difference between a man and himself' (317), to make man be 'unmerciful to himself', to dwell with ruin (215, 218), and to love his ease and comfort more than he loves himself (228). The demonic plays on a self-love which is really a form of self-hate, and seeks to develop a destruction of the self which is consequent on an unhealthy affirmation of the self. On the other hand, a healthy and proper self-love is possible only as corollary to the love of God, issuing in what Milton in *Paradise Lost* called 'self-esteem, grounded on just and right Well manag'd' (VIII, 572–3). It is in this sense that Mercy 'yearned over her own soul', fell 'in love with her own salvation' and followed Christiana 'to seek to live forever' (194, 197, 205). In Augustine's words, 'it is impossible for one who loves God not to love himself'.[6] The love of God above and beyond the self so alters the face of life that it becomes possible to love both neighbor and self, and to seek in heaven the consummation of charity in companionship with immortals (193).

What may have begun in fear, as with Christian, must give place to this determinative love, if it is to attain to the completion of the way. But although fear may tend to set the pilgrim on his way, as Christian clearly feels that it does (160), fear as such is not necessarily a virtue, and may be a serious form of sin. It may be the fear of difficulty which prevents false pilgrims from completing the journey, or it may be the fear of public opinion, what Hopeful called the 'fear of men' (162), that makes man conform to the contemporary norms of society rather than to the eternal norm of Christ. To such temptations all the pilgrims are subjected, some succumbing to them. Worst of all, perhaps, is the fear of punishment, the 'fear of the torments of hell' which Hopeful says makes some men temporarily 'hot for heaven' (162). The difficulty here, as Christian points out, is that 'the fear of the halter' may exist apart from any 'detestation of the offense' which leads to the halter (163). Men so affected 'seem hot for heaven so long as the flames of hell are about their ears, yet when that terror is a little over, they betake themselves to second thoughts' (162). 'From those who fear punishment,' Augustine said, 'grace is hidden.'⁷

But there is another type of fear to which Augustine referred when he wrote that 'piety begins with fear and is perfected in love'.⁸ This is the productive fear which Christian experienced so often in the earlier stages of his journey, and which was one part of his incentive for leaving the City of Destruction. Not all the pilgrims set out from a fear of the consequences of sin, and some experience virtually no sense of fear in the ordinary ways, but for Christian himself, fear is one motive for seeking God. In his experience, as in that of Kierkegaard, it was necessary to have feared God before he could come to love him. Christian's course may be marked in terms of Alfred North Whitehead's three stages in the development of religion : 'It is the transition from God the void [before the allegory opens] to God the enemy [the stage of frustrated fear with which the story begins], and from God the enemy to God the companion, [beginning when Christian enters the Gate].'⁹

None of these fears is merely the common form of reflex or adrenal fear which all men experience, in varying degrees, when faced with impinging danger. Adrenal fear and alarm is common enough in Bunyan's story, but it is not determinative for the true pilgrims, and is always driven out either by a larger and nobler fear or by impetus from the love to which that fear is akin. This noblest fear is the pilgrim's fear of offending against the love of God, and it tends in its turn to 'take away from them their pitiful old self-holiness' (161). The thing that is dreaded is not punishment, but separation from God, whether because of active evil or passive self-righteousness. Fear grounded in guilt is not enough, though it may be a beginning. What is necessary is an entire and radical reorientation and redirection of life. 'When your heart is thus established in Christ,' Luther wrote, 'you are an enemy of sin out of love and not out of fear of punishment.'¹⁰

One further form of fear afflicts Christian, both as he attempts to cross over the Slough of Despond on his way to the Wicket Gate, and as he crosses the final River of Death to the celestial country. This fear is a form of deficient faith, an inadequate reliance on the grace of God which may afflict even the redeemed. It is a final mark of continuing faithlessness, even in the faithful, so that, at the very outset of his pilgrimage, Christian is driven into the Slough of Despond by fear which 'followed me so hard' (16), and again, at the end of his course, he almost goes under the waters of the river out of 'horror of mind and hearty fears that he should die in that river and never obtain entrance' to the heavenly city (167). In each instance, Christian is afflicted by a deeply morbid sense of sin, the retention of which is, in itself, a form of sin even in the Christian whose life has been radically reorientated toward God.

The righteousness of the Christian is never a mere sinlessness, relieved from all blemishes. It is not a thing pure and apart, but is a center of confidence, a direction of aspiration, a basic character of charity, lived within the framework of common liabilities. All Bunyan's pilgrims continue to sin in greater and lesser degrees, and are not to be distinguished from others by the flawlessness of their lives, as much as by the center of their patriotism. The true pilgrims clearly place their loyalties in the heavenly city, and, despite occasional errrings, move in general in that direction. It is this patriotism and loyalty which makes them appear as fools to the citizens of the present world. The criticisms most commonly applied to them are that they are fools and unmanly, not normally human.

The criteria for wisdom and for humanity are under continuous dispute, at least by implication, throughout *Pilgrim's Progress*. Obstinate tells the wayfaring Christian to 'be wise' (13), Vanity Fair calls him a madman (96), and his wife thinks him neurotic (189). In the second part of the allegory, when Christiana sets out to follow her husband, she is called a fool and insane, while Obstinate and Pliable are held up as models of wisdom (193–6). On the question of humanity, Worldly-wiseman warns Christian that the Bible can 'unman men' (20), and Shame tells Faithful that his conscience is 'unmanly' (77). From the Christian point of view, it is held that those who leave the way to the heavenly city to delve in Demas' silver mine will never be 'their own men again' (113), and Christian is said to have 'played the man' in opposing Apollyon (253).

The divergence apparent in these instances, as in many others, is again traceable to the matter of rooted loyalties. For each of the true pilgrims, loyalty is centered in God, and the norm both of manhood and wisdom is discovered in Christ. The ultimate criterion of life is found to reside neither in transience, as with the City of Destruction, nor in human legalism, as with the Village of Morality, nor in popular materialism, as in Vanity Fair, but only in the normative person of Christ. For this reason, the Christians must enter through the Wicket Gate, and so their basic judgments of wisdom and of humanity differ radically from those of all others they meet. The regnant God in the celestial city is the goal of the pilgrim's way, the incarnate Son on earth is the norm of the pilgrim's life and thought. Without the Son there would be no true knowledge of the entry and the way to the Father, so that all who would attain everlasting communion with God must begin by coming in at the Gate. That is an inescapable absolute of the pilgrimage.

II   THE TWO RELATIVISMS

Along with this absolute there is much relativism among the pilgrims. Indeed, relativism is as much found among the true pilgrims as among the false, though the character of one group's relativism differs entirely from that of the other. For the Christian pilgrims, there are marked and highly relative differences of response to the way, but there is also commitment to the way itself. For the pseudo-pilgrims, relativism appears in their various ways of entry and advance, one way being judged as valid as another. After scaling the wall, Formalist and Hypocrisy ask : 'If we get into the way, what matter which way we get in? If we are in, we are in' (43). Similarly, they get out of the way when they come to the Hill Difficulty, and choose the seemingly easier paths marked Danger and Destruction. One route being as good as another, they naturally choose those which appear the more convenient. Later, Christian meets two men who have turned back from the way because of the horrors of the Valley of the Shadow of Death. When Christian persists in going forward along the dangerous road which they have just abandoned, they

comment : 'Be it thy way, we will not choose it for ours' (66).
Other similar examples of secular relativism might be cited, but
these are sufficient : the way is seen as relative to man, determined by man. Viewing the landscape of reality from the perspective of the self, all falls into place in terms of convenience
and acceptability to the individual. In this manner the primary
sin asserts itself again : man is god, the *I* is god, and his own
knowledge of good and evil is determinative. The entrance, the
way, and even the goal, are relative to the individuals who
judge. Thus Ignorance says to Hopeful and Christian : 'Be content to follow the religion of your country, and I will follow the
religion of mine. I hope all will be well' (132).

In all this, the Christian assumptions are not attacked so much
as repudiated by the false pilgrims. Without a recognition of the
primary sin of self-deification, they cannot see the dangers involved in making pilgrimage only to please themselves. Their
relativism is that of the absolute self, by which all else is judged.

The Christian pilgrim's relativism, on the other hand, is that
of the relative self before an absolute God. The way established
by God can neither be short cut, nor made over, nor avoided, but
experience of the one way will vary greatly according to the individual temper of the wayfarers. In this regard, the experience
of various pilgrims may be compared to that of Christian, who is
clearly the most prideful of those who eventually reach the
heavenly city. It is due to his pride, and his inability to meet,
on his own terms, the proud standards which he holds up for
himself, that Christian falls into the Slough of Despond, which
all others among the faithful pass without mishap. So, too, the
Valley of Humiliation is a dreadful place for Christian, while of
this valley the other pilgrims are told that 'here is nothing to hurt
us unless we procure it to ourselves' (249). Mercy and her companions of part two find it a delightful place, and Mr. Great-
heart declares that 'though Christian had the hard hap to meet
here with Apollyon and to enter with him a brisk encounter, yet I
must tell you, that in former times men have met with angels
here, have found pearls here, and have in this place found the
words of life' (251). Similarly with the Valley of the Shadow of
Death : whereas Christian found it a place of horrors, to Faith-

ful it was a sunshine place (80) and it was never quieter than when Mr. Fearing passed through it (265). Of all the pilgrims, Christian, because of his pride, is the least able to pass in peace through the valleys of Humiliation and of the Shadow of Death.

Faithful is a more fleshly man than Christian, less profound perhaps, and certainly less proud. His temptations accordingly differ from Christian's, and as he is less morbidly fearful about his own guilt, he has no difficulty at the Slough of Despond. He does, however, have a tempting encounter with the lustful Madam Wanton outside the Gate, and she promises him 'all manner of content'. He is so strongly attracted to her that, as he says, 'I know not whether I did wholly escape her or no' (73). More humble than Christian, but also more conventional, he is tempted in the Valley of Humiliation not by the massive on-slaughts of Apollyon but by the rather bourgeois appeals of Dis-content and Shame, who taunt him with his violation of con-ventional mores (76–8).

Other individual differences make for varied experiences of the way. Mr. Fearing, utterly unconcerned with outward dangers, has 'a Slough of Despond in his mind, a Slough that he carried everywhere with him, or else he could never have been as he was' (263). Mr. Feeble-mind is 'carried up' the Hill Difficulty over which all the other pilgrims toil (281), and the shepherds in the Delectable Mountains call on each of the weaker pilgrims by name, as they would otherwise be 'most subject to draw back' (299). Each of the principal pilgrims sets out in a fashion somewhat different from that of the others, Christian with a deep, numinous awe, Christiana with middle class direct-ness, the children because they are told to go, and Valiant-for-truth with the forthrightness of the young knight-errant : 'I be-lieved and therefore came out, got into the way, fought all that set themselves against me, and by believing am come to this place' (309).

For all of the true pilgrims, though, 'the way is the way, and there's an end' (250). They may temporarily persuade them-selves, as Christian does, that there is a better path, but always they return to the way itself, to endure there whatever their own failures may procure to themselves until they complete the entrance of the Wicket Gate by entrance into the Celestial Gate. The movement is from earthly disclosure through Christ to heavenly culmination with God. The Kingdom of Heaven must thus be entered through the two gates, the one at the beginning and the other at the end. Between the two is the inescapable road of pilgrimage. To it, Christian is directed at the Wicket Gate : 'Look before thee : dost thou see this narrow way? *That* is the way thou must go. It was cast up by the patriarchs, prophets, Christ, and his apostles, and it is as straight as a rule can make it. This is the way thou must go' (29).

As Reinhold Niebuhr puts it,

The Kingdom of Heaven as it *has come* in Christ means a disclosure of the meaning of history but not the full realization of that meaning. That is anticipated in the Kingdom which *is to come*, that is, in the culmination of history. . . . Thus history as we know it is regarded as an 'interim' between the disclosure and the fulfillment of its meaning.[11]

The Christian accepts the inescapable absoluteness of the disclosure and of the fulfillment, as both are wholly determined by the will of God, and accepts the relativities of the 'interim' through which he passes from the one to the other.

III THE SLOW ADVANCE

Entrance at the Wicket Gate can establish a final commitment to God, but it does not and cannot establish a static relationship. Entrance provides the possibility of growth, and growth precludes a static condition. Thus the naive hope of Mercy is disappointed, and she discovers that by entering upon the way she has not left danger and sorrow behind (208), as she had expected. An apt description of the difficult life of Christian wayfaring comes from Old Honest, who says : 'Sometimes our way is clean, sometimes foul : sometimes up hill, sometimes down hill. We are seldom at a certainty' (289).

In this condition, beset by repeated difficulties within and without, 'seldom at a certainty', the pilgrims 'keep by the pole, and do by compass steer from sin to grace' (298). Holding to their goal of communion with God, they nonetheless do not have the goal always before their eyes, and they move slowly. When Evangelist first directs Christian, it is not for the full journey, and he gives him as his goal not the City of Zion, but the Wicket Gate and the light which he dimly sees shining about it. When Pliable briefly joins Christian, he asks him if he knows the whole way to the 'desired place', and Christian replies that he has only been directed 'to a little Gate that is before us, where we shall receive instructions about the way' (13). So it is again in the second part of the allegory that when one of the children asks the guide, Mr. Great-heart, whether they can see to the end, he is merely told to 'look to your feet, for you shall presently be among the snares' (256). The pilgrimage is long, and must be taken one step at a time. 'Come, let us venture', says Mercy at the Slough of Despond, 'only let us be wary' (198).

The way is always venturesome, and the pilgrim is sometimes not wary. Christian falls into the Slough of Despond, and Pliable deserts him to return to the City of Destruction. Released from the Slough, Christian again takes up his way toward the Gate, but is diverted by Mr. Worldly-wiseman, who persuades him to work out his own deliverance by improving his character, and so Christian sets out for the Village of Morality, to profit from the counsel of Mr. Legality. On the way, however, he becomes afraid that Mount Sinai will avalanche down upon him and so he turns from legalism, and is once more encountered by Evangelist who again directs him to the Wicket Gate. Once entered there, he is directed to the House of the Interpreter, who further instructs him, and sends him on for the next part of his journey. All this while he has been carrying upon his back the great weight of his guilt, and he is relieved of this burden only when he comes to the cross standing above an empty tomb. Beyond this point he is joined by Formalist and Hypocrisy, who soon apostatize, so that he climbs the Hill Difficulty alone and arrives at the House Beautiful on its summit, where he is refreshed and given further instruction. He next descends into the Valley of Humiliation, and passes on through the Valley of the Shadow of Death, after which he joins Faithful for his first Christian companionship on the road. In Vanity Fair, Faithful is martyred, but his example is such that Hopeful now joins Christian on the way. Together they withstand the blandishments of Demas to turn aside to his silvermine, but they themselves shortly seek an easier path by crossing over into By-Path Meadow, and so are imprisoned by Giant Despair in Doubting Castle. Escaping after a harrowing period in the castle dungeon, they make their way to the Delectable Mountains where they are entertained, instructed and refreshed by the shepherds of Emmanuel's Land. They next meet with Ignorance on the way, pass through their final hazard in the Enchanted Ground, and enter Beulah Land, where they are royally welcomed. Finally, they cross the River of Death and are received with great rejoicing into the City of God. The movement is clearly a matter of gradual stages. From House Beautiful, the pilgrim can see only to the Delectable Mountains, from the Delectable Mountains, he can see the glory and the gate of heaven, and from Beulah, he sees the heavenly city itself. The growth of vision is as gradual as is advance along the way, and throughout, the pilgrims must 'look to their feet' (256). As God the Father says in *Paradise Lost*,

> Light after light well us'd they shall attain,
> And to the end persisting, safe arrive.   (III, 196–7)

SOURCE: *God, Man, and Satan: Patterns of Christian Thought and Life in Paradise Lost, Pilgrim's Progress, and the Great Theologians* (Princeton, 1960) pp. 95–113.

NOTES

1. Page references are to the edition edited by J. B. Wharey (Oxford, 1928).

2. John 10 : 1–18, *passim*.

3. *Sermons,* ed. S. Hebgin and F. Corrigan (New York, 1960–1).

4. Sören Kierkegaard, *Attack upon Christendom*, trans. Walter Lowrie (Princeton, 1944) p. 100.

5. *Christian Doctrine*, in *Basic Writings of Saint Augustine,* ed. Whitney J. Oates (New York, 1948).

6. Waldo Beach and H. Richard Niebuhr (eds), *Christian Ethics, Sources of the Living Tradition* (New York, 1955) p. 117.

7. *Basic Writings of Saint Augustine*, ed. Whitney J. Oates, vol. 1 (New York, 1948) p. 503.

8. *Earlier Writings of Saint Augustine*, trans. and ed. J. H. S. Burleigh, Library of Christian Classics, vol. vi (1953) p. 240.

9. Alfred North Whitehead, *Religion in the Making* (Cambridge, 1927) p. 6.

10. Martin Luther, *A Compend of Luther's Theology*, ed. Hugh Thompson Kerr Jr (Philadelphia, 1943) p. 55.

11. Niebuhr, *The Nature and Destiny of Man, A Christian Interpretation*, vol. ii (New York, 1949) p. 288.

Henri A. Talon

SPACE AND THE HERO IN THE PILGRIM'S PROGRESS: A STUDY OF THE MEANING OF THE ALLEGORICAL UNIVERSE (1961)

'It is not fantastic to assert that it was the Puritan culture as much as Bunyan that produced *The Pilgrim's Progress*' (Q. D. Leavis).[1] But this culture could only produce a work of literature after it had formed a life. The direct source of *The Pilgrim's Progress* is Bunyan's own experience. The hero of the book is fashioned in his author's image. The spiritual development which is found in the autobiography, *Grace Abounding*, appears again in the allegory: but the growth of a conscience has become a pilgrimage, the inward action has taken a concrete form, and the invisible ways of the understanding have built a road and paths like those of seventeenth century England. So the incidents in Christian's tale are symbols of his inward life, and the author's imagination was not so free that it could evade the dictates of a peremptory spiritual compulsion : the general movement and the particular incidents of the *story* as they are set before the reader serve an *action* that goes beyond them.

The story gives to the action a peopled setting, fields that are sometimes like those of Bedfordshire, hills that bring the Chilterns vaguely to mind, houses that bear a certain resemblance to English country mansions, and travellers whose remarks, habits, and very prejudices belong to a particular epoch. The story gives the action a live historical reality.[2]

The action deals primarily with a man's relationship with God, but it also involves his relationship with other people. It may be said therefore that this already dates the action and that there is no need of the story to place it historically. The religious and moral outlook of the hero are enough to determine the historical period.

Is not Puritanism 'a closed account', as Roger Sharrock puts it?[3] For my own part, I once wrote that Bunyan had lived in the theological age of Auguste Comte, and another Bunyan scholar, Maurice Hussey, has remarked that 'Christian was not Everyman, but one of the Lord's chosen souls'.[4]

Mr. Hussey wants by this to register a protest against those who read into the 17th century ideas that belong to other periods of history and particularly to the present age, and who in so doing are guilty of an anachronistic way of thinking which modern scholarship was supposed to have rendered impossible.[5] I believe however that we may apply to Mr. Hussey's remark Leibniz's verdict on the sects : true in what they affirm, but false in what they deny.[6] Indeed, though the contemporary *ethos* is different from that of the seventeenth century, and although the protestant faith is no longer confined within the bounds of a narrow Calvinism, yet, among the religious, moral and metaphysical preoccupations of every man there is something independent of all dogmatism, and independent of the particular forms of this belief or that ethical system. A man is never wholly prisoner of his age. Everyman is seen in Christian as in every truthfully imagined character.

So the universal in the hero's inward life can still waken a response in us. And so we can in a large measure share in the action which is the inner life of the book, while we can only watch from a distance the incidents of the story, with its fights, its giants and its monsters. The action transcends the story. Besides, many details of the book were only prompted by Bunyan's responsibilities as a minister, and bear witness to his homiletic talent alone; but the topography of the road and the chief incidents of the pilgrimage were dictated by his concern for psychological realism in the hero, the only kind of realism that is really important in this work. It even seems to me that formerly, following Sir Charles Firth, I laid too much stress on the realism of the background and of certain secondary characters.[7] A hundred or even a thousand realistic features are not enough to give the appearance of reality to the wonderful land where Christian knew suffering and joy.

It is a dream land which rises from the very first sentence of

the book. Mingled and blending into one another, we find, making a new and individual landscape, the worlds of the Bible and
of the folk-tales dear to the author,[8] pictures of his native
country and of the Holy Land, all dominated by the features of
that inner landscape[9] where his conversion takes place, where his
salvation is decided, and where, in short, the lot for his whole life
is cast. And in this sense we may say that the real country is just
precisely this dream land which Bunyan created with that energy
of vision and of faith which is one of the characteristics of genius.
This, as soon as we have understood the spiritual meaning of the
setting, we no longer find, as Coleridge did,[10] that 'the wide field
full of dark mountains' where one of the false pilgrims is lost, is
ridiculous. The mountain chain does not only represent a landscape, but brings to mind Jeremiah and, through him the word
of God : 'Give glory to the Lord your God, before he cause darkness, and before your feet stumble upon the dark mountains.'[11]

The country through which Christian travels is at once
distant and immeasurably close. It transcends the pragmatic distinction between 'here' and 'there'. The reader quickly sees that
this is a country of the soul, where Biblical heroes and the
Pilgrim may meet, and where past and present are fused.

The hero's meeting with God gains a remarkable concrete
quality because the signs of God's will and his conflict with Satan
can be read in the very landscape. Christian's encounters with
objects are no more accidental than his encounters with people.
It is not by chance that he passes by a mountain spitting fire, or
comes 'to a place somewhat ascending' surmounted with a cross.
In the universe of the allegory the circumstantial *data* are not
fortuitous, any more for that matter than, for Bunyan, they
were in early life. He tells us, in *Grace Abounding*, that he fell
in the river at Bedford but was not drowned, that he put his hand
between the jaws of a snake without being bitten, and that he
escaped death during the siege of a town because another soldier
asked to take his place at the last minute. All these seemed to be
signs from the Lord designed to waken his spirit (paragraphs
12–14). The world is a significant whole to which Bunyan, like
his hero, responded with that intensity of all his being which
characterised him.

Thus out of the symbolic vision natural to a Puritan there grew for Bunyan a literary vision,[12] just as the dreamer of *The Pilgrim's Progress* grew out of the dreams on which he had fed daily for years. Viewed in this light the Dreamer no longer seems to be an artificial device or merely a figure of allegory.

God speaks throughout to Christian as he had spoken to Bunyan. *Grace Abounding* shows this constant interchange of words between God and the tinker, now in a wholly personal form ('A voice did suddenly dart from Heaven into my soul, which said, wilt thou leave thy sins and go to Heaven, or have thy sins and go to Hell') (§ 22), and now making Biblical words resound so loudly that he turned his head to find out where the voice was coming from (§ 93). The Puritan faith does not lead to mystical union but to speech with God.[13] It is no paradox to say that Bunyan did not so much *read* the Gospel as *hear* it from his Master's lips, and that by his fervour and imagination he realised that 'contemporaneousness' with Christ that Kierkegaard deemed essential for a true Christian.

Part of himself lived always in the far depths of history. When doubts attacked him, his comforters rose immediately before him from the Bible, not mighty shadows, but like living beings. For him, as for so many other Puritans, 'the whole of Jewish history became', in Emerson's words, 'flesh and blood'.[14] And he saw the world through innumerable Biblical texts, like those marked for reference in the margin of *The Pilgrim's Progress*, texts which had entered so deeply into his life and his language that he came to quote them, as Louis L. Martz has remarked, 'in his own way, binding (them) to his own particular style'.[15] Language and vision are therefore naturally linked, since the style, and indeed the whole conception of the allegory, are determined by his vision and also by his way of judging the world. Christian's flight from the City of Destruction, his refusal to listen to the advice of Mr. Worldly Wiseman and other prosperous men, established solidly and comfortably in this world, his horror at the habits, customs, and profits of *Vanity Fair*, where men sell themselves like objects, the fight with Apollyon, the conjuring up of the Palace Beautiful and many other aspects and events of the story from a real Christian Utopia, seen in a Puritan light. In *The Pilgrim's Progress*, as in so many other allegories, we find, of course, a critical view of reality and, as Edward Honig puts it, 'a re-examination of the objective norms of experience in the light of human ideality. It includes the making of a new version of reality by means of an ideal which the reality of the fiction proves'.[16] And this brings me back once more to the highly individual character of the Pilgrim's native land, where contradictory elements are found in harmony, a land ideal and concrete at once, a dream land which is nevertheless real, a land whose horizons are often familiar, and yet one of which it can be said, in the words with which Bacon concludes his *New Atlantis*, 'for we are here in God's bosom, a land unknown'.

In the end, the pilgrim must not therefore be considered apart from the country which is the projection of his inward landscape and the manifestation in space of his sense of values. Mountains, plains and sloughs have a meaning at once psychological, religious, and axiological. We must look at the man.

What first marks him out is his singlemindedness. In him, feeling and thought unite to dictate an irrevocable decision : he will live according to the demands of his faith, as the first scene illustrates in dramatic fashion. Throughout all his pilgrimage Christian continually recalls this moment in his past, a moment which he has singled out from all others, for he feels that he had never come nearer to realising fullness of being than in that moment, when he was so ardently straining towards his goal. By leaving his family he puts into practice the most terrible of Christ's commands : 'If any man come to me, and hate not his father, and mother, and wife, and children, and brethren, and sisters, yea, and his own life also, he cannot be my disciple.'[17] And the cry he utters repeats the gaoler's question to Paul and Silas : 'Sirs, what must I do to be saved?'

This traditional question and the man's appearance are alone enough to reveal the Puritan : he is 'cloathed with raggs'; rags which are the symbol of the worthlessness of our works, as they had been for Isaiah : 'But we are all as an unclean thing, and all righteousnesses are as filthy rags.'[18]

To begin with Bunyan does not give his character a name.[19]

He is 'a man' or 'he'. We do not know *who* he is but only *what*
he is. For the 17th century Puritan, he is a 'brother' who has
not yet received personal evidence of grace and election, and the
load he carries on his back immediately recalls the words of the
Psalmist : 'For mine iniquities are gone over mine head; as an
heavy burden they are too heavy for me.'[20] For the modern
reader the burden has a more general meaning. The stranger appears to be a tormented man. Everyman casts his shadow behind
the silhouette of the Puritan. A universal symbol is super-im-
posed upon the national symbol, 'the man clothed with rags',
who had been a familiar figure in Protestant England since the
time of Wycliffe.[21] The original meaning, which the reader must
never forget, is enriched by a new meaning, for, like all works
of genius, the book continues to lead an independent life.

This man's decision and effort, by granting him his first meeting with the Evangelist who becomes his guide, wrench him from
his anonymity – he becomes Christian. In one respect *The Pilgrim's Progress* is really the account of all the meetings and dialogues that have directed the hero in the way he has taken, Bible
in hand.

This man of decision is also a genuine man. The way in which
he tackles obstacles reveals the completeness of his responses.
With him, there is no distinction between reality and appearance,
no duality between his being and his existence, and no divorce
between the *'ought'* of his conscience and the way he leads his
life. Bunyan offers us more than the adequate picture of
Puritanism for which Perry Miller has so justly praised him; he
has portrayed 'the religious man' whom we have come to
recognize through Sören Kierkegaard, Martin Buber, and many
others before them.

Christian shows his authenticity not only by decision but by
the courage with which he recognises his weaknesses, just as
Bunyan had the courage to see the evil in his own nature. *Grace
Abounding* shows clearly that if, for Bunyan, sin is often the
transgression of the moral law, it is also a change in his relationship to God, a breach of faith with His love. We see this, for
example, in his fear that he had 'sold' Christ.[22] There is a Hebrew
streak in the spirit of this Puritan. 'The Biblical view of sin',

writes the French philosopher Paul Ricœur, 'concerns itself first and foremost with the sinner's position *before God*. Sin has above all a religious significance, not a moral one; it is not the infringement of an abstract command, not the violation of moral values, but the appearance of a flaw in the sinner's relationship with God'.[23]

For this true pilgrim, hypocrisy is perhaps the most insidious form evil can take. He is continually unmasking hypocrites, Talkative, Bye-Ends, and others, whom he regards as hollow men. Indeed, scattered along the road are men of straw whom he names Mistrust, Formalist, etc., names that are no more than descriptive labels, whereas others such as Christian, Faithful, Great Heart have a deep significance. It is clear that, for Bunyan, to be significant a man must live to the full in mind, emotion, and deed. This is what he calls 'that harmony and oneness of body and soul',[24] which leads the Christian 'to have (his) life squared according to the Scriptures, both in word and practice'.[25]

Bunyan shares this concern for sincerity with all genuine Puritans. Like them all, he recognises true faith by its deeds, alone, and only sets a value on words if the bitter experience of battle and sacrifice has, if I may be permitted the expression, scored their flesh. This is the source of his scorn for Two-tongues, Say Well, and all the other inhabitants of Prating Row or of the City of Fair Speech, whose language and lives alike are, Bunyan would say, as empty of substance as the white of an egg is of savour.

But Christian, the true pilgrim, the knight of the faith, gains in vigour and confidence as he moves forward, despite the anxiety inherent in both Puritanism and the human condition. By the heights he scales, from which he discovers ever more distant horizons, the country symbolises the growth of his moral force and the deepening of his spiritual vision. The bye-paths tempt him, but do not lead him to his ruin, for he is always able to tear himself away from them. The upward path is his destiny. And, as belief in predestination never weakens this pilgrim's sense that he must strive, and as Calvinistic determinism never sapped the Puritan's will, so Bunyan shows unconsciously how free will and fate may be reconciled. The hero's story (like the autobiography) leads to a conclusion foreign to its design, one that may be expressed in Martin Buber's words : 'Only the man who makes freedom real to himself meets destiny. In my discovery of the deed that aims at me – in this movement of my freedom the mystery is revealed to me.'[26]

In order to understand the complete development of religious Man, and to see the whole expansion of the Puritan landscape, we must always consider the hero of the second part, Great Heart, as Christian under another name and at another stage of his growth. He is the fully mature pilgrim. The time of uneasy seeking and perpetual worry about election has passed. Such consciousness of his inadequacy and short-comings as still exists, far from disturbing the stability of his mind, acts as a stimulant. Because he is whole, Great Heart is less reserved towards others than Christian. He shows his strength by being freely accessible : he is at the service of all who call upon him.

Once he has become guide to the weak and undecided he fits his step to theirs. The urgency of the first pilgrim's pace has given place to the slow speed made necessary, if not by the women, at least by the children. The dialogue has changed key. Its solemnity is relieved by a smile. To the irony and the slightly caustic humour which were not lacking in the first part is added a sense of fun. The road is the same, but, because the spiritual temperature and the inward climate of the pilgrims have changed, the landscape appears in a new light. The life of the spirit is no longer a lonely struggle, one continuous tension between fear of God's anger and trust in his love, but is led in the innocence of each successive hour. A valley which was threatening before is now 'as fruitful a place as the crow flies over', the air the pilgrims breathe is 'pleasant', and how cheerful is the light on the 'sun-shine morning' when Mercy decides to travel with Christiana !

Without the second part of *The Pilgrim's Progress* we would only have an unfinished portrait of the Puritan and of man as a religious being.[27] Here he does not pass his whole life with his gaze riveted on a list of prohibitions. He does not abjure the world; on the contrary, he accepts it in order to sanctify it, and in particular, as we must stress because Bunyan himself does, to sanctify it by marriage and family life.

After sacrifice and despair, Christian, Faithful, and Hopeful know a joy which is not of this world. Christiana, Mercy, Great Heart, Father Honest and their companions experience also a fully human joy. *Laetitia* before *Beatitudo*.

SOURCE: *Études anglaises*, XIV (1961) pp. 124–30.

NOTES

1. Q. D. Leavis, *Fiction and the Reading Public* (London, 1932).
2. I am indebted for some suggestions to Henri Gouhier's article 'Intrigue et action', *Mélanges Georges Jamati* (Paris, 1956).
3. *John Bunyan* (London, 1954) p. 14.
4. 'Bunyan's Mr. Ignorance', *Modern Language Review*, XLIV (1949) p. 483.
5. See Hardin Craig, *Literary Study and the Scholarly Profession* (Seattle, 1944).
6. This is not a literal quotation. See Leibniz's letter to Rémond, 10 January 1714.
7. C. H. Firth, *Essays Historical and Literary* (Oxford, 1938).
8. 'Give me a ballad, a news-book, George on Horseback or Bevis of Southampton', *A Few Signs from Hell, Works*, Offor's ed., vol. 3 (Glasgow, Edinburgh and London, 1862) p. 711.
9. See Jacques Blondel's perceptive remark in *Allégorie et réalisme dans le Pilgrim's Progress*, a small brochure (47 pages), Archives des Lettres modernes (Paris, 1959) p. 29.
10. S. T. Coleridge, *Notes on English Divines*, Derwent Coleridge's edition, 2 vols (London, 1853) vol. I, p. 343.
11. Jeremiah 13 :6.
12. See Charles Feidelson's analysis of American puritanism in his remarkable book on *Symbolism and American Literature* (Chicago, 1953), and Phoenix Books.
13. See Friedrich Heiler, *Prayer, A study in the History and Psychology of Religion*, Galaxy Books (original German ed. Munich, 1923).
14. *Works*, vol. x (Boston and New York, 1909) p. 234.
15. Introduction to *The Pilgrim's Progress*, Rinehart, p. xii.
16. *Dark Conceit: The Making of Allegory* (London, 1959) p. 109.
17. Luke 14 :26.
18. Isaiah 64 :6.

19. Although later, when he refers to Christian before he met Evangelist, Bunyan calls him Graceless.

20. Psalms 38 : 5.

21. G. M. Trevelyan, *Clio, a Muse, and other Essays* (London, 1930) p. 52.

22. *Grace Abounding*, § 133 et seq.

23. 'Culpabilité tragique et culpabilité biblique', *Revue d'Hist. et de Philosophie religieuses,* XXXIII (1953) p. 298.

24. *Saved by Grace, Works,* I, p. 342.

25. *A Few Sighs from Hell, Works,* III, p. 720.

26. *I and Thou* (Edinburgh, 1937) p. 53.

27. See some penetrating remarks in Rosemary Freeman, *English Emblem Books* (London, 1948).

Roy Pascal

THE PRESENT TENSE IN
THE PILGRIM'S PROGRESS (1965)

Various uses of the present tense in narrative fiction were analysed in my article 'Tense and Novel' in the *Modern Language Review*, LVII (1962) pp. 1–11. Reading *The Pilgrim's Progress*, I was struck by a use that I had not mentioned and that indicates such stylistic discrimination that it repays closer examination.

Bunyan's allegory follows the established tradition of narrative in being told in the past (preterite) tense. The story is accompanied by marginal notes, and they themselves are worth attention. They indicate an event, provide an exegetical explanation, or give a more general religious or moral comment. The normal plan is that, while the story proceeds in the past tense, these notes are in the present. Occasionally however a note is given in the past tenses – 'Christian missed his Roll wherein he used to take comfort' (p. 43)[1] – and the somewhat more dramatic tone thereby introduced is arresting. That these occasional changes of tense are not haphazard is indicated by the group pp. 137–9, where Hopeful is telling about experiences of his earlier life; here the marginal notes begin and end in the present tense, but the past for the body of his account.

In the narrative of Part 1, I have found only one occasion on which the present tense is used. When Christian and Hopeful enter the grounds of Doubting Castle, we read that Giant Despair 'caught' them and 'put' them into a dungeon. When he goes to bed he tells his wife of the prisoners, and she advises him to beat them without mercy. All in the normal past tense. The narrative continues (p. 114 ff.) :

So when he arose, he getteth him a grievous Crab-tree Cudgel, and goes down into the dungeon to them; and there, first falls to rateing of them as if they were dogs, although they gave him never a word of distaste; then he falls upon them, and beats them fearfully, in such sort, that they were not able to help themselves, or to turn them upon the floor. This done, he withdraws and leaves them, there to condole their misery, and to mourn under their distress : so all that day they spent the time in nothing but sighs and bitter lamentations. The next night she talking with her Husband about them further, and understanding that they were yet alive, did advise him to counsel them, to make away with themselves : So when morning was come, he goes to them in a surly manner, as before, and perceiving them to be very sore with the stripes that he had given them the day before; he told them. . . .

The narrative continues in the past tense, and after a short conversation between Christian and Hopeful, goes on : 'Well, towards evening the Giant goes down into the Dungeon again, to see if his Prisoners had taken his counsel; but when he came there, he found them alive, and truly, alive was all.' – again the past tense takes over. The day leads to another bed-time discussion between Giant and Giantess, and the next morning visit again introduces the present tense : 'So when the morning was come, the *Giant* goes to them again, and takes them into the Castle-yard, and shews them, as his Wife had bidden him.' This is his last visit to the prisoners, for in this night they make their escape; and this is the last time the present tense makes its appearance (it is interesting that the marginal note here uses the past : 'On Saturday the Giant threatned, that shortly he would pull them to pieces').

One notices immediately that the use of the present tense in this episode is anything but arbitrary. It is never used for Christian and Hopeful, nor for the giant's wife. It is used solely for the giant, and only for certain of his actions. It starts with 'getteth him a cudgel and goes to them' and is used for his first beating. It is later used only for the repeated going to them, not for his arguments with them.

This is of course one of the incidents in which Bunyan draws directly on folk-tale. Terror and homeliness are mingled, the dire threat with the conversations in bed, and in the fits that overcome the giant when he is about to kill his prisoners there is the

familiar mixture of terror and laughter. It is the function of the
present tense to recall these associations. The folk-tale itself
could, when told, most readily fall into the present tense for the
type of incident that is established as a ritual, typical, recurrent
event, such as, here, the visit of a giant to his victims. In such a
case it does not make the action more 'present', i.e. more
dramatic, as its occasional use in ballads frequently does. Rather,
it recalls the basic structure of a myth, repeated in so many tales,
something familiar and expected. So Bunyan's usage recalls a
familiar situation by using the familiar tense and manner. But he
is also giving a new content to the traditional situation. The days
are not any successive days, but are named from Wednesday to
Saturday, and we are to know from the beginning that Sunday,
the Lord's Day, will bring the prisoners release. And, while the
first torture, the beatings, can be put in the present tense, since
they are traditional, the later torture, the urging to suicide, the
assault on their souls, cannot tolerate the present tense. It is
unique and significant, an essential part of the religious theme,
and demands the specific past tense. We note that, even in the
midst of the present tense of the beatings, Christian and Hopeful respond in the past tense; for their response is not to be taken
as normal and familiar, however much it is under-pinned by the
familiar successful resistance of the hero of folk-tale.

We can see how sure Bunyan's linguistic sense was if we compare the descriptions of the encounters with other monsters, with
Apollyon for instance, or the Monster of Vanity Fair in Part II.
These are given throughout in the past tense. These monsters are
not fabulous in the same sense, they do not belong to folklore,
they have no traditional behaviour, and therefore cannot be
described in the present tense. It is a remarkable testimony to
Bunyan's literary feeling that when the pilgrims of Part II arrive
at Doubting Castle, again the present tense is used for the giant
(p. 281): 'When they came at the Castle Gate, they knocked for
Entrance with an unusual Noyse. At that the old Gyant comes to
the Gate, and *Diffidence* his Wife follows. Then said he . . .' The
rest, the altercation, battle, and death of giant and giantess, are
in the past tense. Once again the present skilfully conjures up
the familiar, the traditional, but is swiftly replaced by the past in

order that the particular significance should not be swallowed up by the general and vague associations of the folk-tale situation.

Bunyan's use of the present tense in his narrative, exploiting the repetitive function of this tense, evokes the associations connected with a traditional tale. It has little or nothing of the 'historic present' about it; rather, it is used when less attention than usual is attracted to the event involved; these present-tense verbs are deliberately under-emphasized, and are only a prelude to the significant incidents, that are given in the preterite. If there is a temporal element to be felt on these occasions, it consists in a loss of a specific time, a lapse from the historicity of the story into a more general, timeless mode.

The passages I have mentioned contain, so far as I have noticed, the only examples of the use of the present tense in Part I of *The Pilgrim's Progress*. The Second Part uses it sparingly too, but more frequently and more variedly. Thus there is a fairly straightforward use of the historic present in the account of Great-heart's battle with the Giant Maul (pp. 244–5). This is given consistently in the past tense, till with the decisive stroke 'Mr Great-heart seeing that, runs to him in the full heat of his Spirit, and pierceth him under the fifth rib . . .' It is the same when the pilgrims find Mr Honest sleeping (p. 246): 'the old man gets up and stands upon his guard, and will know of them what they were.'

There is a particularly interesting usage of the present when the company of pilgrims, now very numerous and including children and old folk, encounter the difficulties of the Enchanted Ground (p. 296):

Here therefore was *grunting*, and *puffing*, and *sighing* : While one tumbleth over a Bush, another sticks fast in the Dirt, and the Children, some of them, lost their Shoos in the Mire. While one crys out, I am down, and another, Ho, Where are you? and a third, the Bushes have got such fast hold on me, I think I cannot get away from them.
Then they came at an Arbor. . . .

Here the present tense deftly suggests a crowd of simultaneous incidents, befalling indifferently this or that person. None has a special importance, and all the people come through safely.

There is however a recurrent type of present tense, that corresponds to the general character of the style in this Second Part. Domestic and every-day affairs are more prominent in this Part than in the First, and one notices immediately that it is written in a more colloquial and racy style. It is in this context that I place a group of examples of the present tense :

So Mrs. *Timorous* returned to her House, and *Christiana* betook herself to her Journey. But when *Timorous* was got home to her House, she sends for some of her Neighbours. . . . So when they were come to her House, she falls to telling of the story of *Christiana*, and of her intended Journey. And thus she began her Tale (p. 184).

When the Interpreter had done, he takes them out into his Garden again, and had them to a Tree . . . (p. 204).

When Mr Brisk is courting Mercy : 'So the next time he comes, he finds her at her old work, a making of things for the Poor. Then said he, What always at it?' (p. 227). When Gaius the innkeeper entertains the pilgrims : 'Then he went down, and spake to the Cook . . . to get ready Supper for so many Pilgrims. This done, he comes up again, saying, come my good Friends, you are welcome . . .' (p. 259). A little later : 'Now, just as Mr. *Feeble-mind*, and Gaius was thus in talk; there comes one running, and called at the Door, and told . . .' (p. 269).

All these examples (and they complete my list)[2] are embedded in a narrative told in the past tense. At first sight they may seem to belong to the historic present, for they tend to bring the action closer to us; they do not, however, make it more dramatic or vivid, and in any case Bunyan refuses to pursue their dramatic possibilities, since he returns immediately to his past tense. It will be noticed that the verbs in the present tense are all much-used, simple words, 'sends', 'falls to', 'takes', 'finds', and 'comes'; and that the actions they indicate are all extremely usual, the actions one would expect to happen in that situation. The present tense here links up the action with the familiar every-day of the readers; the statement does not need the historic mode, the past, and gains positively by its associations with the experience of the readers. It is true, the present tense in these cases brings the action closer to us; but it is not so much a temporal closeness as a closeness of familiarity (that is of course strengthened by the surrounding colloquialism of phraseology).

This last group of examples is therefore linked with the Doubting Castle group. In the most unobtrusive way (what reader consciously records these changes of tense?) the narrative impinges on our daily experience and builds on its associations. That these grammatical variations are unobtrusive does not mean they are not powerful. Indeed, the processes that the analysis of tense-usage uncovers are all the more effective for seeming so natural; and it is not in the least surprising to find a gifted writer like Bunyan to be so sure and consistent in his grammatical usages.

SOURCE: *Modern Language Review*, LX (1965) pp. 13–16.

NOTES

1. Page references are given to the edition of J. B. Wharey, revised by R. Sharrock (Oxford, 1960).

2. Except for an author's intrusion. Bunyan could in fact dispense with authorial comment in the text, since he had characters to make clear his own intention, and could in addition fall back on his side-notes.

Roger Sharrock

WOMEN AND CHILDREN (1966)

I CHRISTIANA'S PILGRIMAGE

The Second Part of *The Pilgrim's Progress* was published in 1684, six years after the First. As we have seen there is evidence to suggest that the First Part was completed many years before its publication; Part Two, on the other hand, is a new venture inspired by the success of its predecessor. It belongs to a common type in popular literature, the sequel bearing no particular formal or artistic relation to an original story but serving to perpetuate a popular character or situation. Thus the attraction of Falstaff demands that he should be revived for the antics of *The Merry Wives of Windsor*. A new set of prefatory verses again answers the possible objections of pious critics, but the tone is now exultant and confident :

> My *Pilgrim* knows no ground of shame, or fear ;
> City and Countrey will him entertain,
> With welcome *Pilgrim*, yea, they can't refrain
> From smiling, if my Pilgrim be but by,
> Or shows his head in any Company.

> Brave Galants do my pilgrim hug and love,
> Esteem it much, yea, value it above
> Things of a greater bulk, yea, with delight
> Say my *Larks* leg is better than a *Kite*.

As Bunyan had expected, there had been critics of the First Part. A certain T.S. (probably Thomas Sherman), a General Baptist whose sect did not agree with the doctrine of a particular call to salvation that is basic to the lonely pilgrimage of Christian, had published his own Second Part in 1682. He considered that Bunyan had unduly neglected the communal life of the church, and endeavoured, dully and humourlessly, to remedy this. Bunyan was not led to curb his lively fancy and boisterous humour, but he does turn to the outward, social problems of the holy community, and away from the dominating figure of the Christian hero, perhaps because he had already accomplished this transition in his own life and work. Released from prison, he had now become the busy pastor of the Bedford independent congregation and the 'Messenger' or co-ordinator of a scattered confederacy of open-communion Baptist churches in Bedfordshire and the surrounding counties. The passionate cry for personal salvation that is the ground-bass of the original *Pilgrim's Progress* had given way to a preoccupation with external problems of discipline and behaviour.

The structure of the pilgrimage, the king's highway, the places of resort along the route, its giants and perils, provide a framework common to both parts. But imaginatively a great gulf lies between. The Second Part has been perhaps unduly neglected because it lacks the high drama of the First : it has real virtues nevertheless, and it would be wrong to overlook them; it presents a cheerful, teeming picture of the life of a seventeenth-century godly family and of the small separatist community made up of a few such families. It treats family affection and personal relations in a way that was impossible in the story of the isolated, epic individual. And finally it establishes workable links between the humdrum life of ordinary men and women (which in the scornful catalogue of Vanity Fair in Part One had been practically dismissed as sinful) and the call to heroism that may sometimes come to them, so that in terms of religious sensibility, if in no other, it does represent a continuation of the earlier work.

Clearly the atmosphere is much tamer. Especially in the early pages the reader is conscious of an absence of pressure and immediacy. As Monsignor Ronald Knox said : 'Christian goes on a pilgrimage, Christiana on a walking tour.' Sometimes it is actually a conducted tour of former battlefields, since there are monuments to Christian's fights and sufferings to be pointed out to his family at the appropriate places along the route. Bunyan

is here experiencing the problem of the second novel, a problem
that confronts widely differing novelists in many periods. The
first book grows directly out of personal experience, its form
seems inevitable, and it writes itself. By the success of the book
the unknown explorer of a single personal theme finds himself a
writer with a public; the second novel is a writer's book, self-
conscious, the work of an artist with a style (the surprising
legacy of his first) looking for a theme. These elements are present in the Second Part of *The Pilgrim's Progress*, and nothing
illustrates more tellingly the situation of the writer who by being
a writer is to that extent separated from his original subject-
matter than the curious device by which Bunyan attempts to
tell the story of the second pilgrimage through a narrator and
his interlocutor. The dreamer dreams again and in his dream he
meets a Mr. Sagacity who tells him that he has recently visited
the City of Destruction and that the latest news is that Christian's
wife and children have now gone on pilgrimage :

Better and better, quoth I. But what ! Wife and Children and all?
    Sagacity.   'Tis true, I can give you an account of the matter,
for I was upon the spot at the instant, and was thoroughly acquainted
with the whole affair.

Bunyan had used this gossipy, dialogue form in *The Life and
Death of Mr. Badman* (1680). It provides a vehicle for a story
broken down into anecdotes with reflective intervals for moral
comment and explication. What it inhibits is the continuous
flow of a major dramatic action, and Bunyan's curious choice
may have been prompted by a sound critical perception : he saw
that much of his material for the Second Part was social comedy
which could be mediated in this way. On the other hand nothing could reconcile this method to the dream vision and Bunyan
soon saw that the two were incompatible. 'And now Mr.
Sagacity left me to dream out my dream by myself.' Why did he
not realise this incompatibility at the start? The blunder
illustrates more completely than any thing else could his lack of
any critical self-consciousness in relation to the literary methods
he employed. When he begins to develop a full scene, in
Christiana's dialogue with her neighbours who come to dissuade

her from going on pilgrimage, he has to contend with the clumsiness of a dialogue within a dialogue, but even then he does not make the intellectual judgment which would cause him to abandon the device. It is only when his pilgrims reach the Wicket Gate that he does this; then the spell of his old fable reasserts itself; now for the first time he can say again, 'Still as I pulled, it came' : the visual imagination is serenely in control and there is no need of any narrator but the dreamer.

The world of Part One is a testing ground for masculine heroism with little use for women and children. Christian's wife and family are not converted with him and so they must be abandoned. They cry after him, but he runs on with his fingers in his ears crying, 'Life, life, eternal life.' Later 'wives, husbands, children' are listed together with 'whores, bawds, silver and gold' among the merchandise of Vanity Fair. It is the hysterical passion of the tone that gives a vein of Manichaean unorthodoxy to this; what it means is that salvation is purely individual and family ties can be as dangerously diverting as the world and the flesh. Clearly now that the crisis has passed, when Bunyan-Christian has received the final assurance of faith he describes in *Grace Abounding*, and when he has been released from prison and returned to the life of society, it is time for some recompense to be awarded to Christian's wife Christiana and her children. There is also the fact that women had played an important part in the growth of the Bedford church since its early days, as in many other small independent churches, and Bunyan is now ready to recognise this at a stage when his imagination is increasingly informed by his pastoral experience. Persecution had relaxed since the First Declaration of Indulgence, and in 1682–3 the *Bedford Church Book* records regular meetings for prayer and breaking of bread. Mothers of families had helped to hold the church together in difficult times and their prestige was now high. This went hand in hand with an increasing liberalism as to church membership, always prominent in a group which had prided itself on its open-communion principles. Membership was open to all Christians of good life who claimed an awakening faith without insistence on adult baptism or any interrogation into precise beliefs as a condition of acceptance. Joan Cooke

who had moved to London was given permission to join any
congregation she pleased, 'for her edification and the further-
ance of her faith'.[1] The women formed a powerful group who
even demanded a separate prayer meeting; Bunyan, however,
contested, and apparently defeated, this demand in *A Case of
Conscience Resolved* (1683). Church life in general is far more
prominent in Part Two: we find references to the ordinance of
adult baptism by immersion, when at the House Beautiful the
pilgrims are taken out to the Bath of Sanctification and come
out 'not only sweet and clean, but also much enlivened and
strengthened in their joints'; the fine hymns scattered through
the narrative provide an indirect defence of congregational singing which was an issue among the sectaries at this time; and, as
we shall see, a main feature of the work is the study of various
types of tender conscience in the characters who attach themselves to Christiana's family along the way, Ready-to-halt,
Feeble-mind, and so on. These creations give positive expression to the open-communion ideal of reconciling minor
theological differences and gently removing scruples.

II CHRISTIANA AND MERCY

Though Bunyan's characterisation is guided by conventional
seventeenth-century notions of woman as the weaker vessel, at
least this leads him towards an interesting recognition of the differences of feminine psychology especially in respect of a more
acute nervous sensibility. 'Bowels [i.e. pity, tender feeling] be-
cometh pilgrims', says Christiana, and it is the keynote of the
book. Her uneasy conscience for her unkind behaviour to her
husband is described; there is no firm theological structure
governing the psychological changes here, conviction of sin leading on to the fruitless search for a merely human righteousness, and then on to assurance of faith. It is a purely human
psychological motivation which impels Christiana along the
road formerly taken by her husband: 'her thoughts began to
work in her mind; first, for that she had lost her husband, and
for that the loving bond of that relation was utterly broken betwixt them'. Even the token of grace that comes to her from the

King seems highly feminine; it is a letter smelling 'all of the best Perfume'. During conversion she remains a widow and a mother, consoling her children in many tearful scenes and yet contriving to make them weep a good deal too.

The change from a strict theological framework to a humane psychology is shown in her relation to her friend Mercy. The beauty of a purely human friendship is presented as something capable of development into Christian fellowship. There is the same emphasis on affection and the inspiration of another human being; these are the incentives that draw Mercy gradually to her spiritual awakening. Her love for her friend comes first : 'First, her Bowels yearned over Christiana; so she said within herself, "If my Neighbour will needs be gon, I will go a little way with her, and help her." Secondly, her Bowels yearned over her own soul (for what *Christiana* had said, had taken some hold upon her mind).' She has no formal token of grace like Christiana, and at the Wicket Gate, which signifies election, while the others are admitted, she stands in fear and trembling knocking loudly. Knocking on the door is the Gospel metaphor for fervent prayer. She is falling into a swoon when the Keeper of the Gate gently takes her in, reminding her that he prays for all who believe in him 'by what means soever they come unto me'. The Calvinist doctrine of election is here modified in favour of those who have not undergone a twice-born conversion but are drawn to become members of the separated community by the ties of friendship or kindred. Mercy is told later by the Interpreter that she is like Ruth, who left home and parents 'for the love that she bore to Naomi and to the Lord her God'. In this context the very name of Mercy is important as indicating the greater role in the Second Part of the tender emotions at the expense of the will. It would be misleading to think of a relaxation of the earlier dramatic tension between grace and nature, because this would be to pre-judge the religious atmosphere of the book in terms of the crisis-theology of the author's conversion and prison phase. The quality of vision in the Second Part represents not a surrender to humanism but an assured theology of charity which naturally looks at the points of contact between divine and human love for the growing places of the knowledge of God.

We first see Christiana weeping with remorse when she thinks of her past conduct towards Christian. Then she laments of this to her children and they all weep together. Next she has a dream of two 'ill-favoured ones', devils who seek her soul, and awakes sweating and trembling. The scene with Mercy introduces us to more tears and tender-heartedness, and anxiety and depth of feeling are further displayed at the entry to the Gate. A dangerous mastiff (the Devil) strikes terror into the little boys, and a little farther on the ill-favoured ones of Christiana's dream assault the women and attempt to rape them. They are rescued by a Reliever who afterwards expresses surprise that they did not petition their Lord at the outset for a conductor through the dangers of the way. Thus we have a consistent record of sensibility and fear, a brave adherence to the way but a proneness to the weaknesses of women in a man's world. It is as if Bunyan is prepared to grant to Christiana and Mercy as Puritan mother and maiden the most generous possible tribute compatible with an understanding that all their devotion cannot suffice to enable them to accomplish the way alone. The Reliever's criticism is a broad hint that they have overestimated their powers, perhaps as the women of the Bedford congregation did in 1682–3. A male champion is on the way to protect them, an idealised pastoral figure, such a one as Christian saw in emblem in the Interpreter's House.

III A GATHERED CHURCH: TENDER CONSCIENCES

The escort who is deputed to go along with the women is Great-heart and he is said to be a man-servant of the Interpreter; that is to say, he is the true Christian minister who bases his pastoral care on a right reading of Scripture. Christian had been armed at the House Beautiful in order to withstand the dangers immediately ahead but Greatheart is armed all the time with 'sword, helmet and shield' and presents the image of a warrior. He, and some of the companions he meets on the way like Mr. Standfast and Valiant-for-truth, do something to preserve a note of heroic, dedicated purpose in the milder domestic atmosphere of the Second Part. He is a character to admire rather than to identify with, unlike the puzzled, searching Christian; he is a man under discipline, a happy warrior, and all his speeches carry ringing authority : ' 'Tis the Kings High-way that we are in, and in this way it is that thou hast placed thy Lions; but these Women and these Children, though weak, shall hold on their way in spite of thy Lions.' So he speaks to the giant Grim who backs up the lions threatening to keep them from entering the Palace Beautiful. And there are more giant fights in the Second Part; an atmosphere of successful military achievement is established as Greatheart cuts down one after another. Grim, whose other name is Bloody-man, stands for the persecuting power of the civil authority (in *The Holy War*, 1682, Bunyan had represented the revival of prosecutions against the Dissenters by the attacks of the army of the Bloodmen). At the end of the Valley of the Shadow of Death they encounter Giant Maul; him too Greatheart kills and cuts off his head. He is said to have 'spoiled young pilgrims with sophistry', the charge usually levelled against the Jesuits at the time of the Popish Plot. No doubt he stands for the corruptions of Rome, but Bunyan seems to have used the word to reflect his favourite theme of Satan's assaults on the confidence of the penitent : 'The tempted, wherever he dwells, always thinks himself the biggest sinner. . . . This is Satan's master argument . . . I say this is his maul, his club, his masterpiece.'[2]

While entertained at the house of Gaius the male pilgrims are invited to go out on what is practically a giant-hunt. 'Since, as I know, Mr. Greatheart is good at his weapons, if you please after we have refreshed ourselves, we will walk into the fields, to see if we can do any good.' The quarry, Giant Slay-good, is simply a general manifestation of evil; he holds as his prisoner Feeblemind who is released to join the pilgrims; otherwise the episode has no allegorical significance whatsoever. It is an instance among many of the sheer entertainment and diversion that make up the variety of the Second Part. Finally Greatheart and his band slay Giant Despair and pull down his castle, releasing more prisoners. This is the climax of the giant-fights and of the rising optimism of the book : Christians are now not merely surviving

the terrors of pilgrimage but helping to make the world a place
fit for pilgrims to live in.

If it is impossible to take these hunted, doomed giants very
seriously, it is because of the surrounding atmosphere in which
the steady, peaceful life of Christiana and her family from conversion to death is allowed to take its course. The tension in Part
One prevents the journey metaphor from being particularly
transparent; dramatic crises seen *sub specie aeternitatis* do not
convey a sense of the gradual unfolding of a life. But in Part
Two there is quite the opposite effect of the journey-metaphor
being a rather clumsy and ill-fitting image. The company of pilgrims expands into a wide circle of friends and relations; from
being a naughty little boy who eats forbidden fruit, Matthew
grows up and marries Mercy; James, the other son, is married
to Gaius' daughter Phoebe, while Christiana has by this time
become 'an aged Matron'. Clearly many years have passed,
though it would be impossible to work out a definite time-
scheme for the pilgrimage.

There are the same stages on the road, the Interpreter's House,
the Palace Beautiful, the Valley of Humiliation, and so on, but
they have been transformed into scenes of domestic tranquillity.
New houses of resort are added : the inn of Gaius and the house
of 'one Mnason, a Cyprusian' (Acts 21:16); in the latter a
Christian community is found establishing a catacomb in Vanity
Fair itself, moved by the example of Christian and Faithful.
There are long conversations and long halts which breathe the
charm of settled domestic life.

One of these genre pictures is the courtship of Mercy by Mr.
Brisk. We are out of the world of allegory now and looking
realistically at the life of a gathered church, in this case the
problem of marriage with unbelievers. Brisk is a poseur : he
thinks Mercy will make a good housewife, but she is easily able
to get rid of him when she tells him that the needlework which
she is about is intended for the poor. Now he sees her as one
'troubled with ill conditions'. Piety does not prevent Mercy
from taking a proper pride in her personal appearance : 'I might
a had Husbands afore now, tho' I spake not of it to any; but they
were such as did not like my Conditions, though never did any

of them find fault with my Person : So they and I could not agree.'

Another such genre picture is when Matthew, sick from the apples he stole from the Devil's garden, is persuaded by his mother to take physic :

Come, come, said the Physician, you must take it. It goes against my stomach, said the Boy. I must have you take it, said his Mother. I shall Vomit it up again, said the Boy. Pray, sir, said *Christiana* to Mr. *Skill*, how does it taste? It has no ill taste, said the Doctor, and with that she touched one of the pills with the tip of her tongue. Oh Mathew, said she, this potion is sweeter than Hony. If thou lovest thy Mother, if thou lovest thy Brothers, if thou lovest *Mercie* if thou lovest thy life, take it. . . . he took it. . . . It caused him to Purge, it caused him to sleep and rest quietly, it put him into a fine heat and breathing sweat, and did quite rid him of his Gripes.

This is not purely gratuitous social fiction like the episode of Mercy and her sweetheart. This is an allegory, however homely, of original sin; that is the apple which has turned Matthew's stomach : at first Mr. Skill tries on him a purge that is too weak, made from the sacrifices symbolic of the old law of Moses – the blood of a goat and the ashes of a heifer : the successful purge is made '*ex carne et sanguine Christi*' and represents the intercession of Christ the redeemer. But the symbolism sinks under the strength of the domestic scene outlined. The seventeenth-century doctor's sententiousness and his grisly mixtures, the boy's obstinacy, the mother's sentimental but business-like initiative all communicate the definiteness of a Dutch picture. The attempt to link Matthew's bowel troubles with the Fall of Man has a medieval wholeness of approach that makes judgments of good taste seem an affair of modern decadence.

The Valley of Humiliation and other parts of the way have lost many of their terrors. Music and the social arts are much in evidence. A mysterious concert entertains Christiana and Mercy when they have retired to their room in the House Beautiful. 'Wonderful!' Christiana says, 'Music in the house, music in the heart, and music also in heaven, for joy that we are here.' As they leave the birds in the grove sing to them from Sternhold's version of the Psalms. Later the differing temperaments of Christians are compared to the notes of different musical instruments : Mr. Fearing is likened to the sackbut (a kind of trombone) the notes of which are more doleful than those of other instruments. So, as an analogue of the relaxed harmony of the mood, Bunyan draws on the English Puritans' love of music and the practice of music, denied only by their enemies. The songs, too, are more smoothly lyrical than Bunyan's rough-hewn verses usually are, especially that of the shepherd-boy in the Valley of Humiliation :

> I am content with what I have,
> Little be it, or much :
> And, Lord, Contentment still I crave,
> Because thou savest such.

> Fulness to such a burden is
> That go on Pilgrimage :
> Here little, and hereafter Bliss,
> Is best from Age to Age.

The strangers who are added to the band after being rescued, or simply taken up for company when met on the highway, form a closely knit group with a distinct dogmatic implication. They are all persons whose excessive scruples have prevented them so far from joining a recognised religious body. Feeblemind disapproves of theological catechising and of many other things in his brethren, including gay clothes; there is something of the early Quaker in his composition. Despondancie and his daughter Much-afraid, and Ready-to-halt with his symbolic lameness, are afflicted by morbid doubts whether they will be accepted at last, the fears their author knew about so well. The perception of their behaviour is in no way commonplace. Fearing thinks the hobgoblins will have him in the Valley of the Shadow of Death, but in Vanity Fair he is as brave as a lion. None of these hard cases is rejected from Greatheart's gathered church. It is a proud piece of open-communion propaganda, but the psychopathology of religious scruples is moving and convincing.

IV CROSSING THE RIVER

Lest the whole thing should become too relaxed and too easy, Bunyan has reserved till the last a statement of that substratum of heroic faith that is necessary in any Christian culture, however kindly to human values the mood may seem, however far away the days of persecution. The pilgrims cross the River of Death as Christian and Hopeful did in Part One. It is a splendid purple passage, and, uniquely for Bunyan, a consciously arranged and harmonised set piece. Each of the principal pilgrims receives a summons from the King to join him across the River. Each invitation follows a formalised pattern which is repeated with variations; there is the speech of the messenger, an emblematic token to attest the genuineness of the summons (these are symbols from the twelfth chapter of Ecclesiastes, conventionally used at Puritan death-beds) the bequests of the dying pilgrim to his or her friends, and their last words when crossing the River. Valiant-for-truth's last words are perhaps the most memorable, but it is important to see that their effect is part of a musical whole that has already set an enthralling rhythm of cadence and meaning working throughout the long passage :

My Sword, I give to him that shall succeed me in my Pilgrimage, and my *Courage* and *Skill* to him that can get it. My *Marks* and *Scarrs* I carry with me, to be a witness for me, that I have fought his *Battels* who now will be my Rewarder. . . . And as he went down Deeper, he said, *Grave where is thy Victory?* So he passed over, and the Trumpets sounded for him on the other side.

We are returned to the dynamic splendour of conversion, but with a frank recognition of the human side of the equation. Valiant-for-truth's personal striving is characteristic of the humanised Calvinism of Part Two, the pilgrimage of the family.

SOURCE: *The Pilgrim's Progress* (1966) pp. 42–53.

NOTES

1. *Church Book of Bedford Meeting* (London, 1928) p. 70 – 30 March 1682.
2. *The Jerusalem Sinner Saved, Works,* ed. George Offor, vol. 1 (Glasgow, Edinburgh and London, 1862) p. 96.

Roger Sharrock

CHARACTER AND DREAM (1966)

I PEOPLE AND QUALITIES

Bunyan's allegory of the journey of the soul involves one primary consequence in the drawing of character. Particular traits are drained away from Christian and lavished on the various personified temptations and incentives. His tendency to religious relativism is bequeathed to Atheist, his worldliness to Worldly Wiseman, his hopefulness to Hopeful. One would expect the central character to become rather flat and universalised like the *Humanum Genus* of a morality play. It is all the more surprising that this is not entirely what happens : though in Christian we do meet the flatness of portraiture that enables the reader easily to identify himself with him, on occasion he can remain obstinately individual. As in other aspects of *The Pilgrim's Progress,* there is no need to attribute this to some deep-seated plan to blend two approaches to character. Christian is for the great part of the pilgrimage the subject of universal experiences, the wayfaring pilgrim of tradition. When he retains individual qualities they are those which Bunyan was interested in or which corresponded most closely to his own experience.

Though brave at the sticking-point, he can be deeply cast down into the despair that endangers faith; witness the Slough of Despond, and his imprisonment in Doubting Castle : the latter is a full-scale repetition of the former episode in terms of a different allegory. Especially in his terror in the Valley of the Shadow of Death does Christian reflect this aspect of his character where the history of a type has been enriched by Bunyan's autobiographical experience of spiritual doubt :

Thus he went on, and I heard him here sigh bitterly . . . I took notice that now poor *Christian* was so confounded that he did not know his

own voice, and thus I perceived it : Just when he was come over
against the mouth of the burning Pit, one of the wicked ones got
behind him, and stepped up softly to him, and whisperingly suggested
many grievous blasphemies to him which he verily thought had proceeded from his own mind. This put *Christian* more to it than anything that he met with before, even to think that he should now
blaspheme him that he loved so much before; yet, could he have
helped it, he would not have done it : but he had not the discretion
neither to stop his ears, nor to know from whence those blasphemies
came.

Also, Christian is inclined to be impulsive and passionate. He runs
part of the way up the Hill Difficulty, and it is he who, by over-
ruling Hopeful's good advice and taking a short cut, leads them
both into By-Path Meadow and to Doubting Castle. He is too
ready to jump to conclusions, fearing that all hope is gone when
he loses his roll of election in the Arbour, or beginning to sink
when his doubts return upon him in the crossing of the River.

   In his relations with Faithful and Hopeful there is some room
for the play of temperament as well as a generalised picture of
Christian comradeship. Hopeful appears as the young disciple
beside whom Christian, though naturally naïve and reckless,
begins to take on the character of a grizzled veteran; he 'snibbeth
his fellow' and rebukes him for uttering an unsound theological
opinion by saying : 'Thou speakest as one upon whose head the
shell is still to this day.' Their interchanges are not usually as
colourful as this; colour and the exploitation of particularity are
reserved for the episodes with hypocrites and unbelievers where
there is humorous contrast. But in the fairly neutral, quiet
conversation of the fellow-pilgrims there is often a subtlety of
moral analysis. It is not only the passages of theological exposition
(like Greatheart's long dialogue with Christiana on the covenant
of grace in Part Two) that remind us that being a popular writer
is not the same as being a crude or banal one. The theological
passages have a firm intellectual structure, a binding dialectic
comparable to that given by Marxism to some 'uneducated'
writers in the twentieth century; more interestingly, the treatment
of human relations is not at all based on some over-simplified
model of Christian solidarity. This comes out in the scene in By-

Path Meadow : Christian acknowledges his fault, and, checking an initial impulse to crow, Hopeful is generously forgiving; so far the perceptiveness is moving but not extraordinary. But then Christian offers to walk in front to face first the new danger he has incurred, and Hopeful refuses to let him do this on the grounds that with a mind troubled by remorse he is in no fit state to take responsibility :

Christian. No, if you please let me go first; that if there be any danger I may be first therein, because by my means we are both gone out of the way.
Hopeful. No, said Hopeful, you shall not go first, for your mind being troubled may lead you out of the way again.

This admirably suggests the delicate tact necessary to true friendship.

II HYPOCRITES AND OTHERS

We have seen that the form the story takes is the result of a series of happy chances and visionary lucky hits rather than of conscious contrivance. In contrast, in the minor characters something that can be called literary art is displayed in its full subtlety; it is the art of the traditional popular sermon judiciously fusing moral doctrine and dramatic reality into economical vignettes. In the portraits of heretics and backsliders, after we have taken in the introductory catch-word of a moralised name, Ignorance or Ready-to-halt, we slip from allegory to genre studies of flesh and blood. Ignorance is 'a very brisk lad'. Talkative is 'a tall man, and something more comely at a distance than at hand'. Honest sees that Feeble-mind must be closely related to Fearing, 'for you have his whitely look, a cast like his with your eye, and your speech is much alike'. Madam Bubble who tries to entice Standfast is 'a tall comely dame, something of a swarthy complexion' and she 'speaks very smoothly and gives you a smile at the end of a sentence'. Sharp visual details from recognisable human types here take over from conventional moral allegory. Madam Bubble is a good example, because she is a conventional figure in the iconography of the emblem books, standing for the vanity of 'this bubble world' and is depicted in the plates to Quarles' *Emblemes* and other collections much as she is described in Bunyan, with a great bag at her side to contain the riches of the world. But in the woman described by Standfast we have a particularised character, a swarthy, plausible wanton, not a traditional symbol, however much the character may be as we loosely say 'typical'. The same process is at work in the satiric types of Restoration comedy with their generic names like Love-wit and Wishfort.

The skilful, dissecting humour of the portrait of Ignorance may serve to illustrate the quality of all these studies of heretics and backsliders. Ignorance is young and somewhat ingenuous; he is not a corrupt old time-server like By-Ends, or a pompous authoritarian prig like Worldly Wiseman (almost an anticipation of Beckett's Pozzo). If we read carelessly there is a risk that he may be dismissed as one of the few personages in the pilgrimage who are wholly dependent on a theological *parti-pris,* the supremacy of free grace over good works, and can therefore never be sympathetically understood by the majority of modern readers. For he does, after all Christian's arguments, persist in the error of reliance on his own righteousness : 'But is it not a good heart that has good thoughts? And is not that a good life, that is according to God's commandments?' He speaks in the detached, sceptical language of a man of the new age, perhaps of a latitudinarian Anglican, when he speaks of Christian and Hopeful's uncompromising adherence to the doctrine of salvation by grace as 'whimsies . . . the fruit of distracted brains'. Indeed the new age felt a twinge of sympathy for Ignorance, and in the eighteenth century the liberal Presbyterian Edward Foster used to say that none of the characters in *The Pilgrim's Progress* spoke sense except him. But as with the other minor characters Ignorance is a study in temperamental weakness as well as theological error; the heresy is seen as an offshoot of the personal weakness. His words betray him. To begin with, there is his total and shocking complacency : his reliance on the good state of his own religious feelings springs from this unshakeable vanity rather than from any theological argument :

Ignorance.   . . . I am always full of good motions, that come into my mind to comfort me as I walk.

But my heart and life agree together, and therefore my hope is well founded.

Christian. Who told thee that thy heart and life agrees together?

Ignorance. My heart tells me so.

Where By-Ends and his companions had at least tried to rejoin Christian on the road and argue it out with him, the deadly vanity of Ignorance causes him to 'take pleasure in walking alone, even more a great deal than in company'. He is self-sufficient; he will not learn. It is this wilful ignorance that makes him deficient on any view of Christian humility, and not merely in terms of a Calvinist objection to belief in salvation by personal righteousness, and which makes him a character, naïve, articulate, exasperating and pathetic, not a text-book example.

It is the same with all the more important characters met along the road. A living person is presented, striving to realise a particular vice or virtue. It might be said of all of them what Honest says to Greatheart, 'Not Honesty in the abstract, but Honest is my name'. There are of course lesser figures who simply sketch in a type, or who appear to make a single point by the introduction of their names and then disappear again. Such is the man whose name is Help who helps Christian out of the Slough of Despond; such are Faint-Heart, Mistrust and Guilt, who set upon Little-faith and rob him : the symbolic point is quickly made, and we have reached the outer limits of allegory to enter upon a realistic scene of highway robbery : 'So they all came up to him, and with threatening language bid him stand. At this, Little-faith looked as white as a clout, and had neither power to fight nor fly.' Then, in a rather different category, come traditional personifications which Bunyan uses rarely. Prudence, Piety and Charity, in the House Beautiful, while related to the traditional moral and theological virtues, are not carefully distinguished allegorically, and their attractive, glowingly charitable and unpriggish discourse with Christian savours much more of the atmosphere of an ideal Puritan domestic interior than of moral allegory. So again, as with Little-faith and Vanity Fair and the medical consultation with Mr. Skill, we are in the presence of a direct treatment of common life that involves Christian moral types quite naturally. It is no quibble to suggest that this is something different from true allegory, thinking in abstracts and psychological entities and using touches of realism as embroidery. Bunyan's method is what distinguishes the types of Restoration comedy from earlier 'humours' comedy; it is the method which passed on into the secular novel to flower in Fielding. In his novels characters like Allworthy and Heartfree belong to an observed contemporary life which is seen as part of a moral universe.

III   THINE OWN NATIVE LANGUAGE

Bunyan was careful to check in himself the sin of pride, which he felt he was prone to, but in sending forth his Second Part he could not help boasting that it might be distinguished from counterfeits by his 'native language' which 'No man Now useth, nor with ease dissemble can'. The First Part had already established his claim to greatness with readers of every class as a writer of simple, natural prose relying on the native strength of his English. To describe it as colloquial is to run the danger of blurring what we mean to say; the word has enjoyed more than its fair share of critical usage lately. Prose is prose, not speech, however closely based upon the spoken idiom. M. Jourdain was wrong : he had not been speaking prose for more than forty years. But large parts of the *Pilgrim's Progress* are conversation. In these parts the manner runs as close to spoken idiom as would seem possible, the idiom of ordinary people, yeomanry or small middle class, not the mannered repartee of Restoration comic dialogue. Even the longer speeches which extend the story and are not strictly conversational keep this tone and natural rhythm. It can be seen from a not specially remarkable passage like that in which Greatheart describes his guidance of Mr. Fearing :

I got him in at the House *Beautiful,* I think before he was willing; also when he was in, I brought him acquainted with the Damsels that were of the Place, but he was ashamed to make himself much for Company, he desired much to be alone, yet he always loved good talk, and often would get behind the *screen* to hear it; he also loved much to see *ancient* things, and to be *pondering* them in his Mind. He told me afterwards, that he loved to be in those two Houses from which he came last, to wit, at the Gate, and that of the *Interpreters*, but that he durst not be so bold to ask.

The grammatical arrangement is loose but never sloppy, a series of parallel clauses and sentences; if they naïvely run on, they are never allowed to pile up too much and cause confusion. An emphatic pause, like that before the last sentence, serves to make the structure of meaning absolutely clear. The slight but pleasing music of the short clauses, varying in length but only varying a little, creates a transparent medium for dramatic effects. The simpler the prose statement, the more humorous or poignant implications can show through it. Here it is the vignette of the shy Fearful listening to the talk in the parlour from behind the screen that stands out.

The prose has a range extending through this serviceable, fairly neutral medium, to a rough, vivid colour in words and phrases from racy, country speech. The language is studded with popular proverbs; sometimes it is hard to tell whether a phrase not recorded elsewhere is a rare proverb or simply the creation of the proverbial imagination. 'Every fat (i.e. vessel) must stand upon his own bottom', says Presumption. Mrs. Lightmind at Madame Wanton's was 'as merry as the maids'. Some provincial forms occur: we meet 'he all-to-befooled me' and the unstressed spoken form 'a' for 'have' in 'he would a had him gone back for fear of the lions'.

There is little in this prose of the influence of the English Bible, except in a few intenser passages echoing the Psalms: 'Behold, how green this valley is, also how beautified with lilies.' Too much has been made, by Southey and others, of the notion that Bunyan was a man of one book and that one book was the Authorised Version. Its distinctive rhythms and its phraseology, already slightly archaic in 1611 because of the dependence on earlier translations, are not the major force which drives along the prose of *The Pilgrim's Progress.* That force is Bunyan's own speech and tone of voice, modified by the use he had put it to in order to express personal religious experience and by his training as a popular preacher. Where the Bible is dominant is in the thought and structure of the work. First, in the great metaphors of wayfaring and struggle, but also in nearly every important episode. The Valley of the Shadow, Vanity Fair, the houses of entertainment for pilgrims modelled on the life of the apostles in the Acts, the final bourne of the Heavenly City – all by the creative ferment of the naïve imagination expand hints and suggestions into full-scale drama. The dream is frame; it is also the process by which the naïve imagination was able to crack the narrow sectarian pattern and free the Biblical truths to describe the way of the people of God in living terms. It is something that in the twentieth century even theologians, Catholic and Protestant, have only slowly come round to, and it can never be judged by purely literary standards.

SOURCE: *The Pilgrim's Progress* (1966) pp. 54–61.

C. S. Lewis

THE VISION OF JOHN BUNYAN
(1969)

There are books which, while didactic in intention, are read with
delight by people who do not want their teaching and may not
believe that they have anything to teach – works like Lucretius'
De Rerum Natura or Burton's *Anatomy*. This is the class to
which *The Pilgrim's Progress* belongs. Most of it has been read
and re-read by those who were indifferent or hostile to its
theology, and even by children who perhaps were hardly aware
of it. I say, most of it, for there are some long dialogues where
we get bogged down in sheer doctrine, and doctrine, too, of a
sort that I find somewhat repellent. The long conversation, near
the end of Part 1, which Christian and Hopeful conduct 'to
prevent drowsiness in this place'[1] – they are entering the
Enchanted Ground – will not prevent drowsiness on the part of
many readers. Worse still is the dialogue with Mr Talkative.

Bunyan – and, from his own point of view, rightly – would not
care twopence for the criticism that he here loses the interest of
irreligious readers. But such passages are faulty in another way
too. In them, the speakers step out of the allegorical story
altogether. They talk literally and directly about the spiritual life.
The great image of the Road disappears. They are in the pulpit.
If this is going to happen, why have a story at all? Allegory
frustrates itself the moment the author starts doing what could
equally well be done in a straight sermon or treatise. It is a valid
form only so long as it is doing what could not be done at all,
or done so well, in any other way.

But this fault is rare in Bunyan – far rarer than in *Piers Plow-
man*. If such dead wood were removed from *The Pilgrim's
Progress* the book would not be very much shorter than it is. The
greater part of it is enthralling narrative or genuinely dramatic

dialogue. Bunyan stands with Malory and Trollope as a master of perfect naturalness in the mimesis of ordinary conversation.

To ask how a great book came into existence is, I believe, often futile. But in this case Bunyan has told us the answer, so far as such things can be told. It comes in the very pedestrian verses prefixed to Part 1. He says that while he was at work on quite a different book he 'Fell suddenly into an Allegory'.[2] He means, I take it, a little allegory, an extended metaphor that would have filled a single paragraph. He set down 'more than twenty things'.[3] And, this done, 'I twenty more had in my Crown'.[4] The 'things' began 'to multiply'[5] like sparks out of a fire. They threatened, he says, to 'eat out'[6] the book he was working on. They insisted on splitting off from it and becoming a separate organism. He let them have their head. Then come the words which describe, better than any others I know, the golden moments of unimpeded composition :

> For having now my Method by the end;
> Still as I pull'd, it came.[7]

It came. I doubt if we shall ever know more of the process called 'inspiration' than those two monosyllables tell us.

Perhaps we may hazard a guess as to why it came at just that moment. My own guess is that the scheme of a journey with adventures suddenly reunited two things in Bunyan's mind which had hitherto lain far apart. One was his present and life-long preoccupation with the spiritual life. The other, far further away and longer ago, left behind (he had supposed) in childhood, was his delight in old wives' tales and such last remnants of chivalric romance as he had found in chap-books. The one fitted the other like a glove. Now, as never before, the whole man was engaged.

The vehicle he had chosen – or, more accurately, the vehicle that had chosen him – involved a sort of descent. His high theme had to be brought down and incarnated on the level of an adventure story of the most unsophisticated type – a quest story, with lions, goblins, giants, dungeons and enchantments. But then there is a further descent. This adventure story itself is not left in the world of high romance. Whether by choice or by the fortunate limits of Bunyan's imagination – probably a bit of both – it is all visualized in terms of the contemporary life that Bunyan knew. The garrulous neighbours; Mr Worldly-Wiseman who was so clearly (as Christian said) 'a Gentleman',[8] the bullying, foul-mouthed Justice; the field-path, seductive to footsore walkers; the sound of a dog barking as you stand knocking at a door; the fruit hanging over a wall which the children insist on eating though their mother admonishes them 'that Fruit is none of ours'[9] – these are all characteristic. No one lives further from Wardour Street than Bunyan. The light is sharp: it never comes through stained glass.

And this homely immediacy is not confined to externals. The very motives and thoughts of the pilgrims are similarly brought down to earth. Christian undertakes his journey because he believes his hometown is going to be destroyed by fire. When Matthew sickens after eating the forbidden fruit, his mother's anxiety is entirely medical; they send for the doctor. When Mr Brisk's suit to Mercy grows cold, Mercy is allowed to speak and feel as a good many young women would in her situation: 'I might a had Husbands afore now, tho' I spake not of it to any; but they were such as did not like my Conditions, though never did any of them find fault with my Person.'[10]

When Christian keeps on his way and faces Apollyon, he is not inspired by any martial ardour. He goes on because he remembers that he has armour for his chest but not for his back, so that turning tail would be the most dangerous thing he could do.

A page later comes the supreme example. You remember how the text 'the wages of sin is death' [11] is transformed? Asked by Apollyon why he is deserting him, Christian replies: 'Your wages [were] such as a man could not live on.' [12] You would hardly believe it, but I have read a critic who objected to that. He thought the motive attributed to Christian was too low. But that is to misunderstand the very nature of all allegory or parable or even metaphor. The lowness is the whole point. Allegory gives you one thing in terms of another. All depends on respecting the rights of the vehicle, in refusing to allow the least confusion between the vehicle and its freight. The Foolish Virgins, within the parable, do not miss beatitude; they miss a wedding party.[13]

The Prodigal Son, when he comes home, is not given spiritual consolation; he is given new clothes and the best dinner his father can put up.[14] It is extraordinary how often this principle is disregarded. The imbecile, wisely anonymous, who illustrated my old nursery copy of *The Pilgrim's Progress* makes a similar blunder at the end of Part II. Bunyan has been telling how a post came for Christiana to say that she was to cross the river and appear in the City within ten days. She made her farewells to all her friends and 'entered the *River* with a *Beck'n*' (that is a wave) 'of Fare well, to those that followed her to the River side'.[15] The artist has seen fit to illustrate this with a picture of an old lady on her death-bed, surrounded by weeping relatives in the approved Victorian manner. But if Bunyan had wanted a literal death-bed scene he would have written one.

This stupidity perhaps comes from the pernicious habit of reading allegory as if it were a cryptogram to be translated; as if, having grasped what an image (as we say) 'means', we threw the image away and thought of the ingredient in real life which it represents. But that method leads you continually out of the book back into the conception you started from and would have had without reading it. The right process is the exact reverse. We ought not to be thinking 'This green valley, where the shepherd boy is singing, represents humility'; we ought to be discovering, as we read, that humility is like that green valley. That way, moving always into the book, not out of it, from the concept to the image, enriches the concept. And that is what allegory is for.

There are two things we must not say about the style of *Pilgrim's Progress*. In the first place we must not say that it is derived from the Authorised Version. That is based on confusion. Because his whole outlook is biblical, and because direct or embedded quotations from Scripture are so frequent, readers carry away the impression that his own sentences are like those of the English Bible. But you need only look at them to see that they are not : 'Come *Wet*, come *Dry*, I long to be gone; for however the Weather is in my Journey, I shall have time enough when I come there to sit down and rest me, and dry me.'[16] Who in the Old or New Testament ever talked like that?

'Mr. *Great-heart* was delighted in him (for he loved one greatly that he found to be a man of his Hands).' [17] Is that like Scripture?

The other thing we must not say is that Bunyan wrote well because he was a sincere, forthright man who had no literary affectations and simply said what he meant. I do not doubt that is the account of the matter that Bunyan would have given himself. But it will not do. If it were the real explanation, then every sincere, forthright, unaffected man could write as well. But most people of my age learned from censoring the letters of the troops, when we were subalterns in the first war, that unliterary people, however sincere and forthright in their talk, no sooner take a pen in hand than cliché and platitude flow from it. The shocking truth is that, while insincerity may be fatal to good writing, sincerity, of itself, never taught anyone to write well. It is a moral virtue, not a literary talent. We may hope it is rewarded in a better world : it is not rewarded on Parnassus.

We must attribute Bunyan's style to a perfect natural ear, a great sensibility for the idiom and cadence of popular speech, a long experience in addressing unlettered audiences, and a freedom from bad models. I do not add 'to an intense imagination', for that also can shipwreck if a man does not find the right words. Here it is in a descriptive passage :

They are, said she, our Countrey Birds : They sing these Notes but seldom, except it be at the Spring, when the Flowers appear, and the Sun shines warm, and then you may hear them all day long. I often, said she, go out to hear them, we also oft times keep them tame in our House. They are very fine Company for us when we are Melancholy.[18]

And here it is rendering the exact voice of the rustic wiseacre – Mrs Timorous is speaking : 'Well, I see you have a mind to go a fooling too; but take heed in time, and be wise : while we are out of danger we are out; but when we are in, we are in.' [19]

Here you see it turning a point in the narrative, very economical but full of suggestion :

Thus they went on till they came to about the middle of the Valley, and then *Christiana* said, Methinks I see something yonder upon the Road before us, a thing of a shape such as I have not seen. Then said *Joseph*, Mother, what is it? An ugly thing, Child; an ugly thing, said she. But Mother, what is it like, said he? 'Tis like I cannot tell what, said she. And now it was but a little way off.[20]

Can anyone read that without hearing both the voices? Here it attempts, successfully, a higher strain : 'Then *Apollyon* strodled quite over the whole breadth of the way, and said, I am void of fear in this matter, prepare thy self to dye, for I swear by my Infernal Den, that thou shalt go no further, here will I spill thy soul.'[21]

Or here with a more daring image than is usual : 'I fought till my Sword did cleave to my Hand, and when they were joyned together, as if a Sword grew out of my Arm, and when the Blood run thorow my Fingers, then I fought with most Courage.'[22] Any of the epic poets would be glad to have thought of that.

In dialogue Bunyan catches not only the cadence of the speech but the tiny twists of thought. Mr Talkative is not allowed to talk much. But note how, when Faithful has tried to correct him, he replies : 'That is it that I said.'[23]

It is perfect for the unteachable man; whatever you put to him will be taken as an endorsement of the last opinion he has expressed. Or consider this, from Mr Great-heart's long story of Mr Fearing : 'And I will say that for my Lord, he carried it wonderful lovingly to him.'[24] Great-heart is devoted to his Master. He delights to eulogize him. Yet the form of words in which the praise here comes out – 'I will say this for him' – is exactly that with which an honest man would reluctantly concede one, and only one, redeeming feature in an opponent. One could understand this if it were artfully done in the witness box; an apparently reluctant witness impresses the jury. But there is no question of that here. There is some kink in the mind of the English rustic, some innate rhetoric, that makes him talk that way. You may hear it in country pubs any day.

But it is always dangerous to talk too long about style. It may lead one to forget that every single sentence depends for its total effect on the place it has in the whole. There is nothing remarkable about the sentence '*I will pay you when I take my Mony*' and '*I will fight so long as I can hold my Sword in my Hand.*'[25] But in their context they are devastating. For they are uttered by

two men lying fast asleep on the Enchanted Ground, talking in
their sleep, and not to be waked by any endeavour. The final
stroke of the grim irony comes with the words : 'At that, one of
the Children laughed.'[26] How horrifying the joke and the
laughter are is perhaps immediately apparent only to those who
share Bunyan's premises. Yet perhaps not. Even those who think
that the stakes we play for in life are not, as Bunyan believed,
strictly infinite, may yet feel in some degree the uneasiness he
meant us to feel; may wonder whether what we regard as our
firm resolutions, our long industry, and our creditable achieve-
ments, are not all talking in our sleep and dreaming, sleep from
which, though we may talk louder and louder, we shall not wake.
For stakes less than infinite may yet be fairly high.

Part of the unpleasant side of *The Pilgrim's Progress* lies in the
extreme narrowness and exclusiveness of Bunyan's religious outlook. The faith is limited 'to one small sect and all are damned
beside'. But I suppose that all who read old books have learned
somehow or other to make historical allowances for that sort of
thing. Our ancestors all wrote and thought like that. The
insolence and self-righteousness which now flourish most notice-
ably in literary circles then found their chief expression in
theology, and this is no doubt a change for the better. And one
must remember that Bunyan was a persecuted and slandered
man.

For some readers the 'unpleasant side' of *The Pilgrim's Progress*
will lie not so much in its sectarianism as in the intolerable terror
which is never far away. Indeed *unpleasant* is here a ludicrous
understatement. The dark doctrine has never been more horrify-
ingly stated than in the words that conclude Part 1 : 'Then I saw
that there was a way to Hell, even from the Gates of Heaven, as
well as from the City of *Destruction*.'[27]

In my opinion the book would be unmeasurably weakened as
a work of art if the flames of Hell were not always flickering on
the horizon. I do not mean merely that if they were not it would
cease to be true to Bunyan's own vision and would therefore suffer
all the effects which a voluntary distortion or expurgation of
experience might be expected to produce. I mean also that the
image of this is necessary to us while we read. The urgency, the

harsh woodcut energy, the continual sense of momentousness, depend on it.

We might even say that, just as Bunyan's religious theme demanded for its vehicle this kind of story, so the telling of such a story would have required on merely artistic grounds to be thus loaded with a further significance, a significance which is believed by only some, but can be felt (while they read) by all, to be of immeasurable importance. These adventures, these ogres, monsters, shining helpers, false friends, delectable mountains, and green or ghastly valleys, are not thereby twisted from their nature. They are restored to the weight they had for the savage or dreaming mind which produced them. They come to us, if we are sensitive to them at all, clothed in its ecstasies and terrors. Bunyan is not lending them an alien gravity. He is supplying, in terms of his own fundamental beliefs, grounds for taking them as seriously as we are, by the nature of our imagination, disposed to do. Unless we are very hidebound we can re-interpret these grounds in terms of our own, perhaps very different, outlook. Many do not believe that either the trumpets 'with melodious noise'[28] or the infernal den await us where the road ends. But most, I fancy, have discovered that to be born is to be exposed to delights and miseries greater than imagination could have anticipated; that the choice of ways at any cross-road may be more important than we think; and that short cuts may lead to very nasty places.

S o u r c e : *Selected Literary Essays* (1969) pp. 145–53.

NOTES

1. *The Pilgrim's Progress*, ed. James Blanton Wharey, second edition revised by Roger Sharrock, Oxford English Texts (Oxford, 1960) Part 1, p. 136.

2. Ibid. p. 1.

3. Ibid.

4. Ibid.

5. Ibid.

6. Ibid.

7. Ibid. p. 2.

8. Ibid. Pt I, p. 21.
9. Ibid. Pt II, p. 194.
10. Ibid. Pt II, pp. 227–8.
11. Romans 6 : 23.
12. *The Pilgrim's Progress*, Pt I, p. 57.
13. Matthew 25 : 1–13.
14. Luke 15 : 11–32.
15. *The Pilgrim's Progress*, Pt II, p. 306.
16. Ibid. Pt II, p. 305.
17. Ibid. Pt II, p. 291.
18. Ibid. Pt II, p. 235.
19. Ibid. Pt II, pp. 183–4.
20. Ibid. Pt II, p. 241.
21. Ibid. Pt I, p. 59.
22. Ibid. Pt II, p. 291.
23. Ibid. Pt I, p. 76.
24. Ibid. Pt II, p. 251.
25. Ibid. Pt II, p. 298.
26. Ibid. Pt II, p. 298.
27. Ibid. Pt I, p. 163.
28. Ibid. Pt I, p. 160.

F. R. Leavis

BUNYAN'S RESOLUTENESS (1969)

It is possible to read *The Pilgrim's Progress* without any thought of its theological intention. I myself can testify to that. When I read it in childhood, as everyone did (at least we assumed so and there seemed to be plenty of evidence for the assumption), I had not heard of Calvin or of Predestination, Imputed Righteousness, and Justification by Faith, and even if they had been explained to me I should not have seen any point in trying to relate what I could grasp of those doctrines to the book that was so stirring a presence in our imaginative life. I am not for a moment suggesting that the theological significance had not counted immensely in its becoming an established popular classic among English-speaking people. What I am emphasizing is that *The Pilgrim's Progress* was written by a highly gifted, imaginative writer and has the vitality and significance of major art.

This is an emphasis that one finds in place when reading that valuable scholarly book *John Bunyan, Mechanick Preacher*, by William York Tindall. Professor Tindall's theme is that Bunyan was one of a host of preaching tinkers, cobblers, blacksmiths, wheelwrights, tradesmen of all kinds, and field workers – all humble uneducated persons. *John Bunyan, Mechanick Preacher* is a valuable book because Tindall documents his theme so thoroughly, and thus brings out the representative quality of the life and conditions behind Bunyan's art. He provokes us, at the same time, to insist on the distinction of the art – to insist there *is* art, and art of an impressiveness that makes Bunyan for us that rare thing, a creative genius. For Professor Tindall's treatment of the facts he presents has the effect of telling us that Bunyan was *merely* one of an ignorant and fanatical preaching host. But there was only *one* Bunyan, we reply. There were other gifted Puritan 'mechanick' preachers whose talent appears in their

writings, but *The Pilgrim's Progress* stands alone; there is no
rival Puritan classic in the field of creative literature.

Having said this, I wonder whether it is altogether felicitous to
call *The Pilgrim's Progress* a 'Puritan classic'. Certainly it isn't in
the least what 'puritanical' today suggests. Nor does it in the
world and ethos it evokes remind us at all closely of Hawthorne's
The Scarlet Letter. What I meant was that it is a classic produced by English Puritanism of the seventeenth century. And in
saying this I come back to the emphasis on representativeness:
The Pilgrim's Progress has a representative significance such as
is found only in the work of a great creative writer. As I have
testified out of my own experience, it can be read – and having
been so read, leave a profound and lasting impression – as a
dramatic and classically compelling tale innocent of theological
intentions, an imaginative work that holds us by what it is in its
impact as an intensely evoked particular history.

Recognizing in later life, however, that it is something more
than a children's classic, and thinking about the nature of its
power, one sees that the theological intentions unmistakably demand – from anyone interested in the art – a recognition different
in tone and less simple in implicit judgment than is exemplified
by Professor Tindall's commentary. His tone is an ironic dry-
ness. He assumes that the embattled and quarrelsome certitudes
of sectarian Calvinistic theology can, by the modern reader, be
seen only as bigotry, fanaticism, and ignorance. But if one is
interested in the art, one tells oneself that the religious ethos of
The Pilgrim's Progress isn't fairly suggested by an account of
Bunyan's theology as a Particular Open-Communion Baptist,
even though religious ethos and theology can hardly be altogether separated. Bunyan himself, one recognizes as an essential
and very germane truth, would have greeted with astonishment
the distinction just implied. But although (finding, too, the
associated bigotry repellent) one may be unable to regard the
doctrine with any sense of attraction or enlightenment, it is
hardly possible to admire *The Pilgrim's Progress* as a creative
work without being moved by its religious quality and seeing that
this inheres in the power of the art. And to take stock of this complexity of perception and recognition that one finds in oneself is

to acquire a more lively sense of a representative significance in John Bunyan.

The tone of Tindall's commentary, as I have intimated, carries a reductive judgment on the world – or the culture (for the term, we shall see, is appropriate) – to which Bunyan belonged. The force of the adjective 'puritanical', as currently used, doesn't tend to advert us to the need for a fuller and juster sense of that word. But to ponder the vitality and depth of Bunyan's art is to see in *The Pilgrim's Progress* an incontrovertible document of seventeenth-century Puritanism – a representative product the clear human significance of which refutes the too-simple judgments and preconceptions in a most salutary way. And in throwing a revelatory light on seventeenth-century Puritanism, *The Pilgrim's Progress* at the same time gives us an insight into that past of our civilization which is not in time very remote, but that, if we really think of it, we have to think of as a civilization of the past – as not ours, but the civilization that produced Shakespeare.

John Bunyan was born in 1628, near the market town of Bedford. Bedford lies thirty miles to the west along the road that runs a hundred yards from where I write. Fifteen miles northward from here (from Cambridge, that is) lies Huntingdon, county town of the shire where Cromwell farmed. Puritanism was not confined to any part of England; it was pervasive and had many centres, but this eastern region was one where it was notably strong. The Civil War broke out in 1642, and there can be little doubt, though the particular facts of his service are not on record, that when in 1644 Bunyan was enlisted, it was in the Parliamentary army. It seems that he saw no fighting – there was none in the neighbourhood of Newport Pagnell where he was stationed. But this was not garrison duty in a country at peace; among his fellow soldiers there will have been those whose memories of action were both vivid and matter-of-fact and who could communicate to the boy a strong sense of belonging to a fraternity from the members of which, in the natural order of things, the mustering of courage and address for the hazards of armed hand-to-hand encounter would be required. The presence of this adolescent experience in the preacher-allegorist is to be seen in *The Pilgrim's Progress*, where for the most part the terms of the allegory, in which arms and the use of them play a prominent part, obviously belong, in their convincing reality, to the texture of the artist's daily life.

Bunyan the Puritan allegorist *was* an artist; however incongruous a word for him it may seem, it is worth insisting on as a way both of challenging recognition for the nature of great art and of making the point that he might have had his spiritual intensity and steadfastness without having the creative writer's gift that makes him a great name in the history of prose fiction; he might, that is, have had as intense, painful, and undeviating a concern for the certitude of personal salvation. I touch here on a delicate matter for thought, one that cannot be ignored in considering the time-honoured status of *The Pilgrim's Progress*, though I think it would be crass to suppose one can formulate neatly definitive conclusions as the upshot. In shifting, in the sentence before the last, from my first phrase to 'an intense, painful, and undeviating concern for the certitude of personal salvation', I point to something essential in Bunyan that pulls most modern readers up when they become acutely aware of it, for it reminds them that Bunyan's intensity was indeed that of a seventeenth-century Puritan. For Professor Tindall it seems to be at the best something for a pitying smile, being a manifestation of ignorance, bigotry, and fanatical conceit. And actually, though I have meant to be taken as suggesting that Bunyan may properly be seen as representative of seventeenth-century Puritanism, he belonged to a minority even among seventeenth-century Puritans. As W. Hale White says in his *John Bunyan* : 'His awful doubts and fears were not shared by others, not even by "the people of God". "They would pity me and would tell me of the Promises." The "people of God" at Bedford believed in their Calvinism, but they sat in their shops and quietly went about their business untroubled by their creed.'

The way in which Bunyan was, as the voluminous body of his writings manifests, troubled by his creed (and he insisted indefatigably, and with moving conviction, that the people of God cannot but be so moved) is given in what Hale White recalls to us of Samuel Johnson :

It is strange . . . that Johnson resembled Bunyan. His spectres haunted Johnson, and the *History of My Melancholy*, which he once thought of writing but never dared to write, would undoubtedly have reminded us of another history by the author of *The Pilgrim's Progress* which he loved so well. 'You seem, sir,' said Mrs. Adams to Johnson, 'to forget the merits of our Redeemer.' 'Madam,' he replied, 'I do not forget the merits of my Redeemer; but my Redeemer has said that He will set some on His right hand and some on His left.' 'He was in gloomy agitation', adds Boswell, 'and said I'll have no more on't.'

Johnson the High Church Tory was not a Calvinist; we think with sympathetic horror of his suffering in this way, and see it as something to be thought of as coming under the head of pathology. But Bunyan *was* a Calvinist; that in him which leads Hale White to make the comparison with Johnson was something entailed on Bunyan by his taking his creed with the intensity of full belief. How could an imagination possessed by such a creed create a humane classic, for Bunyan's 'puritan classic' *is* that. He, of course, with that paradoxical security registered in the way in which the pilgrim, having escaped from the Slough of Despond, has still Doubting Castle, Giant Despair, and so many hazards of the same significance in front of him, had – as Johnson had not – the assurance of being one of the Elect. But it is hard to think of that relation to the sectarian exclusiveness of his polemical and damnation-dispensing theology as conducive to a generous creative power.

Yet the creative power is beyond question there in *The Pilgrim's Progress*. It is so compelling there that, through reading after reading, one remains virtually unconscious of the particular theology – remains so even when one could, if challenged, offer a fair account of the detailed doctrinal significances of the allegory in which the intention of this is given. Here and there, perhaps, one retains a faint sense of knowing some reason for entering a kind of protest – as, for instance, when, remembering that glimpse through the opened door where 'they also thought that they heard a rumbling noise, as of fire, and a cry of some tormented, and that they smelt the scent of brimstone', we read at the close of the First Part how at the King's command the two

Shining Ones, Christian's and Faithful's conductors, dealt with Ignorance – on whose particular allegorical significance in terms of Restoration controversy Talon,[1] in his standard work, throws an interesting light : 'Then they took him up, and carried him through the air, to the door that I saw in the side of the hill, and put him in there. Then I saw that there was a way to hell, even from the gates of heaven, as well as from the City of Destruction.'

But the clear if paradoxical truth is that one's sense of a religious depth in the book prevails with such potency that particular theological intentions to be elicited from the allegory don't get much recognition for what they doctrinally are, or, if noticed and judged to be incongruous with one's basic response, don't really tell. That is, in considering *The Pilgrim's Progress*, we have to recognize that we do very much need the two words 'theological' and 'religious'. Bunyan's religion, like his art, comes from the whole man. And the man, we can't help telling ourselves as we reflect on the nature of the power of his masterpieces, belonged to a community and to a culture, a culture that certainly could not be divined from the theology. The next step – one that follows necessarily in a critical appreciation of *The Pilgrim's Progress* – is to recognize the force of the obvious truth that seventeenth-century Puritanism considered in the context of English life from which in the concrete it was inseparable looks very different from an abstracted Puritanism, in our sense of which an account of its theological characteristics predominates. In fact, what is apt to predominate is the Calvinistic ethos as Dickens, the incomparable recorder of Victorian civilization, evokes it for us. We have it in Mrs Clennam of *Little Dorrit* – morose, repressive, anti-human, the enemy of happiness, childhood, art, and life. But the Puritanism of Bunyan's England is not to be identified with this. It is worth recalling that Cromwell, the arch-Roundhead, wore long hair and delighted in music. But the sufficient evidence is there in *The Pilgrim's Progress* itself, from which it is plain that the 'people of God' did not in their revulsion against Vanity Fair think it necessary to ban from their lives the humane arts and graces. The place of music, dancing, and the social pleasures of the table in the

Second Part, where a whole party make their pilgrimage together, is especially significant. And the Delectable Mountains are not a symbol that we can think of as belonging to Mrs Clennam's imaginative life.

But I must return briefly to Bunyan's personal history. The youth we left under arms at Newport Pagnell was not, to go by his own account, devout, and certainly not a Puritan; that is why, the record not being specific, some nineteenth-century biographers felt at liberty to conjecture that he might have been in the King's army. He was soon back at Bedford, and there, having married at about the age of twenty, he was 'converted' by the Bedford minister, John Gifford (ex-major of the King's army), and in 1653 baptized. Since Gifford had been a royalist officer, we can accept as fact the account of him as having been before his conversion a reckless profligate. But confessions to such an effect, as Professor Tindall's book brings out, were common form among converts, and without imputing any insincerity to Bunyan we can believe that the wickedness he avowed as having characterized his unregenerate days was less lurid than the profligacy of a blackguard royalist major. The account he himself gives of it seems to make it nothing worse than swearing and bell-ringing (the church bells being in question) and not having obeyed or even listened to the call to become a 'pilgrim'. He now began his career of preaching, which may be said to have been, in one form and another, the main occupation of his life.

His addiction to it was compulsive; it led to his spending a large part of his life in prison. That fate closed down on him in 1660, the first year of the Restoration, when monarchy in the person of Charles II came back to England. Charles had undertaken in the Declaration of Breda that the Nonconformists — the Protestant rebels to the authority of the Anglican church — should be left their freedom of worship, but the promise was not kept and Bunyan was one of the first victims. The Clarendon code of penal laws, together with his obduracy, ensured that he should be an inmate of Bedford jail from 1660 to 1672. He was imprisoned again for some while in 1676, and, dying in 1688, the year of the Revolution, he didn't live to enjoy the established toleration inaugurated then.

Froude's suggestion that Bunyan's imprisonment wasn't for the most part very rigorous, so that we may think of him as slipping out from time to time to preach in the neighbourhood, is not now regarded as well founded. Parted from wife and children, for whose welfare he suffered painful anxiety, he was confined in what was indeed a 'den' – a breeding-place of jail-fever. There was no chimney in it, and we have to think of him as sleeping in straw. Yet in prison as out he was a preacher – a preacher and a shepherd of souls in that given Puritan tradition. Opportunities for the exercise of his vocation were not lacking in prison, and he took them assiduously. Moreover, he wrote immensely, and his themes, as we can see from the great body of his writings, were those of his preaching, and always the same. They were those of his spiritual autobiography, *Grace Abounding to the Chief of Sinners*, and those yielded by a summary of the theological significance of *The Pilgrim's Progress* – those of the Puritan sectarian's intensely fostered Calvinistic preoccupations : the terrifying realization of one's total depravity, conversion and joyful hope, infinitely subtle promptings of the devil, recurrent despair, the paradoxical struggle for faith, the difficulty of keeping the narrow doctrinal way, the assurance of Election and of salvation by Imputed Righteousness – over and again. How could this fanatical treadmill-concentration issue in or be compatible with a generous humane art   a creative presentment of human life that counts for so much (and not the less essentially because not measurable) in the subsequent history of major art achieved in prose fiction? If we think of the uglier characteristics of sectarian controversy, it has to be recorded that Bunyan can't be acquitted of these. His earliest published book was a brutally bigoted polemic against the Quakers.

Yet *The Pilgrim's Progress* was, unquestionably, the work of the preacher – his most successful and popular work; and the more we know of his other writings the more emphatically can we say that, if unique, it was no sport. The best way of approaching the considerations that throw light on the paradox is to read G. R. Owst's *Preaching in Mediaeval England* and *Literature and Pulpit in Mediaeval England*. Owst shows, with an abundant particularity of illustration, that Bunyan as a popular

preacher and homiletic writer was in a tradition that went back
beyond the Reformation, in unbroken continuity, deep into the
Middle Ages. I see an economy in quoting at this point a couple
of sentences that, appealing to Owst's testimony, I have written
elsewhere.[2] 'If one observes that this tradition owes its vitality to
a popular culture, it must be only to add that the place of
religion in the culture is obvious enough. The same people that
created the English language for Shakespeare's use speaks in
Bunyan, though it is now a people that knows its Authorized
Version.' Bunyan, that is, had behind him – or rather, had
around him and in him – that pervasive and potent continuity, a
living culture; it was the air he breathed, the spiritual food
(doctrinal Puritanism being only an element in it) that nourished
him, the more-than-personal sensibility that as a writer he was.
'One writes', D. H. Lawrence late in his life replied to a questioner, 'out of one's moral sense', going on immediately to give
'moral' an intense special force by adding 'for the race, as it
were'. Bunyan the creative writer wrote out of a 'moral sense'
that represented what was finest in that traditional culture. He
used with a free idiomatic range and vividness in preaching
(the tradition he preached in ensured that) the language he
spoke with jailers and fellow prisoners, with wife and children
and friends at home. A language is more than such phrases as
'means of expression' or 'instrument of communication' suggest; it is a vehicle of collective wisdom and basic assumptions, a
currency of criteria and valuations collaboratively determined;
itself it entails on the user a large measure of accepting participation in the culture of which it is the active living presence.

The vigour of Bunyan's prose is more than a matter of an
earthy raciness that consorts happily with biblical turns and re-
sonances. And the way in which the creative writer's art
transcends the intention belonging to the allegory is illustrated
here :

Christian.   Pray, who are your kindred there, if a man may be so
bold?

By-Ends.   Almost the whole town; and in particular my Lord
Turnabout, my Lord Timeserver, my Lord Fair-speech (from whose
ancestors the Town first took its name), also Mr Smoothman, Mr

Facing-both-ways, Mr Anything, and the Parson of our parish, Mr
Two-tongues, was my mother's own brother by father's side; and to
tell you the truth, I am become a gentleman of good quality; yet
my grandfather was but a waterman, looking one way and rowing
another; and I got most of my estate by the same occupation.

Christian.   Are you a married man?

By-Ends.   Yes, and my wife is a very virtuous woman, the
daughter of a virtuous woman; she was my Lady Feigning's daughter,
therefore she came of a very honourable family, and is arrived at
such a pitch of breeding that she knows how to carry it to all, even
to prince and peasant. 'Tis true we somewhat differ in religion
from those of the stricter sort, yet but in two small points : First,
we never strive against wind and tide; secondly, we are always
most zealous when religion goes in his silver slippers; we love much
to walk with him in the street, if the sun shines, and the people
applaud him.

Professor Tindall comments :

To Bunyan the name By-ends connoted ends other than that of
salvation by imputed righteousness . . . By-ends is the product of the
resentment against the Anglicans of an enthusiastic evangelist and
despised mechanick. . . . Bunyan's fortunate discovery that through
these controlled debates between his hero and these caricatured pro-
jections of his actual enemies he could experience the pleasures of
combat without the complications of reality invests *Pilgrim's Progress*
with the character of a controversial Utopia.

The first sentence of this commentary states an unquestioned
fact. One's return comment is that one can respond to the
characteristic power of that passage of Bunyan, and respond in a
critically admiring way, without reminding oneself of the fact,
even though one knows it, and that when one does remind oneself of it there is little difference to register in one's response or
one's appreciation. As for what follows, one can only reply that
while the doctrinal preoccupation, which naturally tended to be
associated with a polemical habit, without doubt sharpened
Bunyan's observation of character and gave vivacity to his
analysis, what strikes one is the rendered observation, its life and
truth and depth. And so far from suspecting Bunyan of trying to
create for himself, with small-minded bigotry, an unreal 'controversial Utopia', one is possessed by the strong sense one has of an

actual reality evoked. The art, one sees, belongs to a popular culture. The names and the racy turns of speech are one with the general style, and the style, concentrating the life of popular idiom, is the expression of cultural habit. What we have is something more than an idiomatic raciness of speech, expressing a naïve gusto of malicious observation : it is an art of social living, with, where the valuation of character is concerned, a fund of experience to draw on and shrewd criteria.

Lively characterization, of course, constitutes a major strength of *The Pilgrim's Progress*. Along with By-ends, everyone remembers Worldly Wiseman and Talkative and Pliable. But the spirit and quality of Bunyan's art in this respect are not adequately suggested in terms of the characters in the book that are observed satirically; there is no lack in his characterization of sympathetic perception and rendering or of warm human feeling. One would know confidently from *The Pilgrim's Progress* that he was a tender husband and father, a steadfast friend, and a man, authoritative in his human insight and his integrity, whom a close neighbourhood of the devout would naturally choose for their pastor – as the Bedford 'people of God' chose Bunyan in 1672, the year of his release from jail. The tradition in which he preached and wrote, together with the culture to which it and he himself belonged, ensured that the qualities and traits glanced at should be strongly present in his imaginative work.

The above considerations do something to explain how it is that even when we tell ourselves from point to point what the allegorical intention is, no consciousness of the allegory in terms of such a gloss as Professor Tindall gives us impedes or alters our fuller response – the inevitable response (we feel) to Bunyan's art; and how it is that we should find ourselves taking a religious significance that is not identical with the theological but transcends it. I confess for myself that the occasions when the doctrinal habit associated with the allegory has to be taken note of for an unsympathetic response are those when I am merely bored a little, rather than balking at something repellently unacceptable offered for acquiescence. I am thinking of those recurrent quasi-dramatic disquisitions and those dialogues in the pastoral mode :

I won't pretend that I return with any eagerness to such things as the conducted and lectured viewing of 'emblems' and tableaux in the house of the Interpreter.

To attempt to say anything positive about the religious quality of *The Pilgrim's Progress* is a delicate matter. One's awareness of a religious significance as distinguished from a theological intention is challenged by that opening to the First Part :

As I walked through the wilderness of this world, I lighted on a certain place, where there was a den . . . and as I slept, I dreamed a dream. I dreamed, and behold, I saw a man clothed with rags standing in a certain place, with his face from his own house, a book in his hand, and a great burden upon his back. I looked, and saw him open the book, and read therein; and as he read, he wept and trembled; and not being able longer to contain, he brake out with a lamentable cry, saying, 'What shall I do?'

The den, we know, is Bedford jail. The dream convention doesn't in the least tend to diminish the intense reality with which the world of external facts belonging with Bunyan's spiritual autobiography is presented. To consider its use is to recognize the way in which the personal intensity gets, in the creative presentment, while being for that none the less intense, a necessary impersonalization. This effect is hardly separable from the sense we have of there being, in the order of reality in which this history is enacted, a dimension over and above those of the common sense world. The events follow one another in a time succession, but now and then, taking it quite naturally, we are referred to a different, or 'normal', reality of time – that left behind by Christian in the City of Destruction, or by the other pilgrims in whatever this-worldly place they came from. I am thinking of the way in which a pilgrim, being overtaken by – or even overtaking – another from the same place, will, on inquiring about family or acquaintance, be given an account of what has happened there since his departure. It is plain in these cases that the two ostensibly parallel passages of time cannot be reconciled as belonging to the same real world, and yet we feel no need to object or question.

Of course, the word 'convention' that I used above can be invoked as a sufficient explanation : we accept the dream convention and are not troubled by these anomalies. But 'convention' is a word, and more can be said by way of recognizing that quality of *The Pilgrim's Progress* to which we are attuned by the opening paragraph, where 'dream' carries no suggestion of relaxation or unreality. There is something irresistible and unanswerable about the steadfastness of inner life (Bunyan's own steadfastness, something so profoundly and essentially disinterested as to make one flinch from talking about it in terms of fanaticism or a 'concern for personal salvation') that carries the pilgrims through defeats, lapses, disasters, and felicities. This, we recognize, thinking of Tom Brangwen in the first chapter of Lawrence's *The Rainbow*, is the effective 'knowing we do not belong to ourselves';[3] and we recognize, though theologies may have become unacceptable or odious and we may feel that we have nothing left that Bunyan could have called 'faith' or 'belief', a change-defying validity. The close to the Second Part, where the pilgrims one by one cross the river, remains, even when we have told ourselves that the timbre or tone of exaltation belongs to Bunyan's world and not to ours, immensely impressive.

Though closing with this supreme exaltation, the Second Part, in which Christiana and her children, along with a whole party, go on the pilgrimage, is more novel-like than the First Part; that is, it suggests more readily that Defoe could have found in it something congenial to the prompting of his own talent (as it was to be found on so large a scale in Bunyan's *The Life and Death of Mr Badman*). Nevertheless, it is astonishing to reflect that Defoe, already nearing manhood, was to be Bunyan's successor as the great popular writer and bestseller. The Second Part of *The Pilgrim's Progress* (the First having come out in 1678) came out in 1684. The Revolution of 1688, the year of Bunyan's death, marks the unequivocal triumph of the new civilization, of which we see Defoe as a formidable representative. He was educated at a Dissenting Academy, and French writers about English literature describe him as '*puritain*'. But there is nothing either theological or what we readily call spiritual in Defoe's Nonconformity. He is Robinson Crusoe, *terre-à-terre*, com-

monsensical, infinitely resourceful – an invincibly sane man of
this world, an adventurer, but not conceivably a pilgrim.

When I say 'man of this world' and 'invincibly sane' I am,
while paying tribute to positive qualities, at the same time
intimating limitations: we cannot pass from Bunyan to Defoe
without a sense of loss. 'Our excellent and indispensable eighteenth century' (Matthew Arnold's phrase) was notably *not*
characterized by something that is strongly present in the great
creative periods. Of course, Dissenter though he was, Defoe's
decent human feeling had no touch of that morose distrust and
rejection of life that we associate with Calvinism – the Calvinism
of *The Scarlet Letter* and of Dickens's Mrs Clennam. But then,
in spite of the doctrine of Total Depravity to which as a
theological expositor Bunyan subscribed, the attitude towards life
and the world he expresses, out of the whole man, in his art, is
as we have seen, no more life-rejecting than Defoe's. True, life
and the world to his sense are much more dangerous than to
Defoe's, for all the shipwreck and the cannibals of *Robinson
Crusoe*; for Bunyan bottomless sloughs and dreadful abysses
menace the pilgrim, mountains seem about to fall on him, and not
to be a pilgrim is to be certainly and eternally damned. But the
hazards and menaces are the negative accompaniments of something positive that is not there in Defoe's world: the concern,
intense and profound, for what, talking loosely, as we *have* to talk
(for no precision is possible), we speak of as the 'meaning of
life'. Such a concern, felt as the question 'What for – what
ultimately for?' is implicitly asked in all the greatest art, from
which we get, not what we are likely to call an 'answer', but the
communication of a felt significance; something that confirms our
sense of life as more than a mere linear succession of days, a
matter of time as measured by the clock – 'tomorrow and tomorrow and tomorrow....'

Bunyan's theological *statement* of the significance he wishes to
enforce is abstract; but the sense of significance that actually
possessed him couldn't be stated, it could only be communicated
by creative means. It might be objected that Bunyan identifies the
significance of life with a belief in a real life that is to come after
death, and that therefore *The Pilgrim's Progress* cannot, for

readers who do not share that belief, have the kind of virtue I
have attributed to it. But these things are not as simple as that.
However naïvely Bunyan, as pastor, might have talked of the
eternal life as the reward that comes after death to the Christian
who has persevered through the pains and trials of his earthly
pilgrimage, the sense of the eternal conveyed by *The Pilgrim's
Progress* and coming from the whole man ('trust the tale', as
Lawrence said, not the writer) is no mere matter of a life going on
and on for ever that starts after death. It is a sense of a dimension
felt in the earthly life – in what for us *is* life, making this
something that transcends the time succession, transience and
evanescence and gives significance.

Such a sense is conveyed with great potency by *The Pilgrim's
Progress*. There it is, an unquestionable reality for us, a vitalizing
reminder of human nature, human potentiality, and human need,
and remaining that for us even though we may find wholly un-
profitable the theology with which Bunyan accompanies it, and,
moreover, may tell ourselves that so confident and exalting a
sense of significance could not have been achieved in our time
and our civilization. One of the things we learn from frequent-
ing the great works of creative art is that where life is strong in
any culture, the 'questions' ask themselves insistently, and the
'answers' change from age to age, but in some way that challenges
our thought; the profound sincerity of past 'answers' will invest
them for our contemplation with a kind of persisting validity.
And what is 'validity'? To that challenge there is no simple reply
– which is very far from saying that it won't repay endless consideration: the nature and the life of the human world (that
which Sir Charles Snow is so blank about when he exalts the
'scientific edifice of the physical world' as the 'most beautiful and
wonderful collective work of the mind of man')[4] are in question.

The play of 'significance' goes in *The Pilgrim's Progress* with
the homely day-to-day reality in the evoking of life that con-
vinces us of Defoe's indebtedness to Bunyan. At this level itself
(so far as it can be separated for consideration) one may
reasonably judge Bunyan superior to Defoe as a pioneer of the
novel. His 'realism' comes from deeper down; his dialogue, in
its homely rightness, is much more subtle and penetrating in its

power of characterization and has an immensely wider range of tones. As for 'homely', that word in its bearing on Bunyan's art must not be allowed to suggest limitations. As I have already remarked, against the penetrating vividness and economy of his satiric portrayals is to be set the tender potency of his sympathetic evocation of day-to-day life. This is especially so in Part Two. The theme is pilgrimage, but the distinctive note is that of a family party, and the rendering yields abundant matter that might have been invoked in illustration by the historian John Richard Green for the enforcement of his once well-known contention : the home, as we think if it now, was the creation of the puritan.

I cannot allow myself to come to an end without insisting once more that 'puritan' must not be taken to suggest a stern or morose austerity, or, in the preoccupation with Grace, any indifference to the graces of life. Bunyan's 'homely' spirituality entails no contempt for the good things of this world. Our satisfaction in the thought of the children enjoying their bread well spread with honey is patently assumed, and the pleasures of the table, socially enjoyed, play an essential part in the culture that is incidentally revealed for our contemplation. So do music and dancing : this puritanism assumes that art is necessary to life. There is some reason for supposing that Bunyan, in prison, made himself both a violin and a flute, and certainly his Christiana plays the viol, his Mercy plays the lute, and his Prudence accompanies on the spinet her own singing. 'Wonderful ! Music in the house, music in the heart, and music also in Heaven' – the exclamation suggests aptly that actual 'unpuritanical' sense of earthly life in relation to the eternal which informs *The Pilgrim's Progress*. This is the religious feeling, the unquestioned spirituality, that the creative work conveys, even though an account of Bunyan's allegorical intention in terms of the theological doctrines (with Total Depravity as the basic note) would convey something very different.

S O U R C E : Written as an 'afterword' to the Signet Classics edition of *The Pilgrim's Progress* (1964); reprinted in *Anna Karenina and Other Essays* (1969) pp. 33–48.

NOTES

1. Henri A. Talon, *John Bunyan: The Man and his Works* (London, 1951).

2. F. R. Leavis, 'Bunyan Through Modern Eyes', in *The Common Pursuit* (London, 1952; New York, reissued 1964).

3. 'But during the long February nights with the ewes in labour, looking out from the shelter into the flashing stars, he knew he did not belong to himself.'

4. A contention I discuss in *Two Cultures? The Significance of C. P. Snow* (London, 1963).

John R. Knott, Jr

BUNYAN'S GOSPEL DAY: A READING OF *THE PILGRIM'S PROGRESS* (1973)

Recently Stanley Fish has argued that *The Pilgrim's Progress* offers only an illusory kind of progress and that it is in fact 'anti-progressive, both as a narrative and as a reading experience'.[1] The linear form of the work constitutes a danger for the reader, according to Fish, because it 'spatializes and trivializes' the 'way' of Christ's 'I am the way.' As Fish demonstrates, Bunyan discredits the assumption of various pilgrims that all they must do to reach the New Jerusalem is to follow an external, readily discernible way. Formal and Hypocrisy err in assuming that they are in the same way of faith that Christian is ('what's matter which way we get in; if we are in, we are in'),[2] as do others such as Atheist and Ignorance that Christian encounters at various points in his journey. But one can note this aspect of *The Pilgrim's Progress* without concluding that it comprises the basic figure of the journey which underlies the narrative. What Fish pictures as deceptive linear form was the sustaining metaphor of Puritan spiritual life in Bunyan's time. To devalue this metaphor by considering it in purely formal terms is to explain away the reason for the extraordinary power of *The Pilgrim's Progress* over the imaginations of actual readers for several centuries.

Both the Apology to *The Pilgrim's Progress* and the verse Conclusion are remarkable for Bunyan's preoccupation with justifying his figurative method to skeptical Puritan readers, whom he imagines objecting, 'Metaphors make us blind.' Bunyan defends his form by pointing to the substance it contains, as in the comparison of his work with a cabinet offered in the Apology ('*My dark and cloudy words they do but hold/*

The Truth as Cabinets inclose the Gold [p. 4]), but he does not
thereby imply that the form is an inadequate means of expressing his message. I would argue, with U. Milo Kaufmann, that
Bunyan was in truth uncomfortable with the Puritan habit of
reducing biblical metaphor to doctrine.[3] The very fact that
Bunyan protests so much in attempting to justify his method reveals the depth of his commitment to 'similitude' as a means of
expressing God's truth. Some of his formulations actually tend
to undermine the conventional distinction between kernel and
husk. In the conclusion, for example, he suggests that the
reader might not be able to 'extract' his gold from the ore in
which it is wrapped and chides: *'None throws away the Apple
for the Core'* (p. 164).

Bunyan's most significant appeals are to scriptural authority,
and underlying these appeals is a conviction about the metaphoric nature of much Biblical truth. Bunyan saw that the
prophets *'used much by Metaphors / To set forth Truth'* (p. 5)
because God's truth could best be comprehended figuratively.
He never suggests a separation between the *'Types, Shadows,
and Metaphors'* of the Bible and the truth that they express. For
Bunyan the light of the Gospel 'springs' from its 'Dark Figures'.
He felt that by employing a similarly 'dark' method he could
make truth *'cast forth its rayes as light as day'* (p. 6). Such
language does not suggest a concern with doctrine and uses
(though Bunyan was of course concerned with showing his
readers how to conform their lives to God's truth) but with con-
veying the kind of joyful illumination that he found in Scripture.
He would make *'The Blind . . . delightful things to see'* (p. 7).

To appreciate the nature of Bunyan's commitment to the
metaphor of the way one must recognize that he used this metaphor in two basic senses, both of which are important. His
genius for exploiting the dramatic potential of biblical metaphor
is perhaps most apparent from his success at holding in suspen-
sion these two senses of his central figure. The way is the path of
all Christians through the wilderness of the world, the way 'From
This World To That Which Is To Come', and simultaneously
the inner way of faith of the individual believer. Without a
strong conviction about *where* the way leads the pilgrim would

never set out at all, yet he cannot arrive at the promised end unless he understands *how* to walk.

Bunyan talks about the second sense of his metaphor, what it means to walk in the way of faith, in *The Holy City*, his commentary on Revelation. He explains : 'it is usual in the Holy Scripture to call the transformation of the sinner from Satan to God a holy way, and also to admonish him that is so transformed to walk in that way, saying, Walk in the faith, love, spirit, and newness of life, and walk in the truth, ways, statutes and judgments of God.'⁴ Here and in *The Pilgrim's Progress* Bunyan draws upon the Old Testament sense of walking in the 'way of the righteous' (Psalm 1:6), in the 'truth' of God, as well as upon the New Testament sense of walking 'in the Spirit' (Galatians 5:16) and 'in newness of life' (Romans 6:4), but of course the New Testament meaning is primary. Faith must be attested by a genuine 'newness of life'.

This sense of the way as determined by the faith of the individual pilgrim coexists with the other sense of the way as a common journey of all the faithful from the City of Destruction to the New Jerusalem. The design of *The Pilgrim's Progress*, and much of its force, depends upon the figurative reading of the experience of the Israelites that Bunyan and countless other Puritans learned from Hebrews.⁵ *The Heavenly Footman* shows more explicitly than its successor, *The Pilgrim's Progress*, the centrality of the figure of the journey to Bunyan's understanding of the Christian life :

Because the way is long (I speak metaphorically) and there is many a dirty step, many a high hill, much work to do, a wicked heart, world, and devil, to overcome; I say, there are many steps to be taken by those that intend to be saved, by running or walking, in the steps of that faith of our father Abraham. Out of Egypt thou must go through the Red Sea; thou must run a long and tedious journey, through the vast howling wilderness, before thou come to the land of promise.⁶

Bunyan saw that he did not speak any less truly for speaking 'metaphorically'. The metaphor, which he saw as embodying God's promise that his saints would succeed in making their way through the wilderness to the 'land of promise', is the key to his conception of *The Pilgrim's Progress* and to the appeal of the work for his Puritan readers. His 'dream' could succeed because the habit of thinking of the world metaphorically, as a wilderness to be journeyed through, was ingrained in his readers, and because they could identify readily with someone who could show them what it meant to follow 'in the steps of that faith of our father Abraham'.[7] The ground of their faith was a belief in the possibility of progress from this world to the next, and Bunyan's work offered them the hope that an ordinary believer, not without weaknesses, might attain the New Jerusalem.

The encounter of Christian and Hopeful with the shepherds of the Delectable Mountains provides a revealing illustration of Bunyan's ability to combine the two basic senses of the metaphor of the way. This episode offers one of the best examples in *The Pilgrim's Progress* of the subjectivity of the individual way of faith:

Christian.   *Is this the way to the Cœlestial City?*
Shepherd.   You are just in your way.
Christian.   *How far is it thither?*
Shepherd.   Too far for any, but those that *shall* get thither indeed.
Christian.   *Is the way safe, or dangerous?*
Shepherd.   Safe for those for whom it is to be safe, *but transgressors shall fall therein.* (p. 119).

The deliberate ambiguity forces one to recognize that the nature of the way – its length and the specific dangers to be encountered – depends upon the faith of the individual pilgrim. The shepherds can assess the spiritual health of the wayfarers at the moment ('You are just in your way'), but this spiritual condition is dynamic and precarious. To give definite answers to the pilgrim's questions would be to ignore the uncertainty with which faith must live. In *The Heavenly Footman* Bunyan says, 'as the way is long, so the time in which they are to get to the end of it is very uncertain; the time present is the only time'.[8] Christian's faith exists only in this 'time present', because faith must be renewed continuously.

Alice's encounter with the Cheshire Cat reads as though

Carroll might have conceived it as a parody of Bunyan's meeting with the shepherds :

'Would you tell me, please, which way I ought to go from here?'
'That depends a good deal on where you want to get to', said the Cat.
'I don't much care where – ' said Alice.
'Then it doesn't matter which way you go', said the Cat.
' – so long as I get somewhere', Alice added as an explanation.
'Oh, you're sure to do that,' said the Cat, 'if you only walk long enough.'[9]

The Cheshire Cat's responses appear nonsensical only because he does not give Alice the kind of certainty she wants. His logic is impeccable, and it serves as an amusing way of pointing up her confusion. One way is as good as another unless she decides the 'ought'. She is bound to get 'somewhere' if she walks 'long enough', but whether she thinks she is 'somewhere' will depend upon her expectations. The response of the shepherds to Christian's inquiries has the similar effect of turning the questions back on the questioner, though they can offer no assurances that Christian will get anywhere at all because they are talking about a metaphorical way that depends upon a faith that may collapse at any moment. Carroll's logical cat would find them incomprehensible, and probably silly.

Yet Bunyan's shepherds are also talking about the one true way that leads to the New Jerusalem (and not just 'somewhere'), and the Delectable Mountains mark a station along that way, as the Interpreter's House and House Beautiful mark earlier stations. Christian's actions describe a progression through stages of spiritual life. This progression is clearer in some places than in other – notably near the beginning and the end of the journey – but its outlines would have been familiar to readers acquainted with Puritan spiritual autobiography. Together Christian's experiences constitute a 'Calvinist soul-history' (to use Sharrock's term)[10] proceeding from an initial conviction of sin that lands him in the Slough of Despond to the instruction in Scripture that he receives in the Interpreter's House (where he is exposed to scenes designed to 'prick him forward' in the way), and through the various trials of the major part of the journey until he finally arrives at the assurance of God's mercy represented by Beulah.

One should not attach too much significance to the order of the temptations that Christian encounters, yet there is some point to the sequence. The more violent, and dramatic, assaults on Christian's faith come early – the most violent, that of Apollyon, soon after he has put on the Pauline armor of the soldier of Christ. The transition from the Valley of Humiliation to the Valley of the Shadow of Death makes sense in terms of Christian's experience; he has just faced the prospect of annihilation in the battle with Apollyon. After escaping the fiends of the Valley of the Shadow, Christian must face the hostile society of Vanity Fair (after an interlude occupied by conversation with Faithful and Talkative). Again the threat is overt and violent, although violence in Vanity Fair is more insidious and contemptible for being sanctioned by social forms. Later Christian encounters more subtle kinds of temptations, involving fraud or deceptive appearances (Demas, By-Path Meadow, Flatterer, the seductive appeal of the Enchanted Ground for the pilgrim nearing the end of his journey).

The Doubting Castle episode proves that Christian can lose the way at a relatively late point in the journey through overconfidence, not that he has failed to grow in faith and understanding. The very intensity of his despair suggests bitter chagrin at having erred so foolishly after having come through so many trials. In Doubting Castle Hopeful appeals to Christian's past victories over Apollyon and the terrors of the Valley of the Shadow ('*remembrest thou not how valiant thou hast been heretofore*' [p. 116]), but valor will not help him in this very different kind of dilemma. In the first instance he had saved himself by continuing to fight, in the second by continuing to walk. In Doubting Castle Christian is baffled and dismayed by the fact that it seems impossible either to defeat his enemy or to get his key. The brilliance of the episode lies in the fact that Bunyan makes escape seemingly so difficult yet paradoxically so easy; Christian has only to remember that Scripture has provided him with his own key, a solution that comes to him as a result of prayer.

Christian again lapses into doubt at the River of Death, this time a paralyzing 'darkness and horror' that causes him to forget temporarily the 'sweet refreshments' he had met with in the way and the assurance they had given him of reaching the 'Land that flows with Milk and Honey' (p. 157). Bunyan's emphasis upon the 'sorrows of death' does not subvert the metaphor of the journey; it merely indicates his acute sense of the dangers of this final obstacle, even for those who have persevered in the way of holiness. Reaching the plane of assurance represented by Beulah does not relieve one of the necessity of making the crossing.

Christian continues to be vulnerable to doubt throughout his pilgrimage because Bunyan believed that faith could never be completely secure in this world. But his doubts are prompted by very different kinds of trials, appropriate to different stages of the journey, and in each case we are reminded of what has gone before. Christiana's journey presents a clearer, less interrupted sense of progress, of course, because her way is so much easier. Giant Despair falls before Great-heart, the last of a succession of giants to suffer such a fate. Christiana receives so much support from her guides and the companies of Christians she encounters that she scarcely has the opportunity to doubt her salvation. After leaving the Delectable Mountains she sings: '*Behold, how fitly are the Stages set! / For their Relief, that Pilgrims are become*' (p. 289).

My point is simply that one can and should talk about stages in the journey that correspond to mileposts in the development of spiritual vitality. Christiana follows the same way that Christian does, though her temptations differ in degree from his, because Bunyan believed that patterns could be found in Puritan spiritual life. Kaufmann has suggested that Christian 'helps to define the road to be walked' and prepares the way for his wife and family; by markers and victories 'he transforms the way he covers' without, however, changing its outlines.[11] One could take Kaufmann's argument a step further and say that by elaborating the metaphor of the way Bunyan ordered and explained the potentially chaotic events of spiritual life for his readers. In describing the Valley of the Shadow of Death and showing Christian passing through it he localized the terrors of death and suggested that they could be overcome.

To understand the nature of Christian's spiritual progress one must look more closely at the stages of his journey, particularly at his experience in such places as the Delectable Mountains and the land of Beulah. Those episodes that mark Christian's growing awareness of divine favor serve to establish the truth embodied in the biblical metaphor of the journey and hence to convince the reader that the goal for which Christian strives is real. Bunyan's narrative works by establishing the credibility of an entire world of spiritual experience, based upon the Word and opposed to the actual world, the world of his readers' everyday experience in which Christian first appears. But Christian, and the reader, can enter this spiritual country only by recognizing the absoluteness of the claim made by the Word and by stripping themselves of the assumptions that govern life in the secular world. One must first understand the form that this process of disengagement takes in Bunyan's narrative.

Christian's sudden recognition of the force of the biblical truth that the world he inhabits belongs to the City of Destruction propels him into what Bunyan in the Apology calls 'our Gospel-day', a time defined by the Word, and in this 'Gospel-day', according to a verse from Corinthians that Bunyan quotes in *Come and Welcome to Jesus Christ* : 'Now is the acceptable time, behold now is the day of salvation' (II Corinthians 6:2). In the perpetual 'time present' of faith it is always 'now', and Bunyan's Christian acts out of a sense of urgency that is incomprehensible to anyone who does not recognize the same biblical imperative. Obstinate speaks for the community when he dismisses him as '*brain-sick*'.

Christian's dramatic flight from his family – with his fingers in his ears and crying, 'Life, Life, Eternal Life' – appears ludicrous from any perspective other than the biblical one that Bunyan labored to establish. Mark Twain had Huck Finn encounter Bunyan at one point in his journey, when he investigates the books in the Grangerford's library : 'One was *Pilgrim's Progress*, about a man that left his family, it didn't say why. I read considerable in it now and then. The statements was interesting but tough.'[12] Huck is an ideal vehicle for Twain's irony. To one schooled in the hard business of survival in the world Christian's way of faith makes no sense at all. Bunyan knew that his message was 'tough', and he chose to emphasize its difficulty so that there could be no mistake about the kind of renunciation that following the way demands. To put it another way, Bunyan knew that biblical truth was 'dark' not only because it is often metaphoric but because it is at bottom paradoxical, riddling (he exhorts Christiana to expound her 'riddles' in the prefatory verses to Part II of *The Pilgrim's Progress*).

The Gospel demands that one lose his life in order to save it (Mark 8:35) and further that one hate his family in order to follow Christ (Luke 15:26). If one chooses the way of Christ, one will necessarily appear foolish in the eyes of the world. The Pauline opposition between the spirit and the flesh that provided the basis for Augustine's conception of rival cities of God and man lies behind Bunyan's sense of a way that inevitably brings the pilgrim into conflict with the world (one must go '*out of the World*' to avoid Vanity Fair) and yet leads him beyond it. Bunyan's narrative insists that the claims of the way and those of the world are mutually exclusive. The pilgrim must set his course '*against Wind and Tide*' (p. 100), as Christian increasingly realizes. Faithful relates that he has learned to ignore the 'hectoring spirits of the world' because he recognizes that 'what God says, is best, though all the men in the world are against it' (p. 73).

Bunyan's account of his own trial dramatizes as clearly as anything in *The Pilgrim's Progress* the unavoidable conflict between the claims of the world and those of the Word. When the magistrate demanded that Bunyan show how it could be lawful to preach, confident that the law against unlicensed preaching left no room for doubt on the subject, Bunyan responded by quoting Peter: 'As every man hath received the gift, so let him minister the same.'[13] They might as well have spoken two different languages, so fundamentally opposed were their ways of ordering their lives. Bunyan went to jail, for a period that stretched to twelve years, because he could no more stop preaching than he could renounce the Word. To be a 'servant in the Gospel', as Bunyan signed himself, meant to act upon it.

The Vanity Fair episode constitutes the most important

statement of the warfare between spirit and flesh in *The Pilgrim's Progress*. By reducing secular society to a fair, Bunyan could imply that the collective opinion and power of 'all the men in the world' are devoted to upholding the economic (and class) system upon which their material well-being is founded. In Bunyan's severe view even family relationships have a commercial aspect (his catalogue of merchandise includes 'Wives, Husbands, Children'), and the end of all human activity, limited by the perspective of the world, is vanity. At his trial Faithful charges that Christianity and the values of the town are *'Diametrically opposite'*. Bunyan heightened the contrast by exaggerating the strangeness of the pilgrims, showing them to be peculiar in dress, in speech, and in their complete indifference to the wares pressed upon them; to the townspeople they are 'fools', 'Bedlams', 'Outlandish-men'. As strangers and pilgrims on the earth, seeking a better country, Christian and Faithful simply have no interest in the town; they *'buy'* the truth, which is to be found only in the Word. Although the justice of the burghers is a cruel farce, they act upon the correct assumption that Faithful's attitude threatens the very basis of their existence. The whole episode illustrates the necessity of choosing between two modes of life that are irreconcilable, between 'carnal sense' and 'things to come', to use the distinction made for Christian by Interpreter.

All the assumptions about the end of human activity that underlie Vanity Fair, and the indulgence of 'fleshly appetite' that they allow, can be comprehended in the term 'carnal sense' (or a comparable one, 'carnal temper', which Evangelist applies to Worldly Wiseman). One can see a similar repudiation of carnality in Christian's rejection of the appeal of Worldly Wiseman, whose patronizing line finally depends upon the assumption that Christian will be attracted by the prospect of a comfortable, secure existence in the Village of Morality. He offers an ordered society based on a respect for law and class distinctions (to accept his gentlemanly authority and that of Legality would be for Christian to admit that he is one of the *'weak'* who meddle with *'things too high for them'*).

Vanity Fair strongly suggests actual fair towns of Bunyan's day, and, with the Village of Morality and the City from which

Christian sets out, it embodies the material attractions of the real world which Christian must put behind him if he is to attain his goal. These places must be distinguished from landscapes that reflect Christian's inner struggles. Although the Village of Morality and the Slough of Despond can both be located along the 'way' that Christian travels, they reflect different orders of experience. The same can be said of the Valley of Humiliation and Vanity Fair. The latter presents the sort of external challenge that the warfaring Christian continually meets in society, and can resist successfully if he only remembers the scriptural language, typically riddling, that enables him to see his life in a heavenly rather than an earthly perspective. To pass through the Valley of Humiliation and other landscapes that dramatize the crises of his inner life Christian must depend upon the action of grace to reveal how the Word will save him. These landscapes appear more perilous because of his uncertainty.

Bunyan's spiritual landscapes have a fluidity that recalls the shifting terrain of *The Faerie Queene*. They are often surreal, more like what one might expect in a dream than the actual landscapes one might encounter in Bedfordshire or anywhere else.[14] The experience of the pilgrim (either Formal or Hypocrisy) who follows the way of Destruction 'into a wide field full of dark Mountains, where he stumbled and fell, and rose no more' (p. 42) suggests the abrupt transitions of dreams. One cannot really explain these strange 'dark Mountains', even by appealing to Bunyan's source in Jeremiah, except to say that the episode provides a commentary on the nature of spiritual blindness. Dangers rise up unpredictably, and one cannot cope with them by native wit.

The spiritual world that Christian enters in setting out for the New Jerusalem resembles the country he knows yet surprises him in strange ways. The Slough of Despond was obviously inspired by the conditions of Bedfordshire roads (and has been taken as an instance of Bunyan's realism), yet this Slough quickly assumes alarming proportions. Pliable cries out *'where are you now?'* (p. 14) as Christian begins to sink and flees, unable to tolerate a hazard that refuses to conform to the limits of his experience. Pliable is the epitome of the practical man, the sort who has to

know exactly where he is going and how, and he cannot follow
Christian into the treacherous spiritual landscape that he has
entered. Christian himself quickly learns that he is helpless without the Word in this world; only by recognizing the '*steps*' it
provides, with the aid of Help, can he get through the Slough.

The Valley of Humiliation, the Valley of the Shadow of
Death, the Delectable Mountains, and the other landscapes that
Christian must traverse define a world that is open only to those
who believe in the Word sufficiently to seek the goal that he does.
These landscapes do not exist for Pliable, who refuses to enter
the spiritual country to which they belong, or for Atheist, who
cannot find it. The topography of this country is determined
largely by Bunyan's experience of Scripture, and the key to
Christian's progress through it is his understanding of the power
of the Word.

Christian's near disaster in his struggle with Apollyon suggests
that this understanding does not come easily. The education in
the Gospel that he has received from Evangelist, Interpreter, and
the inhabitants of House Beautiful prepares him to resist Apollyon's arguments successfully.[15] Yet his failure in the physical
combat that follows suggests that Christian is deficient in faith
and needs the intervention of the Spirit – whose help Bunyan felt
all Christians required to understand the implications of Scripture, and even to pray successfully – to be able to manage his
sword ('the sword of the Spirit, which is the Word of God'
[Ephesians 6:17]). The verse that Bunyan chose to signal
Christian's new grasp of the power of the Word is particularly
suggestive : '*Rejoyce not against me, O mine Enemy! when I fall,
I shall arise.*' It points to the paradoxical nature of Biblical truth
(a difficult lesson for Christian to learn) and thus to his own
providential recovery, and also, typologically, to Christ's resur-
rection and his ultimate victory over Satan (Bunyan would have
regarded the verse from Micah as foreshadowing these truths).

Christian's encounter with Apollyon has meaning only for one
who grants the fundamental truth of Scripture (Atheist would
not conceive of evil in this way). The indefiniteness of the landscape in which Christian meets him can be explained by his
spiritual condition and his sense of Scripture at this point. In his

guilt and fear Christian imagines the power of the demonic forces that oppose God to be greater than it is. It is startling to discover in reading Part II that the Valley of Humiliation is 'fat Ground'; Great-heart tells Christiana, 'Behold, how green this Valley is, also how beautified *with Lilies*' (p. 237). At a comparable stage in his journey Christian lacks the steady spiritual vision that Christiana demonstrates here; he can see only Apollyon coming 'over the field' and then straddling the way. Thus preoccupied with the monstrous appearance of evil, he cannot experience the foretaste of Canaan that his more tranquil, and humble, wife does.

Christian defeats Apollyon by discovering how to use the power over evil inherent in the Word. He conquers the darkness and terrors of the Valley of the Shadow of Death by learning to rely upon the illumination of the Word, which enables him to keep to the path. Bunyan associated the darkness and the confusion of this second Valley with a loss of the sense of God's presence. Like Milton's hell, it offers a desolate, sterile landscape ('*A Wilderness, a Land of desarts, and of Pits, a Land of drought, and of the shadow of death*'), and in this 'very solitary place' Christian experiences a terrifying feeling of aloneness. In one of the passages that inspired the episode Job in his helplessness sees himself as going to the 'land of gloom and deep darkness, the land of chaos, where light is as darkness' (Job 10:22). Bunyan saw that the terror of this 'deep darkness' lay in a loss of the confidence and the sense of order that assurance of the comfort of the Spirit affords. Yet Christian's dilemma is finally simpler than Job's, for he can get through the darkness through prayer and a reassertion of faith ('*I will walk in the strength of the Lord God*'). His ability to believe in the light of the Gospel, unlike the man in the Iron Cage of Despair who has 'sinned against the light of the Word' and so grieved the Spirit that 'he is gone' (p. 34), causes the light and the Spirit to return. Again the passages that Bunyan quotes point to the paradoxical nature of Biblical truth: 'He hath turned the shadow of death into the morning' (Amos 5:8); 'He discovereth deep things out of darkness, and bringeth out to light the shadow of death' (Job 12:22). As in the previous episode Christian's experience adds a new dimension to his understanding, and the reader's, of the power of God to bring forth good out of apparent evil.

In retrospect one can see that Bunyan's use of passages from Job to establish Christian's 'dark and dismal state' implies his release from that state, for other passages from the book describe the way God enables one to conquer the darkness. One can find a similar implication in Bunyan's use of Jeremiah at the very beginning of the episode. The lines that he draws upon come from God's reproach of the Israelites for forgetting their prior deliverance : 'Neither said they, Where is the Lord that brought us up out of the land of Egypt, that led us through the wilderness, through a land of deserts and pits, through a land of drought, and of the shadow of death, through a land that no man passed through, and where no man dwelt? And I brought you into a plentiful country, to eat the fruit thereof and the goodness thereof . . .' (Jeremiah 2 : 6–7). Christian is not deterred by the two men who warn him of the dangers of the Valley ('Children of them that brought up an evil report of the good Land', that is, the spies of Numbers 13), because they in fact confirm that *this is* [the] *way to the desired Haven* (Bunyan cites Jeremiah 2 : 6 again at this point). In other words, Christian can go forward because the Valley makes sense to him in terms of the larger pattern of the journey; he understands that the 'plentiful country' lies beyond it. Although Christian's confidence is eclipsed temporarily once he is in the Valley, Bunyan's readers would have taken the references to the Exodus as an earnest of his, and their, ultimate deliverance. And they would have seen the whole episode – showing Christian's progress through the wilderness, and from darkness to light – as a miniature version of the larger journey.

Thus far I have been concerned with the ways in which Christian, having entered the 'Gospel-day', uses the Word as a means to spiritual survival. It is just as important to consider how the Word sustains him by offering consolation, in the form of anticipations of the rewards of the 'land of promise'. The growth of Christian's capacity to perceive the delights of Canaan is the surest index to his spiritual progress. Bunyan characteristically pictures these delights in terms of Old Testament imagery of fertility, or 'fatness' (usually drawn from the Psalms, Isaiah, and the Song of Solomon). He shows Christian experiencing a foretaste of these delights as early as his stay in House Beautiful. In that hostel, built 'for the relief and security of Pilgrims' (p. 46), Christian is seated at a table 'furnished with fat things, and with Wine that was well refined' (p. 52) and subsequently shown the Delectable Mountains that lie ahead in his journey : 'behold at a great distance he saw a most pleasant Mountainous Country, beautified with Woods, Vineyards, Fruits of all sorts; Flowers also, with Springs and Fountains, very delectable to behold. Then he asked the name of the Country, they said it was *Immanuels Land* : and it is as Common, said they, as this *Hill* is to, and for all the Pilgrims. And when thou comest there, from thence, thou mayest see to the Gate of the Coelestial City, as the Shepherds that live there will make appear' (p. 55).

Although the senses must be repudiated when one is trying to resist the temptations of this world (hence Christian stops his ears with his fingers and looks to heaven when in Vanity Fair), they do have a proper use : in experiencing, or anticipating, the delights of the world to come. In *The Pilgrim's Progress* Bunyan could express metaphorically, in terms of Christian's sensuous awareness, those heavenly delights that Puritan writers and preachers exhorted the faithful to work at imagining.[16] One can trace a progressive awakening of Christian's senses – in the House Beautiful, beside the River of Life, on the Delectable Mountains, and in Beulah – that corresponds to his increasing awareness that he enjoys the favor of God and the growing satisfaction that he derives from this awareness.

The Delectable Mountains constitute a spiritual height attained only by the stalwart ('For but few of them that begin to come hither, do shew their face on these Mountains,' say the shepherds [p. 120]) on which Christian and Hopeful anticipate pleasures to be realized more fully in Beulah. The 'Gardens, and Orchards, the Vineyards, and Fountains of water' serve as tangible proof of God's marvellous bounty. When Christian reaches Beulah the gate of the New Jerusalem is 'within sight' and he is able to solace himself with the delights of the place : flowers, singing birds, 'abundance' of corn and wine, and, not least, the presence of

'shining Ones'. Christiana and her company stay up all night
listening to the bells and trumpets, so 'refreshing' is the place.
Their chambers are perfumed, and their bodies anointed, with
spices that rival those to be found in Milton's Eden. They are able
to experience such sensuous pleasure, paradoxically, because they
have achieved the 'fullness of the Spirit' that Matthew looks
forward to earlier in Part II.

In the early stages of his journey Christian moves through an
inhospitable terrain, where he must take refuge in a way station
such as House Beautiful and where evidences of divine favor are
fleeting and mysterious (for example, the hand that appears with
leaves from the Tree of Life to heal Christian's wounds when he
is in the Valley of Humiliation). By the time Christian and
Hopeful have reached the River of Life the landscape itself
sustains them; it is an oasis where they may *lie down safely* and
enjoy the lifegiving fruit and water of the place. The Delectable
Mountains suggest a large region (Immanuel's land) that
embodies the promise of salvation, Beulah a whole 'country'.
Bunyan's great talent for expressing the marvellous in simple
terms makes these places convincing for the reader. The pilgrims
seem to come upon them quite naturally. When Christian and
Hopeful arrive at the Delectable Mountains, they lean upon
their staves, as might any 'weary Pilgrims', and ask their improbable question (*'Whose delectable Mountains are these?'*) with
a disarming straightforwardness.

The relationship between Bunyan's pilgrims and these sustaining landscapes can be described as reciprocal. The sequence of
landscapes offers increasing evidence of divine grace and simultaneously an increased faith in 'the reality of the things of the
world to come' [17] that grace makes possible. Beulah is there for
Christian, finally, because he wants and believes it to exist. In his
allegorizing commentary on Revelation 22 : 1, *The Water of Life,*
Bunyan interprets the 'pure river of water of life' that flows from
the celestial throne as 'the Spirit of grace, the Spirit and grace
of God'.[18] He goes on to say: 'All men . . . though elect, though
purchased by the blood of Christ, are dead, and must be dead,
until the Spirit of life from God and his throne shall enter into
them; until they shall drink it in by vehement thirst, as the

parched ground drinks in the rain.'[19] In addition to the River of Life the springs and fountains that Christian encounters in his journey, beginning with the spring at the foot of the hill Difficulty, embody the 'Spirit of grace'. As Christian drinks these waters, and eats the fruit of the Tree of Life and of the vineyards of Beulah and the Delectable Mountains, he may be said to grow in spiritual strength and vitality. The process that Bunyan dramatizes would be described in the language of Calvinist theology as 'vivification', the 'quickening of the spirit' that marks the new life of the Christian.[20]

Bunyan relied increasingly on Scripture in describing the landscapes at the end of Christian's journey, skillfully fusing the Old Testament and the New. The Delectable Mountains do not correspond exactly to anything in the Bible. Bunyan placed the shepherds who witnessed the Nativity (as described in Luke) in a landscape that is closer to the Old Testament than to anything else, thereby offering a symbolic confirmation of Isaiah's prophecy about the coming of Immanuel and exploiting, as he does repeatedly, the suggestiveness of the vineyards and fountains of Canaan. Old and New Testaments also blend in Bunyan's account of the River of Life; it is David's River of God as well as the river of Revelation, and the lush meadow surrounding it recalls Old Testament description. Bunyan's most significant effort to reconcile Old and New Testament visions of blessedness comes at the end of *The Pilgrim's Progress,* in the juxtaposition of Beulah and the New Jerusalem. The two episodes give Christian's journey a double climax. The delights of Beulah suggest the high level of spiritual satisfaction that can be attained by the faithful in this life, but Christian must cross the river (a spiritual Jordan) to reach the true promised land. The Old Testament vision must be completed by that of the New.

The prominence that Bunyan gave Beulah illustrates better than anything else in *The Pilgrim's Progress* his strong attraction to Old Testament accounts of the fruitfulness and rest to be found in Canaan[21] and his ability to see in the saving history of the Israelites the special destiny of the saints in his own time. Bunyan confirms Christian's election in the terms Isaiah used to prophesy the salvation of the '*daughter of* Zion'; he is, like Israel,

'*redeemed of the Lord, sought out*'. Beulah is the antithesis of
the Valley of the Shadow of Death for Bunyan, a place where
one can rejoice upon entering a new relationship with God,
expressed metaphorically as that of bride and bridegroom, and
can rest in the assurance of Isaiah's promises : 'Thou shalt no
more be termed Forsaken; neither shall thy land any more be
termed Desolate' (Isaiah 62 :4). Bunyan would have seen the
land as mirroring Christian's righteousness as well as his sense of
election; one implies the other. In reaching this point Christian
has himself become fruitful, bearing 'the fruits of the Spirit, the
fruits of righteousness'.[22]

Bunyan's Beulah takes on some of the characteristics of the
heaven it borders (the sun shines perpetually, 'shining Ones' come
and go) and serves as a preparation for the transition to the New
Jerusalem. The pilgrims learn to bear what Bunyan, in the
language of the Song of Songs, calls the 'sickness' of love for the
divine and, since they are not yet ready to experience the glory
of the New Jerusalem directly, gaze at the city through an
'*Instrument*' designed to protect them from its dazzling bright-
ness. The fact that Christian no longer needs to worry about
relaxing his vigilance (Beulah is beyond the Valley of the Shadow
and Doubting Castle, Bunyan says) or about keeping to the way
(he can wander into the orchards, vineyards, and gardens whose
gates open onto the 'Highway' because they belong to the King)
suggests that his faith is as certain as it can be. This new certainty
is anticipated in Christian's definite response to Hopeful's query
('I would know where we are') as they near the end of the
Enchanted Ground : '*We have not now above two Miles further
to go thereon*' (p. 151).

In the New Jerusalem the pilgrims will be beyond the need
for faith. As Stand-fast puts it in Part ii : 'I have formerly lived
by Hear-say, and Faith, but now I go where I shall live by sight,
and shall be with him, in whose Company I delight my self'
(p. 311). Bunyan's narrative no longer depends upon the riddling
or metaphoric expression of divine truth but uses the descriptive
language of Revelation to establish the reality of the heavenly
country that Christian had set out to find : 'There, said they, is
the Mount *Sion*, the heavenly *Jerusalem*, the innumerable

company of Angels, and the Spirits of Just Men made perfect' (p. 159). 'Now just as the Gates were opened to let in the men, I looked after them; and behold, the City shone like the Sun, the Streets also were paved with Gold, and in them walked many men, with Crowns on their heads, Palms in their hands, and golden Harps to sing praises withal!' (p. 162). Bunyan has carefully prepared the reader for the imaginative leap to the New Jerusalem by foreshadowing the divine reality in the landscapes that lead up to it, but he must interpret a landscape such as Beulah typologically, as an expression of the promise and the fruits of the salvation of individual Christians. In the New Jerusalem he will see God not by the metaphoric light of the Word but in fact: 'In that place you must wear Crowns of Gold and enjoy the perpetual sight and Visons of the *Holy One, for there you shall see him as he is.* . . . There your eyes shall be delighted with seeing, and your ears with hearing, the pleasant voice of the mighty One' (p. 159). The Gospel day will give way to the eternal day made possible by the glory of God.

For all his emphasis on the splendor of the New Jerusalem Bunyan tried to accommodate its glories to his readers' understandings. His angels are simply 'shining Ones', and they offer the pilgrims what Bunyan describes in *The Heavenly Footman,* in the process of reassuring readers who think heaven too grand for them, as a 'hearty good welcome', helping them up the hill and explaining what they will encounter inside the city. These guides describe an approachable God with whom the pilgrims will be able to 'walk and talk' familiarly and ride out in an 'equipage' worthy of the occasion. As Christian and Hopeful approach the gate of the city in the friendly company of the angelic trumpeters they hear bells ringing, as they might on a Sunday in Bedfordshire. One could call such a heaven comfortable.

Yet Bunyan shows his pilgrims, 'transfigured' by their heavenly garments, entering into a state of bliss and rest that surpasses anything they could have known in the world and justifies all the trials they have endured there. The holy joy that they experience can be attained only in the presence of God, in the act of praising him. We last see Christian and Hopeful as they blend into the festive chorus of angels and saints singing : 'Holy, Holy, Holy, is the Lord' (p. 162). One cannot overemphasize the import-ance of this final episode to the structure of *The Pilgrim's Progress* and the experience of its contemporary readers. The emotional intensity of Bunyan's narrative, as it rises to a series of peaks leading up to the moment of Christian's and Hopeful's reception into the New Jerusalem, registers in unmistakable fashion his own estimation of how far his pilgrims have pro-gressed.

Bunyan's rendering of the glory of heaven, and of the prelim-inary delights of Beulah, is one of the great triumphs of the Puritan imagination and the ultimate justification of his use of the metaphor of the journey. The climactic episodes of *The Pilgrim's Progress* bring the reader all the way from the 'carnal' world in which the narrative began up to the contemplation of a transcendant world whose reality is validated by the Word. In the terms of Bunyan's narrative one can gain entrance to heaven only by learning to understand the visible world of ordinary experience in the metaphoric terms established by the Word : as an alien, and ultimately insubstantial country through which God's people must journey until they attain the ultimate satis-faction of communion with God. To accept this mode of thought is to see in the Exodus a pattern explaining and assuring the deliverance of the faithful of all times.

SOURCE: *English Literary Renaissance*, III (1973)
pp. 443–61.

NOTES

1. In *Self-Consuming Artifacts* (Berkeley and Los Angeles, 1972) chap. IV, 'Progress in *The Pilgrim's Progress*', pp. 224–64, a slightly expanded version of an article that appeared in *English Literary Renaissance*, I (1971) pp. 261–93. My argument implicitly questions two assumptions upon which Fish's claim that *The Pilgrim's Progress* is a 'self-consuming artifact' depends. The first is that Bunyan con-tinually frustrates expectations aroused in the reader by the linear form of his work and hence disqualifies the work 'as a vehicle of the insight it pretends to convey' (p. 225). This position depends upon

the unstated assumption that Bunyan was interested only in exposing his reader's limitations. To maintain it Fish must ignore Bunyan's climactic celebration of the joys of Beulah and of the New Jerusalem and the various signs that point to these joys along the course of Christian's journey. The other major assumption that I mean to question is that 'in *The Pilgrim's Progress* there is an inverse relationship between visibility and reliability' (p. 240). This depends upon the further assumption that all Christian's experiences should be regarded as occurring in the 'carnal' world in which Christians must learn to distrust the evidence of their senses. Such assumptions will work for Vanity Fair but not for the Delectable Mountains or for Beulah, landscapes from which Christian derives sensuous enjoyment that is a sign of spiritual progress. Some of what I have to say, particularly about the subjectivity of the individual way of faith, complements Fish's discussion, but where he looks to a tension between normal habits of perception and the demands of faith to explain the dynamics of the work I look primarily to Bunyan's understanding and use of his source, the Bible.

2. John Bunyan, *The Pilgrim's Progress*, ed. J. B. Wharey, 2nd ed. rev. by Roger Sharrock (Oxford, 1960) p. 40. Quotations from *The Pilgrim's Progress* are taken from this edition.

3. In *'The Pilgrim's Progress' and Traditions in Puritan Meditation* (New Haven, 1966). See especially pp. 3–15. Kaufmann suggests that Bunyan's efforts to prove that his metaphors are unambiguous (*logos*) arise from a need to satisfy the expectations of his audience and finds that other aspects of his Apology, especially the concluding lines, reveal a sense of his narrative as *mythos*, appealing to his audience in non-rational ways. My intention is to extend Kaufmann's argument, though without using his terms.

4. *The Works of John Bunyan*, ed. George Offor, vol. III (Glasgow, 1859) p. 437. Hereafter cited as *Works*.

5. See Brainerd Stranahan, 'Bunyan and the Bible : Uses of Biblical Materials in the Imaginative Structure of *The Pilgrim's Progress*', diss. (Harvard, 1965) for a very full discussion of Bunyan's biblical sources. Stranahan notes the high frequency of references to Hebrews in *The Pilgrim's Progress* and *Grace Abounding*.

6. *Works*, vol. III, p. 382.

7. Such readers would have seen references linking the pilgrims with the saving history of the Israelites as putting the authority of the Word behind the metaphor of the journey. The Shining Ones confirm Christian's identity as a spiritual descendant of Abraham

when they prepare him for entering the New Jerusalem : 'You are going to *Abraham*, to *Isaac*, and *Jacob*, and to the Prophets' (p. 159). Secret tells Christiana before she sets out that God 'will feed thee with the Fat of his House, and with the Heritage of *Jacob* thy Father' (p. 179). Christian interprets his journey in the light of Old Testament history, identifying himself as 'of the Race of *Japhet*, whom God will perswade to dwell in the Tents of *Shem*' (p. 46), thereby associating himself with the favored line that will have dominion over Canaan according to God's promise to Noah in Genesis 9 : 27. When he loses his roll, he recalls the trials of the Israelites : 'Thus it happened to *Israel* for their sin, they were sent back again by the way of the Red-Sea' (p. 44). Bunyan again invokes the Exodus in Part II when he describes the seal with which Interpreter marks the children of Christiana as 'the contents and sum of the Passover which the Children of Israel did eat when they came out from the Land of Egypt' (p. 208).

8. *Works*, vol. III, p. 382.

9. *The Annotated Alice*, ed. Martin Gardner (New York, 1960) p. 88.

10. Roger Sharrock, *John Bunyan: The Pilgrim's Progress* (London, 1966) p. 26. See also Kaufmann, pp. 106–17, on the unity of Puritan religious experience.

11. Kaufmann, p. 115.

12. *Adventures of Huckleberry Finn*, ed. E. S. Bradley, R. C. Beatty, and E. H. Long (New York, 1961) p. 83.

13. See *A Relation of the Imprisonment of Mr. John Bunyan*, in *Works*, vol. I, pp. 50–2.

14. Henri Talon has commented on the dreamlike quality of Bunyan's landscapes. He describes the country through which Christian travels as a 'dream land', a 'country of the soul', which becomes 'real' for Christian. See 'Space and the Hero in *The Pilgrim's Progress*', *Études Anglaises*, 14 (1961) pp. 124–30. The article constitutes part of the introduction to Talon's anthology of Bunyan's works, *God's Knotty Log* (New York, 1961).

15. Both Kaufmann and Roland Mushat Frye have commented on Christian's education in scriptural truth. In *God, Man, and Satan* (Princeton, 1960) Frye argues : 'Throughout, there is a deepening of understanding on Christian's part, a vitally progressive revelation' (p. 138).

16. See Kaufmann, pp. 133ff., for a discussion of the 'heavenly-mindedness' of much Puritan meditation and the use of the senses

in evoking the joys of heaven. William Madsen, in *From Shadowy Types to Truth* (New Haven, 1968) pp. 166ff., argues that critics have neglected the imagistic, and sensuous, character of much Puritan writing.

17. In *The Strait Gate* Bunyan exhorts his readers to 'strive for the faith of the Gospel, for the more we believe the Gospel, and the reality of the things of the world to come, with the more stomach shall we labour to possess the blessedness' (*Works*, vol. I, 369).

18. *Works*, vol. III, p. 540.

19. *Works*, vol. III, p. 552.

20. See John Calvin, *Institutes of the Christian Religion*, ed. John T. McNeill (Philadelphia, 1960) vol. I, p. 595. See also vol. I, p. 600; vol. II, pp. 1307, 1456.

21. See for example, Exodus 3 :8, 13 :5; Leviticus 20 :24; Numbers 14 :8; Deuteronomy 8 :7–9, 11 :8–12; Joshua 1 :13–15.

22. *Works*, vol. III, p. 567. The phrase, a composite of Galatians 5 :22–23 and Philippians 1 :11, appears in Bunyan's elaboration of the parable of the fig tree in Luke 13 : *The Barren Fig Tree, or The Doom and Downfall of the Fruitless Professor.*

SELECT BIBLIOGRAPHY

RECOMMENDED TEXTS

John Bunyan, *The Pilgrim's Progress*, ed. J. B. Wharey, rev. Roger Sharrock (Oxford, 1960; rev. ed., 1968). Based on the first editions of 1678 (first part) and 1684 (second part) this edition gives a full account in its introduction and commentary of all the changes and revisions made in Bunyan's lifetime.

Grace Abounding to the Chief of Sinners and The Pilgrim's Progress, ed. Roger Sharrock (Oxford, 1966). A student's edition including Bunyan's spiritual autobiography as well as the allegory, with very brief introduction and notes.

The Pilgrim's Progress, ed. Roger Sharrock (Harmondsworth, 1965). A text in modernised spelling without the marginal scriptural references but with a critical introduction.

Apart from those represented in this collection, the following books and articles devoted in whole or part to *The Pilgrim's Progress*, may be found useful.

BOOKS

The Narrative of the Persecution of Agnes Beaumont in 1674 (London, 1929). Contemporary account of a scandal involving Bunyan and a member of his congregation.

Jacques Blondel, *Allégorie et réalisme dans le 'Pilgrim's Progress'* (Paris, 1959).

John Brown, *John Bunyan, His Life, Times, and Work* (London, 1928). A revision of the standard Victorian biography with small corrections and additions.

S. E. Fish, *Self-Consuming Artifacts* (Berkeley and Los Angeles, 1972). Contains a chapter on 'Progress in *The Pilgrim's Progress*'.

F. M. Harrison, *A Bibliography of the Works of John Bunyan* (Oxford, 1932).

U. M. Kaufmann, *The Pilgrim's Progress and Traditions in Puritan Meditation* (New Haven, Conn., 1966).

F. R. Leavis, *The Common Pursuit* (London, 1952). Contains an earlier essay on Bunyan than that contained in this book.

Louis Macneice, *Varieties of Parable* (London, 1965). Includes a chapter comparing Bunyan and Spenser as allegorists.

'Mark Rutherford' (William Hale White), *John Bunyan* (1905; new ed. London, 1933). The view of a nineteenth-century Nonconformist intellectual.

Roger Sharrock, *John Bunyan* (London, 1954; Macmillan Papermac, 1968).

Henri A. Talon, *John Bunyan, the Man and His Works* (London, 1951). A translation of the French edition (Paris, 1948).

W. Y. Tindall, *John Bunyan, Mechanick Preacher* (New York, 1934).

Dorothy Van Ghent, *The English Novel: Form and Function* (New York, 1953).

Owen C. Watkins, *The Puritan Experience* (London, 1972). A collection of Puritan writings on spiritual experience which forms a useful introduction to the Puritan mind.

J. B. Wharey, *The Sources of Bunyan's Allegories* (Baltimore, 1904).

O. L. Winslow, *John Bunyan* (New York, 1961). A straightforward biographical account.

ARTICLES

David J. Alpaugh, 'Emblem and Interpretation in *The Pilgrim's Progress*,' *English Literary History*, XXXIII (1966) pp. 299–314.

James F. Forrest, 'Bunyan's Ignorance and the Flatterer'; A Study in the Literary Art of Damnation', *Studies in Philology*, LX (1963) pp. 12–22.

——, 'Mercy with her Mirror', *Philological Quarterly* (1963) pp. 121–6.

Daniel Gibson Jr, 'On the Genesis of *Pilgrim's Progress*', *Modern Philology*, XXXII (1935) pp. 365–82.

Joyce Godber, 'The Imprisonments of John Bunyan', *Transactions of the Congregational Historical Society*, XVI (1949) pp. 23–32.

Roger Sharrock, 'Spiritual Autobiography in *The Pilgrim's Progress*', *Review of English Studies*, XXIV (1948) 102–20.

——, 'Personal Vision and Puritan Tradition in Bunyan', *Hibbert Journal*, LVI (1957) pp. 47–60.

H. G. Tibbutt, 'The Pilgrim's Route', *Bedfordshire Magazine*, VII (1959) pp. 66–8. Examines rival claims for a realistic topography in the work.

NOTES ON CONTRIBUTORS

ROBERT BRIDGES (1844–1930), poet, man of letters, and friend of Gerard Manley Hopkins; his works include the long poem *The Testament of Beauty* (1929).

SIR CHARLES FIRTH (1857–1936), historian of the period of the English Revolution whose works include *Cromwell's Army* (1902), *The Last Years of the Protectorate* (1909), *Essays Historical and Literary* (1936), and *Oliver Cromwell* (1958).

ROLAND MUSHAT FRYE is Professor of English at Emory University. He has published much on the relations of literature and theology including *Shakespeare and Christian Doctrine* (1965).

MAURICE HUSSEY is a Senior Lecturer at the Cambridgeshire Polytechnic. Apart from articles on Puritanism he has published much on Renaissance drama including an edition of Ben Jonson's *Burtholomew Fair* in the New Mermaid series.

JOHN R. KNOTT JR. is Associate Professor of English in the University of Michigan, Ann Arbor.

F. R. LEAVIS, literary critic and founder of the journal *Scrutiny* (1932–53); formerly Fellow of Downing College, Cambridge and at present Visiting Professor of English in the University of York. His works include *New Bearings in English Poetry* (1928), *Revaluation* (1936), and *D. H. Lawrence, Novelist* (1955).

C. S. LEWIS (1898–1963), English scholar and religious writer, moved from Magdalen College, Oxford, to Magdalene College, Cambridge, where he was Professor of Medieval and Renaissance Literature. Among his principal works are *The Allegory of Love* (1936), *The Screwtape Letters* (1942), and *English Literature in the Sixteenth Century* (1954).

ROY PASCAL is Professor of German in the University of Birmingham. As well as his work on German literature he has published a study of the general problems of autobiographical narrative.

ROGER SHARROCK is Professor of English Language and Literature in the University of London, King's College. His publications include *John Bunyan* (1954), editions of *The Pilgrim's Progress* (1960) and *Grace Abounding* (1962), and the *Pelican Book of English Prose* (1970; in collaboration with Raymond Williams).

GEORGE BERNARD SHAW (1856–1950), playwright, social thinker and controversialist, was a lifelong admirer of Bunyan whom he associated with the type of 'prophetic artist' to which he himself claimed to belong. His principal works include *Plays Pleasant and Unpleasant* (1898), *Man and Superman* (1903), *Saint Joan* (1924), and *The Intelligent Woman's Guide to Socialism and Capitalism* (1928).

INDEX